JESUS *the* STRANGER

KENNETH J. COLLINS

JESUS *the* STRANGER

A DAILY LENTEN READER

Copyright 2021, Lent edition 2024 by Kenneth J. Collins

All rights reserved. No part of this publication may be reproduced, stored in a retrieval system, or transmitted, in any form or by any means—electronic, mechanical, photocopying, recording, or otherwise—without prior written permission, except for brief quotations in critical reviews or articles.

All Scripture quotations, unless otherwise indicated, are taken from the Holy Bible, New International Version®, NIV® Copyright © 1973, 1978, 1984, 2011 by Biblica, Inc.™ Used by permission of Zondervan. All rights reserved worldwide. www.zondervan.com. The "NIV" and "New International Version" are trademarks registered in the United States Patent and Trademark Office by Biblica, Inc.™ All rights reserved worldwide.

Scripture quotations marked NRSV are from the New Revised Standard Version Bible, copyright © 1989 National Council of the Churches of Christ in the United States of America. Used by permission. All rights reserved.

Scripture quotations marked CEB are from the COMMON ENGLISH BIBLE. © Copyright 2011 COMMON ENGLISH BIBLE. All rights reserved. Used by permission.

Scripture quotations marked ESV are from the ESV® Bible (The Holy Bible, English Standard Version®), copyright © 2001 by Crossway, a publishing ministry of Good News Publishers. Used by permission. All rights reserved.

Scripture quotations marked NASB are taken from the New American Standard Bible® (NASB), Copyright © 1960, 1962, 1963, 1968, 1971, 1972, 1973, 1975, 1977, 1995 by The Lockman Foundation. Used by permission. www.Lockman.org.

Printed in the United States of America

Cover art and design by Nate Farro
Page design and layout by PerfecType, Nashville, Tennessee

Collins, Kenneth J.
 Jesus the stranger : a daily Lenten reader / Kenneth J. Collins. - Franklin, Tennessee : Seedbed Publishing, 2024, ©2021. Lent edition.

 pages ; cm.

 ISBN: 9798888001103 (paperback)
 ISBN: 9798888001110 (epub)
 ISBN: 9798888001127 (pdf)
 ISBN: 9798888001134 (DVD)
 OCLC: 1468563370

 1. Jesus Christ--Person and offices. 2. Jesus Christ--Biography.
 3. Bible. Gospels--Biography. 4. Lent--Meditations. I. Title.

BT203.C644 2024   232/.9   2024949999

SEEDBED PUBLISHING
Franklin, Tennessee
seedbed.com

For Kathy Armistead,
With Appreciation

Contents

Introduction   1

Day 1: The True Light   7
Day 2: Simeon   12
Day 3: Herod the Great   18
Day 4: John the Baptist   24
Day 5: The Devil   29
Day 6: Hometown Folk   37
Day 7: The Family of Jesus   42
Day 8: The Scribes   48
Day 9: The Pharisees   54
Day 10: The Teachers of the Law   61
Day 11: Simon, the Pharisee   67
Day 12: The Pharisees Again   73
Day 13: One of the Teachers of the Law   80
Day 14: The Jews   88
Day 15: The Jews in the Temple Courts   95
Day 16: Simon Peter   102
Day 17: The Sanhedrin   108
Day 18: Chief Priests, Teachers of the Law, and Elders   115
Day 19: Jesus   123
Day 20: The Crowd in the Temple Courts   130

Day 21: Herod Antipas	136
Day 22: Disciples Then and Now (Part One)	142
Day 23: Disciples Then and Now (Part Two)	150
Day 24: Disciples Then and Now (Part Three)	156
Day 25: The Crowd	164
Day 26: Jesus and the Apostles	170
Day 27: Sinners	176
Day 28: Judas	183
Day 29: Caiaphas, the Chief Priests, and the Sanhedrin	189
Day 30: Peter	196
Day 31: Pilate	202
Day 32: Herod Antipas	210
Day 33: Barabbas	216
Day 34: The Governor's Soldiers	225
Day 35: The Chief Priests and Their Officials	231
Day 36: The Chief Priests, Teachers of the Law, and Elders (Part One)	239
Day 37: The Chief Priests, Teachers of the Law, and Elders (Part Two)	247
Day 38: Jesus (Part One)	256
Day 39: Jesus (Part Two)	264
Day 40: Joseph of Arimathea and Nicodemus	271
Day 41: Mary Magdalene	277
Day 42: A Couple of Disciples	285
Notes	295
Acknowledgments	311

Introduction

My current habit is to run about five miles three times a week. It's exhilarating. I always pray when I run. Images from a careful reading and study of the Gospels, stories about Jesus and others, and reflections on my own current experience flood my prayers and make them intuitive, passionate, and thick. In these prayers, which are informed by so many sources gushing in, I have come to see a picture of Jesus, multifaceted and inviting, but one that is seldom reflected in current cultural depictions of the man from Galilee. Indeed, Jesus of the Gospels is a far more complex and intriguing figure than the distortions that are bandied about today. The ongoing and deepening contrast between the Jesus of the Gospels and recent popular cultural misconfigurations is the principal reason I have written this book. Jesus is far more beautiful than many have imagined. It all has to do with love, but not just any kind of love—holy love.

What This Book Is Not

Let me start, first of all, by pointing out what this book is not. It is unlike most devotionals—although some people will invariably read this work in precisely this way. Many devotionals, even popular ones, change the topic or theme, if not every day, at least very often in accordance with the shifting passages under consideration which may be ordered by any number of criteria. This book is not like that—not at all. It is not a compilation of forty (plus two) different stories. It is *one* story that is told in forty-two different parts or chapters. Indeed, readers will have to be aware of what happened earlier in the story to comprehend what is being offered *now*.

Second, this book is not a commentary, although some will read it in this way as well. It does not focus simply on one gospel, say the Gospel of Luke for example, but on the voices of all four Gospels in terms of the larger theme of the book. And even in terms of our very carefully selected texts,[1] not every verse of each passage will be explored in the reflections, though most are. Moreover, I am not a biblical scholar (but I am grateful for these scholars in terms of the very good work that they do), and this book has not been written for scholars but for laypeople—that is, for those folks who know how to appreciate the gripping power of a narrative that revolves around a central figure and who, therefore, know how to get caught up in a good story.

By inclination and training, I am a theologian and historian who will, therefore, bring to bear a number of different frameworks to the text, but in a way that should be easily understood by average readers. While the givenness of the text is king,[2] and that's how most readers will approach and receive it, I hope to engage the imagination along the way as well. That's not a dirty word. Indeed, it has very much to do with truth—yes, truth.[3]

What This Book Is

If this book is neither a devotional nor a commentary, then just what exactly is it? It is a narrative journey, a thematic presentation, of the suffering, alienation, and rejection of Jesus Christ by a host of people, those for whom Jesus was "the other," and in many respects, therefore, a stranger. Jesus is presented in this grand constructed narrative, carefully laid out and composed of key gospel texts, against the backdrop of a cast of oppositional characters who unwittingly help to portray Jesus in his utter goodness, deep humility, and abiding love. With such a well-developed and ongoing focus, the work inevitably invites a participatory reading, either by individuals privately or by groups publicly, that will entail grappling with key texts and struggling with reflections along the way. Such labor should lead to genuine transformation, especially in terms of understanding Jesus in a new and richly satisfying way, in which both the heart and the mind will be engaged. As a consequence of all of this (so it is hoped), understanding ourselves anew as well. That's where imagination will handsomely come into play.

For one thing, the exclusionary and disciplinary mechanisms employed by groups are different for those who are recognized members than they are for those who are not members at all and are perhaps currently seeking admission. In terms of the former—that is, recognized members—practices such as disfellowshiping, expulsion, and excommunication are the order of the day.

Reading Strategies

Given the nature of this book, this journey of discovery, it is not recommended to read it either quickly or simply in three or four sittings as some readers may like to do. Far too much will be missed. Instead, it is best to walk along this path slowly in the way that it has been laid out: with texts, reflections, and a few questions along the way. Let life happen in the interim, an element that will inevitably prove to be part of the larger narrative as well. It's that kind of story as noted earlier; it's both participatory and engaging. It invites our attention on so many levels, given the kind of people that we are with hearts, minds, and souls—and with passions!

As we read the gospel texts and engage the reflections, it will be helpful, by way of analogy, to employ both a close-up lens and a wide-angle one. We are so used to thinking that we understand something when we break it down into its constituent parts and then analyze them. We think we're done when actually we're not. To be sure, this first, close-up lens offers us necessary information that, reflected upon, will result in knowledge. The problem, however, is such information is not sufficient. This is precisely the approach that some devotionals, by and large, take with a focus on each day and then it's quickly off to the facts, the details, and the passages of the next. No larger structure is ever offered. That approach simply won't work here.

Having understood the parts—that is, each step of the journey—we must then drop back and try to see the whole—the entire constructed narrative in which everything has its place in the grand theme. When this is done properly, just like human life itself in terms of our own personal stories, some things that were so prominent on the up-close level will fade away, and other things not recognized earlier will become much clearer and far more prominent. Consider Salvador Dali's lithograph *Lincoln in Dalivision*, which hangs in the Dali Museum in St. Petersburg, Florida. Up close, the face of Lincoln can hardly be seen; it's lost in the variegated shapes and colors of the work, but the backside of a naked woman is clearly visible with her head almost in the center of the composition. Stand back, however, about twenty-five feet or so, and the woman drops out, along with her earlier eye-grabbing nakedness, and Lincoln's face suddenly appears all by itself. Such will be the case here as well.

A Final Word Before We Begin

You are about to embark on an exciting journey. Think of it as going on a long, multiday hike across a challenging terrain with a guide. The "I" will drop out on this journey. It will soon become "we." I will be your caring and ever-attentive guide. I have been on this journey before. It all came together for me one evening on a long-distance run. I saw it all in a flash, and I was overwhelmed. May this Lenten season prove to be one in which we freshly encounter Jesus, not necessarily as we received him, but as he truly is. May the strangeness of Jesus from Galilee reorient us once again as we encounter him as the Light of the world.

Day 1

The True Light

JOHN 1:9–13 *The true light that gives light to everyone was coming into the world. He was in the world, and though the world was made through him, the world did not recognize him. He came to that which was his own, but his own did not receive him. Yet to all who did receive him, to those who believed in his name, he gave the right to become children of God—children born not of natural descent, nor of human decision or a husband's will, but born of God.*

Consider This

Stories can be enthralling. We read a few lines here, pick up some engaging and puzzling biographical detail there, and suddenly we're hooked. We can't put it down; we've entered a new world. And when we think of recent master storytellers such as J. R. R. Tolkien and C. S. Lewis—both of whom at one time were professors of English literature at Oxford—we can easily understand their own appreciation of the Gospels, which unveil through gripping narrative the greatest story of all. Though the Gospels contain many matter-of-fact details, such as eating, washing, selling, and paying taxes, those many details are caught up in a grand narrative that is flush with meaning—the kind of meaning that captivated the well-worked imaginations of both Tolkien and Lewis.

The depth, the expanse, the heightened dimension, even the narrative roominess of the Gospel of John, our current text, can be seen in its central character, Jesus of Nazareth, precisely in terms of *who* he is and just what happens to him. In fact, the "who he is" is so important to John that not only does he describe this one, this person, in terms of both God and light, filling out crucial background and interpretive context along the way, but he also doesn't even specifically mention the name "Jesus" until verse 17. Simply put, Jesus is not just any human being. John wants us to know that. He's someone special—wonderfully special.

John's affirmation that the "true light that gives light to everyone was coming into the world," is rich with meaning on so many levels. First of all, this statement reveals that the light identified with Jesus, the Word made flesh, exists prior to coming into the world. Elsewhere, John declares: "In the beginning was the Word, and the Word was with God, and the Word was God" (v. 1). These statements could not rightly be made in terms of any other human being. Think about that for a while. Second, observe that John writes of "the true light," implying that false lights, pretend lights, misguided lights also exist and that they can lead many people astray. Third, note also that Jesus, as the true light, gives light to everyone, to all people, to white, black, rich, poor, male, female, young, old, middle-aged, Christian, non-Christian, theist, atheist. All really does mean all here (v. 12); none are excluded from this illumination whose source is none other than the "light of the world" (John 8:12). It is this light that was "with God, and . . . was God" (John 1:1).

Various Christian traditions have grappled with the meaning of this universal illumination. Some consider it along the lines of general revelation—in terms of a created order embedded in the things that have been made, reminiscent of what the apostle Paul had written in Romans 1:20: "For since the creation of the world God's invisible qualities—his eternal power and divine nature—have been clearly seen, being understood from what has been made, so that people are without excuse." Others, however, view this illumination not only externally, in terms of the things that have been made, but also internally with respect to such things as conscience, knowledge of the moral law, and even a basic, if primitive, intuitive knowledge of God. The larger point here—and it's an important one—is that all of this illumination has Jesus as its source. He, and he alone, is the true light that illuminates all of humanity whether he is celebrated or not or even recognized or not.

John is only a few short verses into his gospel and he already introduces remarkable irony. Given who Jesus is, we would naturally expect he would be recognized by the world since the world itself, and all that is in it, has been made through the Word. Instead, we get exactly the opposite: not recognition, but neglect; not reception, but rejection. Who is this Jesus that I should pay attention? What's so special about him? When the light or Word came to that which was his own—meaning the Jewish people—he was not welcomed or received. However, such a frosty attitude, suggesting perhaps a hardness of heart, was not shared by all first-century Jews, though it was found among their religious leaders. (And there were exceptions even here; think of Nicodemus, for example.) In fact, not only was Jesus himself Jewish, but every one of his disciples was as well. We must never forget that.

The irony of verses 10 and 11 is heightened in one of the largest contrasts ever offered in literature, *any* literature. Consider this: the light that has entered the world is none other than the Word who is God. Accordingly, the Word, the Most High, the one greatly to be exalted, will not only be met with stupefying neglect and unwelcoming attitudes, but also, as John will later tell us, outright torture, mocking, and murderous intent. This vast difference, this huge chasm, between the glorious heights of who this light is, in terms of his essential being, and the wretched depths of his rejection manifested in the evil practices and the murderous designs of those who reject this light, both Jew and Gentile, is without parallel. Indeed, this difference, which again is colossal, is one of the reasons why the gospel story is unlike all other stories. It is and remains unique, distinct, and set apart. It offers the grandest narrative of all, from the highest heights to the lowest depths, an invitation to a world much larger than our own workaday world, a reality far deeper than we have—or ever could have—imagined.

To be caught up in such a story, then, to be engaged in this matchless narrative, is an invitation to discovery and transformation, to a new way of being, to participating in what is nothing less than a new world, an enchanting world, one that is full of light precisely because God is light. We enter that world, John tells us, not through our own self-will or strength, not in any natural way, but through the very gift of the new birth, graciously given to us, whereby we become something absolutely amazing: the very children of God (John 1:13).

The Prayer

Heavenly Father, I accept your invitation to this special journey of discovery and transformation, centered on the life and love of your Son, Jesus Christ. May your great story become my story, as I confess his name and receive the right to be called your child.

The Questions

Why does John use the metaphor of light to describe Jesus? What does this reveal about the person and character of Jesus?

Day 2

Simeon

LUKE 2:25–35 *Now there was a man in Jerusalem called Simeon, who was righteous and devout. He was waiting for the consolation of Israel, and the Holy Spirit was on him. It had been revealed to him by the Holy Spirit that he would not die before he had seen the Lord's Messiah. Moved by the Spirit, he went into the temple courts. When the parents brought in the child Jesus to do for him what the custom of the Law required, Simeon took him in his arms and praised God, saying:*

> *"Sovereign Lord, as you have promised,*
> *you may now dismiss your servant in peace.*
> *For my eyes have seen your salvation,*
> *which you have prepared in the sight of all nations:*
> *a light for revelation to the Gentiles,*
> *and the glory of your people Israel."*

The child's father and mother marveled at what was said about him. Then Simeon blessed them and said to Mary, his mother: "This child is destined to cause the falling and rising of many in Israel, and to be a sign that will be spoken against, so that the thoughts of many hearts will be revealed. And a sword will pierce your own soul too."

Consider This

Jesus had been conceived in a special way—in a manner suitable to the Word being made flesh. As the Gospel of Matthew states: "His mother Mary was pledged to be married to Joseph, but before they came together, she was found to be pregnant through the Holy Spirit" (1:18b). Being good Jews, faithful to the requirements of Jewish law, Joseph and Mary had a number of obligations to fulfill in terms of the birth of Jesus. Leviticus 12:1–3 lays out one of the more important responsibilities:

> The LORD said to Moses, "Say to the Israelites: 'A woman who becomes pregnant and gives birth to a son will be ceremonially unclean for seven days, just as she is unclean during her monthly period. On the eighth day the boy is to be circumcised.'"

At the time of circumcision, the child would also be named, as was the custom, but Jesus had already been given a name that had been chosen for him by neither Joseph nor Mary. Earlier an angel of the Lord had appeared to Joseph in a dream and declared: "You are to give him the name Jesus, because he will save his people from their sins" (Matt. 1:21b). Although Shakespeare claimed in his play *Romeo and Juliet*, "a rose by any other name would smell as sweet," the name given to Jesus did, indeed, make a difference. It had already identified him, even before he was born, as the one whose life would be emblematic of "salvation" or "deliverance"— the very meaning of the name *Jesus*, derived from Greek, or in Hebrew, *Yeshua*.

While at the temple courts in Jerusalem, Joseph and Mary were fulfilling another obligation of Jewish law, by *presenting* the child to God, the Holy One of Israel. While in this sacred environment, they encountered a man named Simeon who was "waiting for the consolation of Israel," which means that he was likely anticipating the coming of the Messiah. From the available evidence, Simeon seemed to be something of a prophet because, as our text reveals: "the Holy Spirit was on him," he was "moved by the Spirit," and "It had been revealed to him by the Holy Spirit that he would not die before he had seen the Lord's Messiah." This man, apparently unknown to Joseph and Mary, took the child away from them, held Jesus in his arms, and exclaimed in what has been called the Song of Simeon: "Sovereign Lord, as you have promised, you may now dismiss your servant in peace. For my eyes have seen your salvation, which you have prepared in the sight of all nations: a light for revelation to the Gentiles, and the glory of your people Israel."

Simeon's proclamation, "For my eyes have seen your salvation," reveals that to see Jesus is to see redemption. In other words, to look upon a person—in this case, an infant—is to view God's plan of deliverance. The Most High, interestingly enough, starts out small. That's unexpected. In the fifth century, Augustine had described such prophetic seeing as that undertaken by the heart, a deep, intuitive, and emotive seeing, and it was to be distinguished from the seeing rendered by the eyes.[1] Moreover, notice how "seeing" and "light" make up the substance of Simeon's proclamation and in a way similar to how John had described Jesus earlier in the prologue of his own gospel. Wherever Jesus is, there is light, revelation, and unveiling. It's unavoidable. This is fortunate for the saints but troubling for others.

What makes Simeon's words in their setting so ironic is that his pronouncement that Jesus is the salvation that God has "prepared in the sight of all nations: a light for revelation to the Gentiles" underscores the universality of redemption—embracing both Jew and Gentile precisely at the place, the Jewish temple, where it had been thought by so many that salvation was focused simply on the Jewish people as the chosen of God. The "glory of your people Israel," then, would be the delight, the abundant joy, that this people would express as they realized that the love of their God embraced all peoples, the entire earth. If the problem of sin way back in Genesis 3 had been universal, the solution—redemption—would have to be universal as well.

But all was not light and roses in this holy setting, for Simeon also announced to Mary that not only will a sword pierce her own soul (no doubt because of her love for her son) and that of Jesus as well, but also that "this child is destined to cause the falling and rising of many in Israel, and to be a sign that will be spoken against, so that the thoughts of many hearts will be revealed." Even today many people have difficulty with this last statement, and they, therefore, fail to embrace its full meaning: Jesus, the Savior, *precisely because of who he is*, necessarily invites vigorous opposition and is at the heart of an abiding division within Israel and beyond, among both Jews and Gentiles alike, a division that has lasted for millennia. Put another way, Jesus is a stumbling stone for some, over which they trip and fall, but a stone of ascent for others. How one relates to him, then, makes all the difference.

Moreover, that Jesus is "a sign that will be spoken against," indicates that his life, what he values, and even the very good that he does, will be rejected by those religious leaders of his own time who are animated, even agitated, in their opposition to him. They will curse, slander, and bear false witness against Jesus, all the while thinking that they are doing the very will of God. What lies ahead, then, is an inverted world where at times good is evil and evil is good—and popularity ensures virtually nothing. What's so fascinating about this being "spoken against," as noted by Simeon, is that in their rush to condemn, to engage in all manner of evil speaking, the detractors of Jesus reveal just who they are in the very thoughts of their hearts, the deepest recesses of their being. What was once hidden will, after all, be revealed. Even in this dark place, the light of truth will break through in an undeniable revelation.

Since Jesus as the Word of God has come into this world from eternity, there can only be rising and falling in terms of him; that is, indifference is not really an option. How is this so? If, in Jesus, an enormous good is being presented to humanity—salvation, as Simeon had exclaimed—then to be indifferent to this gift, to not care, or to be preoccupied with other distracting concerns is to lose out on what is truly being offered. What is this but to fail to realize in one's life an enormous and precious good that is actually in the offering? We cannot pretend that the offer has not been made; that's bad faith. Our indifference to the gift of who Jesus is meets the definition of evil as a privation of the good (*privatio boni*, as Augustine described it); in other words, as a genuine lack of the good which should be in place. Now there is only rising and falling: "the cornerstone" (Eph. 2:20) or "a rock that makes them fall" (1 Peter 2:8a). Jesus is a real game changer.

The Prayer

Jesus Christ, whose name indicates God's promise to save, I confess you as the cornerstone upon whom I depend. Move me from indifference to fully embracing you as the person to whom I belong and to whom I offer my allegiance. Jesus, I belong to you.

The Questions

How can Jesus be "destined to cause the falling and rising of many in Israel" (Luke 2:34b), being both a stumbling stone and a stone of ascent—"a rock that makes them fall" (1 Peter 2:8) and the "cornerstone" (Eph. 2:20)—at the same time?

Consider the ways in which Jesus is "a light for revelation to the Gentiles" (Luke 2:32a). How does this reference to light in Luke's gospel compare with the employment of light as found in John's gospel: "The true light that gives light to everyone was coming into the world" (John 1:9)?

Day 3

Herod the Great

MATTHEW 2:1–16 *After Jesus was born in Bethlehem in Judea, during the time of King Herod, Magi from the east came to Jerusalem and asked, "Where is the one who has been born king of the Jews? We saw his star when it rose and have come to worship him."*

When King Herod heard this he was disturbed, and all Jerusalem with him. When he had called together all the people's chief priests and teachers of the law, he asked them where the Messiah was to be born. "In Bethlehem in Judea," they replied, "for this is what the prophet has written:

> *"'But you, Bethlehem, in the land of Judah,*
> *   are by no means least among the rulers of Judah;*
> *for out of you will come a ruler*
> *   who will shepherd my people Israel.'"*

Then Herod called the Magi secretly and found out from them the exact time the star had appeared. He sent them to Bethlehem and said, "Go and search carefully for the child. As soon as you find him, report to me, so that I too may go and worship him."

After they had heard the king, they went on their way, and the star they had seen when it rose went ahead of them until it stopped over the place where the child was. When they saw the star, they were overjoyed. On coming to the house, they saw the child with his mother Mary, and they bowed down and worshiped him. Then they opened their treasures and presented him with gifts of gold, frankincense, and myrrh. And having been warned in a dream not to go back to Herod, they returned to their country by another route.

> *When they had gone, an angel of the Lord appeared to Joseph in a dream. "Get up," he said, "take the child and his mother and escape to Egypt. Stay there until I tell you, for Herod is going to search for the child to kill him."*
>
> *So he got up, took the child and his mother during the night and left for Egypt, where he stayed until the death of Herod. And so was fulfilled what the Lord had said through the prophet: "Out of Egypt I called my son."*
>
> *When Herod realized that he had been outwitted by the Magi, he was furious, and he gave orders to kill all the boys in Bethlehem and its vicinity who were two years old and under, in accordance with the time he had learned from the Magi.*

Consider This

Shortly after Jesus was born, he was already under a death sentence. Few children have entered the world in this way. Joseph had been warned in a dream that Herod was searching for the child in order to destroy him. This was the same Herod, known as "the Great," who had undertaken the massive building project of renewing and expanding the second temple, a work that had begun around 20 BC.

Our text reveals Herod as a disturbed and deeply dishonest man. He hid, for example, his real motivation from the Magi in seeking the child, and they were warned in a dream not to return to him. Though Herod pretended that he, too, would like to worship this one who had been born king of the Jews, he actually had other plans, much darker ones in mind, which were fueled by both anxiety and fear. As a powerful man who would tolerate no rival to his authority, Herod had already executed his two sons, Alexander and Aristobulus, in 7 BC because he had thought they were plotting against him.[1] Such violence was nothing new to Herod, as he had already dispatched their mother, Mariamne I, much earlier in 29 BC.[2] Continuing this pattern, shortly before he died in 4 BC or so, Herod executed yet another son, this time Antipater, who had been born of his wife Doris.[3] It is this man, this monster, who had his eyes on the baby Jesus.

How could Joseph, a decent but obscure man, know anything of the designs of a powerful and corrupt king who would not even reveal them to the Magi? No one less than almighty God, then, would have to intervene in this awful situation in what looks like a contest between a very powerful king, on the one hand, and a nearly helpless infant, on the other. With things so out of balance, so out of whack, in terms of power configurations, the Almighty tipped the balance and sent an "angel of the Lord"—a spiritual intelligence not limited to the confines of time and space—to Joseph, this lowly man, in order to warn him in a dream: "Get up, . . . take the child and his mother and escape to Egypt." The matter must have been urgent because Joseph took the child and his mother, Mary, and left for Egypt right away, at night. There was little to be gained by delay and much to lose.

The descent of Jesus, Mary, and Joseph into Egypt, which was about seventy-five miles or so from Bethlehem, is a powerful biblical image and calls to mind the vision of an earlier journey when Jacob, at his son Joseph's request, and due to suffering from the famine then in Canaan, made his way to the land of the

Pharaohs. Since the small and struggling family during Herod's reign was forced to flee their own land to escape persecution, then they are rightly described as refugees. Think of it: Jesus had barely learned to walk, and his family was already on the run.

The Egypt of the time of Jesus was a much different place than the country Jacob and his sons had entered much earlier. The land had been conquered by Rome in 30 BC, and it was made a province with an accompanying civic order and legal structure for which Rome had become famous. In other words, the land was now a remarkably hospitable place for most people, and a city such as Alexandria had a large population of Jews.[4] In short, it was a great place to hide. The sojourn in Egypt was, of course, brief since Herod died in 4 BC or possibly 2 BC. Dionysius Exiguus, otherwise known as Denis the Small, a sixth-century monk (470–544), tinkered with the old Julian calendar and arrived at dates that do not match our expectations with the result that Jesus, believe it or not, was likely born around 5 BC.

With the death of Herod, the old saying from the prophet Hosea, "out of Egypt I called my son" (Hos. 11:1b), received new meaning, as it was now applied by the author of Matthew to Jesus himself. Originally, during the eighth century BC, Hosea had viewed the referent as Israel: "When Israel was a child, I loved him" (v. 1a). However, the two circles of meanings offered by Hosea and Matthew are not in conflict, but are in a typological relation to one another. That is, Hosea recalled the historic exodus when the Holy One of Israel delivered the ancient Israelites from Egyptian bondage. Matthew is well aware of these meanings and affirms them, but sees their fulfillment in the exodus of Jesus out of Egypt, a deliverance that will underscore that the God and Father of Jesus will set his people free in remarkably new ways. All of the historic meanings of Hosea's prophecy are affirmed. Nothing in the life of Jesus calls for their diminishment in the least or for their rejection. Rather, his life gathers up all of these ancient meanings and they then find their completion, their perfection, in his own life in a deliverance that he and his Father will bring about through the later giving of the Holy Spirit. Such a new exodus, brought about by God's Messiah, will deliver not simply from physical bondage (as great as this is), but also from the far greater spiritual bondage, the captivity of sin that oppresses all people, both Israelite and non-Israelite alike.

Observe also in this passage from Matthew that the Almighty is an evocative God, the one who calls forth, who addresses those in relation to him to follow in obedience the divine will and design. This relationship of obedience and trust, evidence of a lively faith, characterizes the life of Jesus as well, who as a true human being submitted his will to that of the Father.

The Prayer

Almighty God, I hear you calling to me in the saving acts of your Son, Jesus. In his life all the ancient prophecies and promises find their completion. I offer you my trust and my obedience, even when one comes more easily than the other.

The Questions

In what way does our text indicate how God the Father acted providentially in the life of Jesus? How does this overarching providence and care inform the story of Jesus? In what ways has God acted providentially in our own lives?

Day 4

John the Baptist

JOHN 1:29-34 *The next day John saw Jesus coming toward him and said, "Look, the Lamb of God, who takes away the sin of the world! This is the one I meant when I said, 'A man who comes after me has surpassed me because he was before me.' I myself did not know him, but the reason I came baptizing with water was that he might be revealed to Israel."*

Then John gave this testimony: "I saw the Spirit come down from heaven as a dove and remain on him. And I myself did not know him, but the one who sent me to baptize with water told me, 'The man on whom you see the Spirit come down and remain is the one who will baptize with the Holy Spirit.' I have seen and I testify that this is God's Chosen One."

Consider This

Our text about John the Baptist is preceded by the Pharisees questioning him as to why he was baptizing at all since he claimed that he was not the Messiah (vv. 24–25). "Among you stands one you do not know" (v. 26), came the cryptic reply. John himself was likewise a mysterious figure who spent much of his time in Judea, in the wilderness, and he preached a message of a coming judgment which required repentance—a turning around, a change of heart. As a prophet he was at times perceived as antisocial, especially due to his directness, since he warned Herod the tetrarch, for example, that he could not sleep with his brother's wife

(Matt. 14:3–5). Such a warning had infuriated the adulterous Herodias and such anger ultimately led to John the Baptist's death.

In our current text, John the Baptist hailed Jesus as "the Lamb of God, who takes away the sin of the world," and the following day, when he was with two of his own disciples, and in seeing Jesus pass by, John proclaimed again: "Look, the Lamb of God!" (vv. 35–36). What does such a phrase mean? Although this language has a biblical ring to it, as if it occurs often in Scripture, nevertheless, it is actually difficult to determine its exact referent. To illustrate, the author of the book of Revelation employs the image of a lamb, powerfully and often, but such usage celebrates triumph and victory over the enemies of God, whereas the Baptist underscores both sacrifice and suffering. Again, the book of Exodus describes the Passover lamb, another powerful image, but the lamb in that historic setting was not a sacrifice for sin, but was slain so that the angel of death might pass over the Hebrew houses whose lintels (a horizontal beam spanning the top of a door opening) had been sprinkled with blood. Also bear in mind that bulls, not lambs, were offered for the sacrifice of sins in Leviticus, though there is mention elsewhere of a lamb being offered on the altar in the morning and at twilight (Ex. 29:38–39), and so it is not clear that such usage corresponds to the meaning John the Baptist had in mind.

It may be that, in employing the phrase, "the Lamb of God, who takes away the sin of the world," John was a visionary and wonderfully prophetic. In other words, the life and death of Jesus of Nazareth would be so significant, brimming with meaning, that it would gather up the old understandings of the Hebrew faith (see Isaiah 53, especially vv. 7 and 10) and add to them new ones as well, ones never envisioned before, in a fullness that would be deeply and richly satisfying. Such newness is already evident in the very words that follow the pronouncement of the Lamb of God: "who takes away the sin of the world!" Indeed, the Gospel of John has underscored the universality of this *provision* in the often-quoted verse: "For God so loved *the world* that he gave his one and only Son, that whoever believes in him shall not perish but have eternal life" (John 3:16, emphasis added). The Gospel of John also taught that the Samaritans—kept at a distance by the Jews of the first century for numerous reasons, and thereby in many ways alienated, estranged, from the chosen people—came to know that they, too, were the beloved of God and that Jesus was referred to by them not simply as the Savior of the Jewish people but more broadly as, "the Savior of the *world*" (4:42, emphasis added).

When John the Baptist exclaimed, "I myself did not know him" (1:31a, 33a), meaning Jesus, we have to be careful in order to understand in what sense this statement was meant. Since Elizabeth, John the Baptist's mother, and Mary, the mother of Jesus, were relatives, perhaps cousins, then John could not have meant that he did not know Jesus at all, for that would not have been truthful—and prophets always tell the truth. Even though the two boys grew up about ninety miles away from each other—John in Judea and Jesus in Galilee—they would have likely heard family stories that would have filled out some helpful details. So, then, what would it mean to know Jesus in the way that John the Baptist had in mind?

If we could go back to the first century and meet Jesus, he would undoubtedly look like so many of the other young Jewish men of his day. He probably had a beard, although he might have been somewhat leaner than most due to rounds of fasting. His likely profession as a carpenter's son (Matt. 13:55), his level of education, his ethnicity, his religion, his customs, along with his economic class—all of this would have made him virtually indistinguishable from so many other men of his time. Indeed, in terms of all of these characteristics, Jesus would seem to be just another man: obscure, easily passed over, even invisible. And yet John's statement, given his background and the way he posed it, suggests that Jesus was different; he was exceptional.

Knowing Jesus in an all-too-human way would take John only so far. He quickly realized that. There was a limit, a border, that could not be crossed. Again, knowing Jesus in a fresh way would require nothing less than a revelation from on high: "the one who sent me to baptize with water told me, 'The man on whom you see the Spirit come down and remain is the one who will baptize with the Holy Spirit.'" Notice the difference here, because it is huge: John baptized with water but Jesus "will baptize with the Holy Spirit" and the Gospels of Matthew and Luke add: "and with fire" (Matt. 3:11; Luke 3:16). John's baptizing with water was something that any humble prophet calling the people to repentance could do. It was in the realm of human possibilities. But baptizing with the Holy Spirit, communicating the very presence of the Most High to the hearts and minds of those who are baptized, now that's something only God can do.

It's that "more" that describes who Jesus is, in terms of his basic identity, and one that John had come to know through the revelation entailed in the Spirit coming down upon and remaining on Jesus. It is then and only then that John the Baptist had been enlightened, and thereby empowered, to proclaim: "I have seen and I testify that this is God's Chosen One." Other translations of this verse are even more emphatic: "this is the Son of God" (John 1:34 NSRV). John came to this deeper knowledge by seeing the Spirit come down and remain upon Jesus. That same knowledge is promised to us today, not by nature of course, but by grace, for those who can see with the eyes of faith.

The Prayer

Lord Jesus, you were chosen by God and anticipated by the prophets, including your cousin John. Baptize me with your Holy Spirit and put testimony on my lips that you are God's chosen one, reconciling the world to yourself.

The Questions

What does John the Baptist mean by the phrase, "the Lamb of God" (John 1:29)? What are the characteristics of lambs, and how could they be understood to describe who God is in some sense?

Day 5

The Devil

MATTHEW 4:1–11 *Then Jesus was led by the Spirit into the wilderness to be tempted by the devil. After fasting forty days and forty nights, he was hungry. The tempter came to him and said, "If you are the Son of God, tell these stones to become bread."*

Jesus answered, "It is written: 'Man shall not live on bread alone, but on every word that comes from the mouth of God.'"

Then the devil took him to the holy city and had him stand on the highest point of the temple. "If you are the Son of God," he said, "throw yourself down. For it is written:

> *"'He will command his angels concerning you,*
>> *and they will lift you up in their hands,*
>> *so that you will not strike your foot against a stone.'"*

Jesus answered him, "It is also written: 'Do not put the Lord your God to the test.'"

Again, the devil took him to a very high mountain and showed him all the kingdoms of the world and their splendor. "All this I will give you," he said, "if you will bow down and worship me."

Jesus said to him, "Away from me, Satan! For it is written: 'Worship the Lord your God, and serve him only.'"

Then the devil left him, and angels came and attended him.

Consider This

The Gospel of Matthew, chapter 3, has already described the baptism of Jesus in the following way: "As soon as Jesus was baptized, he went up out of the water. At that moment heaven was opened, and he saw the Spirit of God descending like a dove and alighting on him. And a voice from heaven said, 'This is my Son, whom I love; with him I am well pleased'" (vv. 16–17). In the following chapter, our current text, readers learn that this very same Spirit who had descended upon Jesus like a dove at his baptism now led him into the wilderness to be tempted by the devil. So quickly comes the transition from a time of glory and revelation to a time of temptation and testing.

Though the Spirit led Jesus into the wilderness, notice it is the devil who will actually tempt him. As the epistle of James points out: "When tempted, no one should say, 'God is tempting me.' For God cannot be tempted by evil, nor does he tempt anyone" (1:13). To be sure, God would never tempt a man or woman with evil because the very nature of the Almighty is good, purely good, without any hint of evil at all. Put another way, precisely because of *who* God is, the Most High only wills the good for all creatures: "Do I take any pleasure in the death of the wicked? declares the Sovereign LORD. Rather, am I not pleased when they turn from their ways and live?" (Ezek. 18:23). Accordingly, the agent of the temptation in this setting was the devil, the accuser, the one who is described in this gospel as "the tempter" in verse 3 and as Satan, the adversary, in verse 10. The devil is a fallen creature, a filthy, perverted spirit who is ever in opposition to God. This scene in the desert, then, will be dramatic. The cast of characters, so to speak, could hardly be more weighty.

Some commentators on this passage, however, immediately empty out the drama of this narrative by claiming that Jesus was not really tempted at all.[1] It's all a show. Though the Greek word used in our text, *peirazō* (vv. 1, 3), can mean either "temptation" (as in 1 Cor. 7:5; James 1:13–14) or "testing," many interpreters much prefer the latter term. In other words, this was not a contest of sorts, but merely a demonstration. The wilderness scene with its forty days of fasting was simply the occasion, a wonderful opportunity, for Jesus of Nazareth to reveal who he was as a person in proper relation to God. Put another way, the devious schemes of the devil in this barren land were not actually temptations—no, not at all. Instead, they became for Jesus merely suitable occasions in which he could demonstrate his character in three different ways.

Though such an interpretation of our text is popular among commentators, we believe it is theologically problematic for two key reasons. First of all, the entirety of the New Testament reveals Jesus of Nazareth to be the God/Human, that is, as a person who has not one but two natures, both divine and human. Granted, we all know that the divine nature of Jesus cannot be tempted with evil. That's a given once we reflect on the very nature and being of God as we have just briefly done. However, though Jesus is fully divine, he is not *only* divine. He is also a *real* flesh-and-blood human being, and human nature can be tempted, after all, to break faith with God, to go contrary to the divine will. If one contends that such a temptation is not a possibility at all for Jesus— in other words, this option is excluded immediately by definition—then that's just another way of affirming that the divine nature of Jesus overshadows or, better yet, overpowers the human nature. The question could then be raised: Is Jesus really a human being like us with the one exception that he was and remains without sin?

Second, such a troubled interpretation detracts from the incarnation in terms of its extent—that the Word became flesh and descended to the very depths of human existence, where the possibility of temptation was real, not fiction. Again, if the divinity of Jesus prevented him from experiencing the anguish, the pain of temptation, then how could he comfort those who face on a daily basis the challenge and threat of genuine, annoying temptation? Opportunities for demonstrations of character hardly entail suffering.

In contrast, however, the author of the book of Hebrews has understood the two natures of Jesus properly, each in its place, and each fully, not partially, acknowledged. He understood that the extent of the incarnation (the Word becoming human) was so thorough that Jesus can commiserate, that is, be compassionate in terms of the suffering of all humanity as it is tempted with evil: "Because he himself *suffered* when he was tempted, he is able to help those who are being tempted" (Heb. 2:18, emphasis added). In fact, the author of the book of Hebrews is so insistent that this basic truth of proper teaching about Jesus be affirmed that he maintained that Jesus had been tempted *just like we are* with but one exception—he was and remained without sin: "For we do not have a high priest who is unable to empathize with our weaknesses, but we have one who has been tempted in every way, just as we are—yet he did not sin" (4:15).

The first temptation comes in the form of truth mingled with an appeal to doubt: "If you are the Son of God, tell these stones to become bread." Earlier in Matthew 3:17, a voice from heaven had declared: "This is my Son, whom I love; with him I am well pleased." The devil picked up that basic truth, but tried to get Jesus to question that reality by beginning with the little word *if*. Such a word choice is reflected in most modern translations of this passage, though the Common English Bible employs the word *since*.[2] This last word has the devil not casting doubt upon, but actually affirming, the sonship of Jesus. However, this is not a helpful interpretation of the larger truths being articulated here, especially when we remember how Jesus described the devil: "When he lies, he speaks his native language, for he is a liar and the father of lies" (John 8:44b).

Furthermore, the transition from "if " to "since" empties out the deceitfulness of the devil's ruse, props him up to make him a truth teller, and is unable to explain the larger dynamics in play. Indeed, the treachery of the devil in this setting is reminiscent of the serpent's temptation of Eve in which this liar mingled truth with falsity in order to get the woman to doubt: "Did God *really* say, 'You must not eat from any tree in the garden'?" (Gen. 3:1b, emphasis added). The parallels here are instructive but whereas the woman, along with the man, had failed the test put before them, Jesus succeeded. He would neither doubt his sonship nor would he attempt to prove it by making bread. Wisely, he took up "the sword of the Spirit, which is the word of God" (Eph. 6:17b), and quoted Deuteronomy 8:3b: "man does not live on bread alone but on every word that comes from the mouth of the Lord."

Any temptation can be strengthened by repetition and so, not surprisingly, the devil was at it again: "If you are the Son of God . . ." This time the father of lies had Jesus stand on the highest point of the temple, perhaps in a vision, and he suggested that Jesus throw himself down in a spectacular, awe-inspiring display: "For it is written: 'He will command his angels concerning you, and they will lift you up in their hands, so that you will not strike your foot against a stone.'"

Yes, Satan can quote Scripture (are we surprised?), and much, though not all, of Psalm 91:11–12 is cited here, though such quoting is always done with an evil design or purpose. In effect, this evil spirit had invited Jesus, as a true man, who has ever submitted his own will to that of the Father, to disrupt that holy relationship by testing God, by calling the Most High into account. Put another way, the command of the devil to Jesus to "throw yourself down" was an invitation to engage in reckless and foolish behavior that attempted to force the very hand of God. Jesus would have none of this, and so he rebuked Satan once more by citing Scripture: "Do not put the Lord your God to the test as you did at Massah" (Deut. 6:16). Interestingly enough, this reference was to the wilderness wanderings of the ancient Hebrews, who broke faith with the Holy One of Israel by their ongoing complaining and stubborn unbelief. Whereas the people had failed the test of their forty years of wilderness wanderings (remember only Caleb and Joshua of the original generation entered the promised land), Jesus passed his test of forty days by leaning on the Word of God in his time of trial.

In the third and last temptation of Jesus, the devil mixed it up a bit and abandoned the ploy of "If you are the Son of God." Instead, he took Jesus to a very high mountain, once again perhaps in a vision, and showed him all the kingdoms of the world and their splendor. All of this would be given to Jesus (can this promise, however, even be trusted?) but with one stipulation. This condition, tucked away at the end of a string of temptations, was remarkable but not in the way that we might initially expect. The artfulness of the devil—and the devil is indeed artful and cunning—most often consists in mixing truths and lies, in deception and deceit, in pretense and trickery, and yet here the evil one has come out into the open, into the light of day, to *reveal* his true design, what this period of trial, these manifold temptations, had been about all along. What is this singular condition? It is none other than "if you will bow down and worship me." There it is in full view. Satan, now out in the open, wanted that very thing that can belong to God alone, and so Jesus picked up the sword of the Spirit once more, in this case Deuteronomy 6:13a, and commanded: "Away from me, Satan! For it is written: 'Worship the Lord your God, and serve him only.'"

Neither power nor riches, neither kingdoms nor splendor, can ever take the place of the enormous good, beyond imagining, that is God. Jesus, in another context, said it well: "What good will it be for someone to gain the whole world, yet forfeit their soul? Or what can anyone give in exchange for their soul?" (Matt. 16:26).

The Prayer

Holy One of Israel, you who resisted the temptations of the devil by depending wholly on the Word of God and the presence of the Spirit, strengthen me so that I may also remain steadfast in you. I abide in you so that neither power nor riches, neither kingdoms nor splendor, will ever take your place in my heart.

The Questions

What's the difference between temptation and testing? Think of times when someone could be tested but not tempted. Think of other times when they would be outright tempted. How are these times different?

Day 6

Hometown Folk

MARK 6:1–6a *Jesus left there and went to his hometown, accompanied by his disciples. When the Sabbath came, he began to teach in the synagogue, and many who heard him were amazed.*

"Where did this man get these things?" they asked. "What's this wisdom that has been given him? What are these remarkable miracles he is performing? Isn't this the carpenter? Isn't this Mary's son and the brother of James, Joseph, Judas and Simon? Aren't his sisters here with us?" And they took offense at him.

Jesus said to them, "A prophet is not without honor except in his own town, among his relatives and in his own home." He could not do any miracles there, except lay his hands on a few sick people and heal them. He was amazed at their lack of faith.

Consider This

In the early chapters of the Gospel of Mark, Jesus had focused his ministry in and around Capernaum in Galilee, where he healed many people and taught them through the use of parables. Now he was around twenty-five miles to the southwest in his hometown of Nazareth, although Mark does not specifically mention the name of the town. Jesus was not alone, but was accompanied by his disciples. This was much more than the loose grouping of an entourage, for his disciples were deeply committed to Jesus. He entered the town then, from all appearances, as a gifted teacher, a rabbi, and he, therefore, headed for the synagogue.

The hometown folk who gathered in their familiar place of worship had heard many rabbis before, but on that day, Jesus was someone different, set apart. In listening to him, the people were amazed at his teaching; however, they simply couldn't put it all together. Astonished that a hometown boy could speak in such a way, and hearing reports of his miracles, the people raised six questions that expressed their puzzlement. Remarkably, these questions fall neatly into two distinct groups. The first three questions, for example, express the surprise of the local people, some of whom were perhaps Jesus's neighbors as he was growing up, as to where he got such a teaching. In other words, what was the source of such insight? Beyond this, they marveled at both his wisdom and the miracles he had done. His reputation had apparently preceded him.

If we were to stop this account with the first three questions then we could never understand why the local folk "took offense at him," as our text declares in verse 3. The Greek verb for "took offense" in our passage is the root from which the English word *scandalize* is derived. That's an unusually strong and negative reaction that could hardly be explained by the raising of these first three questions. Indeed, by themselves the initial queries should have led at least some of the people from his hometown to become the followers of Jesus, if not his disciples. What then scandalized the people? It was not the first three questions, but the second three.

The first question of the second set, "Isn't this the carpenter?" actually begins to reveal some of the prejudices of the people. If Jesus was a carpenter, or more generally speaking a craftsman of sorts, then how could he enjoy the time, the leisure for study, that is normally required for the wisdom he had uttered? It takes many years of concentrated study to become a rabbi, even in the first century. Besides, Jesus as a carpenter would be associating with "the wrong sort of people" in his daily environment, in his workaday world. The bias of the people, mistaken in so many respects, is demonstrated in their judgment that, in effect, working-class people, common laborers, cannot be wise. In this very narrow and diminished world, people are immediately and flippantly judged; that is, they are limited, even imprisoned, in their social roles. Jesus, however, always baffled the prejudiced.

The second and third questions of the second set have to do with the family heritage of Jesus, a network of familial relations that would, of course, be known by the hometown folk: "Isn't this Mary's son and the brother of James, Joseph, Judas and Simon?" Again, "Aren't his sisters here with us?" However, how many people, then as now, are so very different in some important respects from the members of their own households in which they grew up? Grounded in a setting of love and support (though sometimes perhaps not so much), family members can build on this and yet chart new courses as they find their own path in life. Again, much like a chosen occupation, an early familial setting is not destiny. It doesn't define us as people. In short, men and women cannot be adequately understood by simply referring to their family tree or their occupation. Such a prejudice, in a slightly different form, even marked

Nathanael, a disciple of Jesus, who questioned on one occasion: "Nazareth! Can anything good come from there?" (John 1:46).

The second set of questions has resulted in a much different response from the people than the first set would have ever done: "they took offense at him." What was the scandal? Considerations in terms of both occupation and family gave the townsfolk a false sense that they actually knew who Jesus was. In their minds, at least, they had him all sized up; they had him in a box. They *already* knew him. Here, as in so many other instances, "familiarity breeds contempt." We think we know someone if we know their occupation, their class, their likely income level, their family heritage, where they grew up—but we actually don't. We're only fooling ourselves. We mistake image for reality, outward appearances for what actually is. A person, a living soul created in the image and likeness of God, is far greater than such things. Accordingly, Jesus had the audacity, at least in the minds of the people at the synagogue, to speak and act in ways well beyond what limits they had already conjured up in their minds. He had transgressed their expectations. You can almost hear the additional, derisive comments and complaints, not recorded by Mark, that likely surfaced on that day: "Who do you think you are?" "What makes you so high and mighty?" Put another way, in this honor-and-shame culture, the people were likely ruminating, "He thinks he's better than us! We'll remind him where he came from."

Unable to get out from under the pile of prejudices that they had stacked up, the local folk were deeply troubled, for they couldn't make sense of the identity of Jesus—and it disturbed them. He baffled them at every turn. Mistaking familiarity for genuine knowledge, the people "didn't know what they didn't know," as the saying goes. For them, Jesus was and remained a stranger.

The Prayer

Holy God, I trade mere familiarity with you for intimacy with you. I not only marvel at your words, but receive them as the way to eternal life. Transform every recess of my heart from darkness to light, and may I radiate your goodness as you help me on my way to salvation.

The Questions

Have you ever had the experience of family members putting you in a box because of something that happened when you were young and, in their minds at least, you can never get beyond this image? How does that make you feel? What is the way forward?

Day 7

The Family of Jesus

MARK 3:20–21; 31–35 *Then Jesus entered a house, and again a crowd gathered, so that he and his disciples were not even able to eat. When his family heard about this, they went to take charge of him, for they said, "He is out of his mind." . . .*

Then Jesus' mother and brothers arrived. Standing outside, they sent someone in to call him. A crowd was sitting around him, and they told him, "Your mother and brothers are outside looking for you."

"Who are my mother and my brothers?" he asked. Then he looked at those seated in a circle around him and said, "Here are my mother and my brothers! Whoever does God's will is my brother and sister and mother."

Consider This

These two passages from the Gospel of Mark clearly belong together and form bookends around material that will be taken up in the Day 8 entry. Since these two passages are strongly connected, then this means that the family described in the first one can now be identified with the mother and brothers of Jesus in the second one. Such a connection has been difficult to acknowledge for some interpreters because in each of these passages Jesus's own family, his flesh-and-blood relations, have trouble understanding just who he is.

Though Jesus was still in the early phases of his ministry, he nevertheless challenged the authority of the

Pharisees, religious leaders who called for the rigorous observance of the Jewish law as they were interpreting it. His family probably heard reports of this controversial activity, so when they learned in addition that Jesus and his disciples were so caught up in ministry they were not even able to eat, they decided to take action: "they went to take charge of him." The Greek verb used here is strong and suggests decisive action on the part of his family. For example, when Mark employs this same verb elsewhere, in Mark 6:17, for example, it is translated into English as "arrest."

Why was the family of Jesus so concerned? The obvious answer, judging from the text, is that Jesus and his disciples were neglecting their basic bodily needs in not eating. However, this issue alone hardly seems sufficient to explain the strong-minded action on the part of his family. What else might be involved here? For one thing, first-century Israel was an honor-and-shame culture. Perhaps the members of his family feared many of the actions of Jesus, along with his increasing popularity, would eventually pose significant social problems for them with regard to their reputations, especially their networks of family, friends, and synagogue. Or perhaps they were concerned about Jesus leaving behind his stable occupation as a carpenter, passed along to him by Joseph, only to take up the drifting life of a wandering preacher. Who knows?

At any rate, the subsequent charge that "He is out of his mind," which forms the climax of the first passage, cannot be explained by an appeal to skipping a meal or two. Something else was going on here. It probably had to do with the person of Jesus, his basic identity, and how he had chosen to live his life. Already Jesus had given abundant evidence in his baptism and subsequent ministry that he was utterly dedicated to the worship of the Most High by proclaiming the kingdom of God: "'The time has come,' he said. 'The kingdom of God has come near. Repent and believe the good news!'" (Mark 1:15). The entire family of Jesus likely shared this value as well, but perhaps not (at least at this point) in the same way that Jesus did. Such a difference in how a value is held may be a prescription for trouble or at least for misunderstanding. It is one thing to have a constellation of values; it is quite another thing to make the hard judgment calls that are involved in the process of ranking those many values (work, family, reputation, bodily needs, etc.) where one, and only one, emerges as preeminent.

It appears from our passage that Jesus had placed such an emphasis on the worship of God, through the proclamation of the kingdom, that he, as well as his disciples, were willing to let go of other lesser needs for a while due to the considerable importance that Jesus attached to the glorification of God above all. The distance between the highest value of Jesus (worship of the Father, see John 6:38 and 14:31) and the next value in his ranking was far greater, much broader, than what would be entailed in the judgments of his family. Indeed, what the members of his family found so offensive, so much so that they claimed Jesus was "out of his mind," was the unswerving focus, the energetic intensity, and the enthusiastic zeal of a man who was so utterly dedicated to God. But that's Jesus.

Our second passage reveals that Mary and the brothers of Jesus finally arrived, but notice that they did not enter the room where Jesus was. Instead, they sent someone else inside to call him. This person, whoever it was, did not speak directly to Jesus, but to the crowd who surrounded him. Indeed, it was the crowd, likely made up of the disciples of Jesus given what he subsequently said about them, who informed him: "Your mother and brothers are outside looking for you." The response of Jesus, in receiving this information, is surprising, for he asked: "Who are my mother and my brothers?" What could such a question possibly mean? Jesus quickly offered an answer in looking at those seated around him and exclaimed: "Here are my mother and my brothers! Whoever does God's will is my brother and sister and mother."

Observe once again in this second passage, and in a way similar to the first, that Jesus gives evidence of a commitment to a preeminent value—to the worship of God above all else, and it holds priority over every other value, even over the strength of family relationships and blood ties. Later in Mark's gospel, for example, Jesus will declare: "No one who has left home or brothers or sisters or mother or father or children or fields for me and the gospel will fail to receive a hundred times as much in this present age: homes, brothers, sisters, mothers, children and fields—along with persecutions—and in the age to come eternal life" (Mark 10:29–30). If we compare this passage with a similar one found in Matthew, "Anyone who loves their father or mother more than me is not worthy of me; anyone who loves their son or daughter more than me is not worthy of me" (10:37), we see once again the unwavering focus of Jesus on the will of God, which is now clearly identified with him—a focus that takes precedence over everything else, even over such things as family, clan, tribe, and nation.

This teaching of Jesus was nothing less than revolutionary for first-century Israel on both a social and a religious level. In fact, it was perceived by some in that society as disruptive of the way things ought to be. It not only decentered family life, with its matter-of-fact blood relations, pointing it to something higher, but it also challenged a religious order that had grown presumptuous in thinking that family trees and proper ancestry necessarily guaranteed divine favor. Being a literal descendant of Abraham (if such lineage could even be proved in the first century) did not assure a privileged status in the sight of God. It, too, has now been decentered in the teaching of Jesus to make room for a larger and more embracing vision, one that will ultimately include Gentiles as well. Put another way, the consequences of doing the will of God, as Jesus so clearly affirmed, are far greater than both family ties as well as some of the mistaken judgments embedded in the religious order of the day. Such a teaching, then, would bring enormous hope to the masses.

The Prayer

God of Israel, in whom there is neither Jew nor Gentile, slave nor free, male nor female—thank you for welcoming me into your family and claiming me as your own. May your kingdom come and your will be done in my heart, home, church, and community, and any other allegiance be rightly ordered around your loving reign.

The Questions

Why is the proper ordering of our loves so necessary for the glorification of God and for the love of our neighbor?

In what way is the value of worshiping God unlike all other values? How does this value, if rightly held, decenter all other values?

Day 8

The Scribes

MARK 3:22–30 *And the teachers of the law who came down from Jerusalem said, "He is possessed by Beelzebul! By the prince of demons he is driving out demons."*

So Jesus called them over to him and began to speak to them in parables: "How can Satan drive out Satan? If a kingdom is divided against itself, that kingdom cannot stand. If a house is divided against itself, that house cannot stand. And if Satan opposes himself and is divided, he cannot stand; his end has come. In fact, no one can enter a strong man's house without first tying him up. Then he can plunder the strong man's house. Truly I tell you, people can be forgiven all their sins and every slander they utter, but whoever blasphemes against the Holy Spirit will never be forgiven; they are guilty of an eternal sin."

He said this because they were saying, "He has an impure spirit."

Consider This

Jesus had been ministering in the general area of Galilee, and he cast out an impure spirit in the town of Capernaum. This healing, in conjunction with others, and with the teaching of Jesus clearly on display in the local synagogue—all of this created astonishment and wonder among the people. Not surprisingly, news about Jesus spread quickly throughout the region and crowds began to follow him.

Jesus had sparked such interest among the people, both near and far, that the teachers of the law, also known as scribes, got wind of it and decided to make the three-day trip from Jerusalem to Galilee. Perhaps they were representatives of the Sanhedrin who were now curious or maybe even a little bit jealous. We don't know for sure. At any rate, these scribes from Jerusalem, unlike the crowds, were singularly unimpressed with the signs and wonders that Jesus had brought about. Such miracles simply left them cold and with a very critical spirit. In their minds, at least, Jesus was likely a magician of sorts who was fooling the masses, a view that emerged much later in the writing of the Babylonian Talmud in the sixth century AD.[1]

Even before speaking a single word with Jesus, the scribes from Jerusalem were ready to pronounce their judgment on both him and his ministry—and it was harsh. First of all, they claimed that Jesus was possessed by Beelzebul. The exact origin or etymology of this odd-sounding word is difficult to determine. It could possibly refer to the Canaanite deity Baal in which Baal-Zebul would then refer to the "lord of the house or temple."[2] Or perhaps this may not be the case at all. In any event, our current passage shows us at least this much: the scribes, themselves, associated Beelzebul with "the prince of demons," and Jesus apparently identified it in his subsequent parable with Satan. Either way, this was very bad company indeed.

Second, the scribes contended that in his ministry Jesus was employing "the prince of demons" as his major instrument or tool to drive out the lesser demons. The Gospel of Matthew, unlike Mark, records the likely incident that led to this mistaken judgment: "Then they brought him a demon-possessed man who was blind and mute, and Jesus healed him, so that he could both talk and see" (Matt. 12:22). The people who witnessed this miracle were so astounded that they exclaimed, "Could this be the Son of David?" (v. 23). But the scribes would have none of this.

Evil persons, revealed through the ongoing manifestation of prejudice or animosity, have little to do with the truth. Operating out of a strong aversion and a commitment to ill will, such persons not only fail to see what light is right in front of their eyes—such that they become, in effect, blind—but they also involve themselves in embarrassing contradictions that render their judgments both confused and ultimately worthless. As a careful thinker, Jesus naturally picked up on all of this as it played out in the contorted reasoning of the scribes.

What's so unexpected about the reply of Jesus to the religious leaders is that he took a very pastoral, indirect, and even a non-defensive approach to them. For example, Jesus could have started out with himself in a very defensive posture and complained: "How dare you say such things about me!" "Who are you to say that I am possessed by Beelzebul?" "Don't you know who I am?" or "Don't you realize who my Father is?" Jesus, however, did none of this. Instead, he took up the accusation of casting out demons by the prince of demons. Sensing something of the great emotional distance between himself and the scribes on this allegation, Jesus offered an analogy as a bridge through which the religious leaders could realize the grave error entailed in their own thinking along with its mistaken judgments.

In his response, Jesus considered the charge, "By the prince of demons he is driving out demons," by setting up a comparison between the prince of demons and lesser demons on the one hand, and kingdoms and houses respectively, on the other hand. Just as a kingdom divided against itself cannot stand, and just as a house divided against itself cannot stand, so, too, Satan divided against himself cannot stand. When a war is waged against one's own household, then everyone is defeated. The reasoning here is careful, orderly, and thoroughly convincing.

Now consider this: the scribes had already acknowledged that Jesus was, after all, casting out demons; there's no argument here. Moreover, after the initial stages of the reasoning of Jesus, in the form of an analogy, the religious leaders should have understood that Satan cannot cast out Satan. It's absurd to think so. If that's the case, then the next obvious question would be: "Who, then, is actually casting out the demons?" Jesus continued the analogy so that the scribes could learn this truth for themselves. It is the one, and only the one, who ties up the strong man and then plunders his house. Who does this tying up and plundering? It is none other than Jesus. The Gospel of Matthew's account of this same incident is revealing: "But if it is by the Spirit of God that I drive out demons, then the kingdom of God has come upon you" (12:28). The scribes had conjured up the kingdom of Satan in their imaginings. That's all they saw. Jesus's actions through the Spirit of God brought about the kingdom of God, not as some imagining, but in reality. It's difficult to draw a stronger contrast.

In the earlier chapters of the Gospel of Mark, Jesus had already exercised great authority that underscored his divine nature. For example, he not only forgave the sins of the paralyzed man as he healed him (2:5), but he also proclaimed that "the Son of Man is Lord even of the Sabbath" (v. 28). In a similar vein, Jesus subsequently affirmed in our present passage that all sins and blasphemies (or slanders) can be forgiven humanity with but one exception. That affirmation itself is wonderful news for anyone who has ever suffered under the heavy burden of guilt. What, however, is that one exception that has no forgiveness? It is only the blasphemy against the Holy Spirit that constitutes an eternal sin.

Throughout the history of the church, some have suffered needlessly in thinking that they have committed this unpardonable sin. However, the mere fact that they are concerned about this matter, that their consciences are troubled or even on fire, so to speak, is a sure sign that they have not committed this sin at all. Indeed, this is not a common sin but a very rare one. It entails identifying the Holy Spirit as evil. That's a terrible thing to do; in fact, it's downright wicked. Since the Holy Spirit is the one who leads sinners to repentance, then that possibility is now cut off. Notice, however, it's not because God does not want to forgive sins. God remains loving and desires the salvation of all (1 Tim. 2:4). It's because those who commit this grave sin don't want to receive the forgiveness that is so graciously offered through the ministrations of the Holy Spirit. If that same Holy Spirit is rejected at the outset, called evil, then how could forgiveness ever be received? It's a nonstarter. In such a case there is no hope; there is only despair.

Once again, however, Jesus surprises us. He responded to the scribes because they had been claiming that he had an impure spirit. Did Jesus condemn them? Did he curse them? No, instead Jesus, like a good physician, cautioned them strongly. He warned them of the grave danger entailed in attributing to the very Spirit of God what could only pertain to Satan. Sometimes it is what we judge to be the simple things that are actually the most important of all. It is ever a mark of honesty, abundant sincerity, and deep spiritual wisdom to be able to call the good, "good" and evil, "evil." In fact, it takes great courage to do so especially in a corrupted age, one oriented toward lies.

The Prayer

Dear Holy Spirit, you are the empowering presence of God in our world. I honor you for giving me good gifts that sustain me daily. Protect and preserve me from every kind of danger, including those of my own heart, from this broken world, or from spiritual darkness. Align me with your purposes so that I might recognize and participate in your gracious acts.

The Questions

What harm is done to both ourselves and to others when we demonize our enemies or use defamatory language? Why should Christians, in particular, take special care in this area, as James 3:5–6 warns?

Day 9

The Pharisees

JOHN 9:13–34 *They brought to the Pharisees the man who had been blind. Now the day on which Jesus had made the mud and opened the man's eyes was a Sabbath. Therefore the Pharisees also asked him how he had received his sight. "He put mud on my eyes," the man replied, "and I washed, and now I see."*

Some of the Pharisees said, "This man is not from God, for he does not keep the Sabbath."

But others asked, "How can a sinner perform such signs?" So they were divided.

Then they turned again to the blind man, "What have you to say about him? It was your eyes he opened."

The man replied, "He is a prophet."

They still did not believe that he had been blind and had received his sight until they sent for the man's parents. "Is this your son?" they asked. "Is this the one you say was born blind? How is it that now he can see?"

"We know he is our son," the parents answered, "and we know he was born blind. But how he can see now, or who opened his eyes, we don't know. Ask him. He is of age; he will speak for himself." His parents said this because they were afraid of the Jewish leaders, who already had decided that anyone who acknowledged that Jesus was the Messiah would be put out of the synagogue. That was why his parents said, "He is of age; ask him."

A second time they summoned the man who had been blind. "Give glory to God by telling the truth," they said. "We know this man is a sinner."

He replied, "Whether he is a sinner or not, I don't know. One thing I do know. I was blind but now I see!"

Then they asked him, "What did he do to you? How did he open your eyes?"

He answered, "I have told you already and you did not listen. Why do you want to hear it again? Do you want to become his disciples too?"

Then they hurled insults at him and said, "You are this fellow's disciple! We are disciples of Moses! We know that God spoke to Moses, but as for this fellow, we don't even know where he comes from."

The man answered, "Now that is remarkable! You don't know where he comes from, yet he opened my eyes. We know that God does not listen to sinners. He listens to the godly person who does his will. Nobody has ever heard of opening the eyes of a man born blind. If this man were not from God, he could do nothing."

To this they replied, "You were steeped in sin at birth; how dare you lecture us!" And they threw him out.

Consider This

Earlier Jesus had healed this man born blind by placing mud on his eyes and ordering him to wash in the pool of Siloam. His neighbors could hardly believe that this person, whose sight had been restored, was the same man who used to sit and beg. They, therefore, brought this man to the Pharisees for some questioning, for they likewise were very curious about this matter.

The religious leaders had a basic problem given the judgments that they had already made. In their eyes, since Jesus did this miracle on the Sabbath, then he had to be a sinner because the faithful keep the Sabbath by avoiding work. This judgment, however, only led to further difficulties for the Pharisees, for if Jesus was judged to be a sinner, then how could such a person do this marvelous work? In fact, some among the Pharisees raised this very question: "How can a sinner perform such signs?" revealing something of the division even among them. The religious leadership then asked the man born blind: "What have you to say about him?" He responded, "He is a prophet." Not content with this answer, they then turned to his parents who affirmed that their son was indeed born blind, but they did not understand how he could now see. Fearful of perhaps being cast out of the synagogue, the parents then moved all responsibility over to their son, "Ask him. He is of age."

All of this was getting nowhere, and so the Pharisees began a second round of interrogation—and that's what it was—by inviting the man to "give glory to God." The use of this particular phrase was another way of saying that the religious leaders did not believe the account of the miracle, again since it had been performed on the Sabbath, and they were, therefore, urging the man to come clean with the truth. A similar phrase, "give glory to the LORD," is employed in Joshua 7:19 in which Joshua exhorted Achan to confess the evil he had done.[1]

The Pharisees then exclaimed, speaking out of their own assumptions and presuppositions, "We know this man is a sinner." The healed man replied by stating the clear and unshakable fact from which he would never depart in this dialogue: "One thing I do know. I was blind but now I see!" Not content with this answer, the Pharisees asked the man yet again: "How did he open your eyes?" Clearly frustrated by this point, the man born blind had the audacity to shoot back, "I have told you already and you did not listen. Why do you want to hear it again? Do you want to become his disciples too?" Undoubtedly angry at being spoken to in this way, the Pharisees hurled insults at the man and declared: "You are this fellow's disciple! We are disciples of Moses!"

Who would have ever imagined that this brief passage in the Gospel of John is the doorway to a great debate, a portal to one of the greatest contests possible? It's as if we've stumbled onto a particular door in a very large building and entered a hallowed hall in which the debaters are already seated. We hurry to our seats, embarrassed that we are slightly late. On the one side are several religious leaders who are finely dressed, reflecting their power and status. On the other side is a single man who has spent almost his entire life begging, and so he evidently could not afford what many people would consider to be the proper attire for the occasion.

The Pharisees laid out their argument for the audience in the following way:

- Keeping the Sabbath requires doing no work.
- Jesus healed the man born blind on the Sabbath.
- In healing the blind man, Jesus did work on the Sabbath.
- In doing work on the Sabbath, Jesus broke the Sabbath.
- Since Jesus broke the Sabbath, he is, therefore, a sinner.

The conclusion of this thinking from which the religious leaders never departed was that Jesus was a rank sinner. Since sinners cannot do great signs and wonders whose source is God, that's why the Pharisees spent so much of their effort trying to explain away the miracle itself with their rounds of questioning. Either the man wasn't actually blind from birth, but had a temporary condition that could be remedied, or else Jesus was a charlatan. But were there other options to be considered?

The man born blind, who was likely poor and obviously intelligent, argued much differently. Unlike the Pharisees, with their years of education, he had a very important fact on his side, and facts can be very powerful things even if you're poor and have very little status. He knew beyond question that Jesus had healed him. In other words, his starting point was much different from that of the religious leaders. He began with the reality of the miracle and then branched out from there. He thought about the implications of the miracle for the identity of Jesus himself. From that vantage point, he then chipped away at the assumption of the Pharisees that Jesus was a sinner. Such a judgment just wouldn't hold up; he knew that. The blind man showed this in two key ways.

First of all, he reasoned: "We know that God does not listen to sinners." It's not that God doesn't hear the prayers of repentant sinners, those who are heartily sorry for their sins. Of course, the Most High hears such humble prayers. To forgive is, after all, divine. It's rather that God will not work in a favored way, such as to perform a miracle, through someone who is set against the divine will through a life of stubborn, willful sin. Second, the healed man argued: "If this man were not from God, he could do nothing." Since, however, Jesus did, in fact, do something—perform a miracle—then he must be from God. Observe that the miracle Jesus brought about was not something similar to what the ancient Egyptians had performed, during the time of Moses, through their use of magic when they, too, turned water into blood or called forth a colony of frogs (see Exodus 7:14–8:7). No, the miracle of Jesus was in an entirely different category. Never before had a person *born* blind been so wonderfully healed. The miracle of Jesus was simply stupendous.

At the end of this great debate the two different sides drew their conclusions and lived into them, so to speak. In terms of the blind man, he was evidently by now a disciple of Jesus, for he knew that this miracle worker was from God, and he would later worship him (John 9:38). For their part, the Pharisees maintained the fiction that Jesus was a sinner (utterly discounting the miracle) and they then turned around and made this judgment a plank of what it meant to be a disciple of Moses. Here was a genuine though unnecessary parting of the ways. From henceforth, being a disciple of Jesus and being a disciple of Moses would be presented as two different, even contradictory, things. In fact, as Gary Burge points out in his own observation on this passage: "In modern-day Israel, a Jew can give up everything about his or her faith, even becoming an atheist, and still be considered a Jew in order to take up Israeli citizenship. The one thing that invalidates 'Jewishness' is belief in Jesus. The deep irony is that an atheist is still Jewish, but a 'messianic Jew' is not."[2]

But what if, back in the first century, the Pharisees had come to doubt some aspects of their own theology, that is, how they thought about God? What if they had recognized that healing a man born blind from birth on the Sabbath was not the work of a sinner but the work of the Holy One of Israel?

The Prayer

Jesus, you who mercifully gave us the Sabbath as a time of rest and healing, thank you that your grace extends to every hour of every day. Help us to celebrate truth wherever we find it, promote goodness in every opportunity, and behold beauty as you designed it.

The Questions

The Gospel of John works with the powerful images of light and darkness, sight and blindness. In what ways does the blind man have sight? In what ways are the religious leaders blind? How does sight and blindness relate to the issue of truth?

Day 10

The Teachers of the Law

MARK 2:1–12 *A few days later, when Jesus again entered Capernaum, the people heard that he had come home. They gathered in such large numbers that there was no room left, not even outside the door, and he preached the word to them. Some men came, bringing to him a paralyzed man, carried by four of them. Since they could not get him to Jesus because of the crowd, they made an opening in the roof above Jesus by digging through it and then lowered the mat the man was lying on. When Jesus saw their faith, he said to the paralyzed man, "Son, your sins are forgiven."*

Now some teachers of the law were sitting there, thinking to themselves, "Why does this fellow talk like that? He's blaspheming! Who can forgive sins but God alone?"

Immediately Jesus knew in his spirit that this was what they were thinking in their hearts, and he said to them, "Why are you thinking these things? Which is easier: to say to this paralyzed man, 'Your sins are forgiven,' or to say, 'Get up, take your mat and walk'? But I want you to know that the Son of Man has authority on earth to forgive sins." So he said to the man, "I tell you, get up, take your mat and go home." He got up, took his mat and walked out in full view of them all. This amazed everyone and they praised God, saying, "We have never seen anything like this!"

Consider This

Jesus had been traveling throughout Galilee, and he now returned to Capernaum, a city where he often stayed when he was in the north. Word of mouth announced his arrival and a crowd gathered around the house in which he was preaching, possibly that of Simon and Andrew,[1] such that even the entrance was blocked with people. Determined that a paralytic man would have an audience with Jesus, four men dug a hole in the likely mud-and-thatch roof, one that could be easily repaired. They then lowered the man into the presence of Jesus.

What Jesus did next, in seeing the faith of all involved, the paralytic included, no doubt surprised the people at that time just as it continues to astonish us today. That is, Jesus did not immediately heal the man (which, for us, seems to be his most obvious need); instead, he declared: "Son, your sins are forgiven." What could this statement possibly mean? Among the Jews of the period, there was indeed a strong association of sin and illness. In fact, even the disciples of Jesus had already raised this question in terms of the man born blind: "Rabbi, who sinned, this man or his parents, that he was born blind?" (John 9:2). Jesus replied, however, "Neither this man nor his parents sinned . . . but this happened so that the works of God might be displayed in him" (v. 3).

We have to be very careful in this area so that people who are already burdened with disease or illness are not further burdened by negative judgments that are both uncalled for and very inappropriate. Granted, some sin is strongly associated with disease: promiscuity, laziness, and poor stewardship of the body, especially in terms of eating and drinking, but not all disease or illness is connected with sin as its generating source. It just doesn't work that way. Even today, doctors and other medical staff are baffled in terms of the causes of some diseases. Pathogens do not follow a hard-and-fast moral order. They don't follow an ethical trajectory, but a biological one. Catching the flu, COVID-19, or some other virus is not necessarily the occasion for repentance. The book of Job should have already taught us such things.

Again, take note of what Jesus did. He declared to the paralytic that his sins were forgiven, thereby highlighting the specific authority of Jesus himself, and not simply the more general authority that even a Jewish priest would enjoy in pronouncing forgiveness on behalf of God. How do we know this? It is evident from the text, because the teachers of the law, or scribes, thought to themselves that Jesus was blaspheming. In their minds, at least, Jesus was exercising a power—indeed, a prerogative—that rightly belonged to God alone. Lines of properly established religious authority may also be in the mix here, because Jesus had just skirted the authority of the priests, the Sadducees, as the ones who were duly ordained to pronounce the forgiveness of sins in the name of the Almighty. Simply put, the directness of Jesus, going around the usual channels, was patently offensive to the scribes. Once again, we can almost hear the internal rumblings among the teachers of the law, "Who does he think he is?" that now comes in the form of their actual question: "Who can forgive sins but God alone?"

Accepting this challenge to his authority, Jesus, in turn, posed a question to the religious leaders that on its surface appeared to be easy and straightforward, but upon further reflection it was actually not the case at all on both counts. Let's take a look at this more carefully. Notice that Jesus raised a *comparative* question in the following way: "Which is easier: to say to this paralyzed man, 'Your sins are forgiven,' or to say, 'Get up, take your mat and walk'?" Before we open up this question with its several parts, kindly keep in mind that the question also implies that there is a distinction between *saying* something and *doing* something. Indeed, we are already very familiar with this distinction in the old adage, "Easier said than done."

Let's just explore for now the first level of *saying* something. Is it easier to say, "Your sins are forgiven," or to say, "Get up, take your mat and walk"? On the one hand, if Jesus said to the paralytic that his sins were forgiven, then how would we know that his sins were indeed forgiven? Would there be any evidence of this? If not, it seems that this is easy to say for how could such a declaration be refuted? On the other hand, if Jesus said to the paralytic, "Get up, take your mat and walk," then how would we know that this saying was true or that it demonstrated real authority? Would there be any evidence of this? The answer is yes. Evidence would come in the form of the paralytic actually doing what Jesus had commanded, that is, getting up and walking. So then, this second saying appears to be harder because the evidence for its fulfillment should be readily observed. Notice also the question of Jesus was already moving in the direction from *saying* something to *doing* something as important elements that will help to confirm his authority.

Now Jesus already knew that he would heal the man. He also, however, wanted to demonstrate his authority to forgive sins, a forgiveness that does not always have clear signs when it occurs. He could accomplish all of this by raising the comparative question to the teachers of the law by drawing a relation between the forgiveness of sins, on the one hand, and the healing of a paralyzed man, on the other hand. Why would this be so helpful? Jesus assumed that to heal such a man, with all its evidence of getting up, taking your mat, and walking, would be received as *the act of God* that it is. With his comparative question in place, then all who witnessed this miracle, this powerful sign and wonder, could then make the transition from doing something to saying something, from healing a man to declaring that his sins were forgiven. The power of God would be the common denominator; it was entailed in each instance.

Though Jesus as a good teacher likely set up this comparison as an aid to belief, for both the scribes and for those assembled around him in the house, the focus of attention was not actually on the deeds themselves, as great as they were, but on *the doer* of the deeds and his authority which is simply divine. After all, it may actually be harder to forgive sins (and so forgiving sins is, after all, an action as well and not simply a declaration) than it is to raise up a paralyzed man—and we think that it is. Doing the one, then, would not necessarily imply the other—although in this case it did. Why was this so? It is because Jesus, through this miracle (as well as through several others), demonstrated quite clearly his *authority and trustworthiness* and, in this particular case, his divine nature as well. The "who" here was far more important than any "what."

The Prayer

Heavenly Father, thank you that your Son has both the authority to forgive sins as well as the desire to heal us of sickness. May your kingdom come and your will be done here on earth, in all of its fullness.

The Questions

In what ways is sin associated with suffering? In what ways is sin not associated with suffering? Can one be a sinner and avoid much suffering? Can a sinful life lead to lasting happiness?

Day 11

Simon, the Pharisee

LUKE 7:36–50 *When one of the Pharisees invited Jesus to have dinner with him, he went to the Pharisee's house and reclined at the table. A woman in that town who lived a sinful life learned that Jesus was eating at the Pharisee's house, so she came there with an alabaster jar of perfume. As she stood behind him at his feet weeping, she began to wet his feet with her tears. Then she wiped them with her hair, kissed them and poured perfume on them.*

When the Pharisee who had invited him saw this, he said to himself, "If this man were a prophet, he would know who is touching him and what kind of woman she is—that she is a sinner."

Jesus answered him, "Simon, I have something to tell you."

"Tell me, teacher," he said.

"Two people owed money to a certain moneylender. One owed him five hundred denarii, and the other fifty. Neither of them had the money to pay him back, so he forgave the debts of both. Now which of them will love him more?"

Simon replied, "I suppose the one who had the bigger debt forgiven."

"You have judged correctly," Jesus said.

Then he turned toward the woman and said to Simon, "Do you see this woman? I came into your house. You did not give me any water for my feet, but she wet my feet with her tears and wiped them with her hair. You did not give me a kiss, but this woman, from the time I entered, has not stopped kissing my feet. You did not put oil on my head, but she has poured perfume on my feet. Therefore, I tell you, her many sins have been forgiven—as her great love has shown. But whoever has been forgiven little loves little."

Then Jesus said to her, "Your sins are forgiven."

The other guests began to say among themselves, "Who is this who even forgives sins?"

Jesus said to the woman, "Your faith has saved you; go in peace."

Consider This

This account of an anointing of Jesus by a woman is similar to those that are found in Matthew 26:6–13, Mark 14:3–9, and John 12:1–8. However, the differences between Luke's story and the others are so significant in detail (Luke's narrative is set in Galilee; the others in Bethany, for example) that it is safe to conclude Luke's rendering is unique, a different story.

The invitation to dine at the home of Simon shows that not all Pharisees were opposed to Jesus. In fact, Luke recounts two other occasions when Jesus was welcomed into the homes of Pharisees (Luke 11:37 and 14:1). The acceptance of this invitation by Jesus demonstrates that he was quite willing to associate with Jewish religious leaders, that is, with those who were open to or were at least curious about his teaching. Though Simon did not even go so far as to acknowledge Jesus as a prophet, nevertheless, he did recognize Jesus as a teacher or rabbi.

This story, though brief, contains many of the elements for a formidable revelation of character for all involved. Such an unveiling begins to emerge once the woman entered the home of this Pharisee who could only view her as an intrusion and as spoiling this environment with her supposed impurity, given her past. In Simon's world, one's past is utterly determinative. No possibility exists for a change in status. In short, there is no exit; the gate has already been shut. Remarkably, in this setting this woman who was so negatively judged by the Pharisee spoke not a word. In her deep humility, she was silent throughout. Instead, it was her actions with respect to Jesus that evoked such a strong response from Simon as well as an extended commentary by Jesus that he offered in the form of a parable.

With Jesus reclining at the table, with his feet directed away from the food, the woman, obviously emotionally distraught, shed tears upon his feet, wiped them with her hair, kissed them, and then poured perfume on them. That Jesus allowed all of this to happen to him, to be touched by such a woman, even to the point of kissing, was simply intolerable to Simon with his Pharisaical understanding of holiness and its strong demands for separation from those deemed both unworthy and unfit. The Pharisee then thought to himself that Jesus could not be a prophet because he didn't know the kind of woman who was touching him. In Simon's eyes, at least, this made Jesus ritually unclean as well. The contagion had been communicated through the touch of a woman. Whatever respect he had for Jesus was likely slipping away.

The woman, mysterious in some respects, is obviously a catalyst in this story, and her actions helped to set up two strong contrasts. The first one was between herself and Simon. Jesus recognized this contrast as well, but in a much different way than had the Pharisee. As a good teacher Jesus helped Simon, on some level, to appreciate this difference by telling a parable whose major truth was that those who are forgiven more love more. That's a difficult teaching for some people to accept even today, especially by those who mistakenly think that they have little need for forgiveness. The truth is that we are all in God's debt and that debt is undoubtedly broad and wide—once we begin to understand just who God is. To fail to realize this is also to fail to appreciate the awe-evoking glory of the Most High manifested in the radiant beauty of holiness.

Jesus was about to apply this parable to Simon and the woman, but just before he did this, he turned toward the woman and posed a telling question to Simon: "Do you see this woman?" The obvious answer was no, for he had not seen this woman at all; indeed, she was invisible to him. This Pharisee couldn't recognize any person with whom contact would render him ritually impure. His mistaken understandings about holiness and righteousness, likely passed along to him under the banner of tradition, removed whole classes of people and their problems from his vision—anyone he and his companions deemed unworthy. The need to preserve his own purity, a strong motivation, was perverted into a stilted self-righteousness that failed to realize that God's love could be embraced and enjoyed precisely by those folks he had excluded and reviled.

The second contrast the woman helped to bring about as a catalyst was between Simon and Jesus. On the one hand, the Pharisee stressed the moral and spiritual distance that he had perceived between the woman and himself, thereby ostracizing her in his own house. He played his part in creating an atmosphere of both alienation and separation. Simon failed to grasp the significance of the woman's actions with respect to Jesus. He had no sense of what such actions were revealing about who the woman really was, on the one hand, and who Jesus was, on the other. All Simon could see were masks—ones very much of his own construction: one for the woman and one for Jesus. However, Jesus comprehended the meaning of the woman's actions immediately. He, therefore, sought not to exclude this woman or to set her apart for public scorn. Instead, he welcomed her back into the community, with its tender graces of love and fellowship, by pronouncing that her sins have been forgiven as evidenced by her great love for Jesus himself. How could Simon have missed, great religious leader that he was, the demonstration of such a humble and beautiful love? The contrast between the ostracizing Pharisee and the welcoming Jesus could hardly be stronger.

One very puzzling aspect of this story, and Luke's account does not help us very much here, is how did this woman know who Jesus was? Had she heard reports from the disciples of John the Baptist or perhaps even from the disciples of Jesus? Had she possibly heard Jesus preach? We simply don't know. One thing the text does reveal, however, is that the woman had remarkable, actually stunning, insight into the identity of Jesus that had evidently escaped Simon. To such a woman whose faith led to the tangible actions of love, Jesus declared:

"Your sins are forgiven." In response to this pronouncement, the dinner guests of Simon, no doubt surprised, asked the question: "Who is this who even forgives sins?" What the woman had known all along was now being revealed to all.

The Prayer

Heavenly Father, continue to reveal the nature of your Son and the scope of his love to me. I offer my heart and life as one great act of love to you.

The Questions

How did the faith of the woman save her? In whom was her faith placed? In what ways have we played the ostracizing role of the Pharisee in our own lives toward others?

Day 12

The Pharisees Again

MATTHEW 9:9–13 *As Jesus went on from there, he saw a man named Matthew sitting at the tax collector's booth. "Follow me," he told him, and Matthew got up and followed him.*

While Jesus was having dinner at Matthew's house, many tax collectors and sinners came and ate with him and his disciples. When the Pharisees saw this, they asked his disciples, "Why does your teacher eat with tax collectors and sinners?"

On hearing this, Jesus said, "It is not the healthy who need a doctor, but the sick. But go and learn what this means: 'I desire mercy, not sacrifice.' For I have not come to call the righteous, but sinners."

Consider This

After Jesus had healed a paralyzed man, he was on the move again and spotted Matthew sitting at a tax collector's booth. Such a profession, which entailed charging fees on goods that passed between the territories of Herod Antipas and Herod Philip,[1] made Matthew an unpopular figure among many first-century Jews. Some of the money he collected in the form of taxes and levies found its way into the coffers of unpopular Roman authorities, who made sure that they got their share of the take, and still other money made it into Matthew's own bag as a commission on what were already exorbitant fees.

With large sums of money passing through his hands, from all sorts of sources, Matthew hardly seemed to be a suitable prospect to become a disciple of Jesus. As a traveling preacher who was announcing the coming kingdom of God, Jesus often had "no place to lay his head" (Matt. 8:20b). The contrast between these two men in terms of their lifestyles, then, could hardly be greater. At the very least, they would likely be incompatible in terms of their desires, values, and basic goals in life. And yet in what was probably the shortest job interview ever conducted in history, Jesus simply called to Matthew, "Follow me," and the erstwhile tax collector got up and followed Jesus immediately. Since the cost of becoming a disciple of Jesus for Matthew was severe (unlike the disciples James and John, the Zebedee brothers, Matthew would not be able to return to his profession), he likely was already familiar with the teaching, miracles, and character of Jesus well before he ever got up.

In their accounts of this same story, both the Gospels of Mark and Luke refer to "Levi son of Alphaeus" (Mark 2:14) and simply "Levi" (Luke 5:27), names that the subsequent tradition has identified as Matthew. This identification is significant because it not only reaffirms that Jesus chose his disciples from among tax collectors, but it also illuminates the contrast between Jesus, on the one hand (and his choice of both a disciple and dinner guests for the evening), and the Pharisees, on the other hand, who expressed strong disapproval on both counts. It's a connection, a relationship between Jesus and others, that rings true and is very much a part of this larger story.

The dinner at Matthew's house, made up of Jesus, tax collectors, and sinners, posed a number of problems for the Pharisees. In their minds the table fellowship of a shared meal implied a closeness, an intimacy, that was reserved for those who were deemed worthy enough to sit among a distinguished religious leadership who in some sense had been chosen by God. The numerous human traditions that these leaders had helped to create over the years in fact demanded it. To illustrate, tax collectors and their like were barred from the synagogues as being unfit. They were also not surprisingly excluded from the tables of religious leaders, the rabbis. Indeed, the repeated contact of tax collectors with Gentiles, through the operations of their trade, made them ceremonially unclean and, therefore, ill-suited to be the dinner guest of any Pharisee. So understood, the gathering at Matthew's house was motley and disreputable. Pharisees dared not to enter such a house; otherwise, they, too, might become defiled.

Precisely because the Pharisees would not enter such a house, they posed their curious question not directly to Jesus, who was already inside, but to some of his disciples who were evidently still outside, perhaps about to make their way in: "Why does your teacher eat with tax collectors and sinners?" Behind this question was perhaps a loveless form of self-righteousness, shiny on the outside but dark within, a strain of self-love that used the forces of alienation and separation as walls to keep the proper social and religious distance in place in order that—imagine this—God might be rightly honored. In their minds at least, because Jesus had entered this den of contagion, with its tax collectors, thieves, and perhaps even a few prostitutes, he, too, had now become defiled and, therefore, unholy—at least in their eyes. In short, Jesus had done something that no Pharisee would ever do: he had crossed a line. He was now an outlier.

We need not be either impressed or, worse yet, misled by all of this in-group and out-group ordering, for this same pathetic and mistaken judgment plays out in numerous high schools around the world even today, although in an admittedly different fashion. That is, those who identify with social outcasts, by showing them even the first elements, the rudiments, of basic human decency, are often deemed to be outcasts as well in what some have termed a double degree of separation. Not only are the supposed pariahs of life rejected, but also those who show them any kindness or compassion are rejected as well. This is a very ugly business, and it has nothing to do with the love of God and neighbor, though when this script occasionally plays out in a religious context, ancient or modern, human tradition and social power insist that it does.

Recognizing that the Pharisees had already descended to low levels of darkness, abandoning the prudent counsels of love (and completely unaware of this, however, in their self-constructed righteousness), Jesus, as a good pastor to all, to friend and foe alike, had to act decisively in order to dispel the fog of this illusion. And that's exactly what he did. His declaration, "It is not the healthy who need a doctor, but the sick," probably seemed like a splash of cold water in the face of those ill-prepared to receive it. Such a statement, to change the analogy, perhaps came as a shock to those who had already divided up the world into good and evil, healthy and sick, insider and outsider, beloved and outcast. What more was there to learn? Much indeed! For the moral world that the religious leaders had constructed, which placed themselves ever at the center, proved to be a frustrating impossibility for all outsiders. How was this so? In this odd and unforgiving world, sinners such as tax collectors and prostitutes had to become righteous *first* in order to be accepted. The problem, however, was that such people were continually rejected, cut off from the sweet love and gentle graces of the very community in which righteousness supposedly dwelled. How, then, would they ever become righteous? The social and religious arrangements of the Pharisees, mistaken for a holy tradition, were put in place not for the welcoming of sinners but for the glorification of the Pharisees themselves. And all of this had worked remarkably well—until Jesus came along.

Appealing to a rabbinical sense of learning in the form of rigorous study, Jesus cautioned the Pharisees once more and urged them "to go and learn what this means," pointing to a truth that they had obviously neglected but that had been recounted by the prophet Hosea earlier: "I desire mercy, not sacrifice." The parallels between these two ages are strong. The quote was, therefore, perfect. In his own day, during the eighth century BC, Hosea had confronted the people of Israel with a warning to repent. Indeed, many in Israel had become satisfied with their own religious rituals though these practitioners, for all their doings, remained displeasing to God.

Put another way, the people whom Hosea addressed had mistaken the form of religion and external matters for the power thereof. That is, they may have been careful in the keeping of ritual precepts, but their hearts were far removed from a God of holy love. Hosea understood that. The jolt of a prophetic warning was, therefore, necessary. Jesus hoped the Pharisees would draw the parallel to their own age and get the same message.

"I have not come to call the righteous, but sinners," was the last thing that Jesus declared in order once again to break the illusion, to dispel the mirage. In a very pastoral way, Jesus took up the self-understanding of the Pharisees, themselves (that is, that they were supposedly righteous), and he challenged them in order that they might begin to see things in a remarkably new way. As it stood, this statement, this declaration, was indeed puzzling. After all, why wouldn't Jesus call the righteous? Isn't that precisely what one sent by God would do? Doesn't God love the righteous? Doesn't the Almighty love those who obey the law and keep the traditions? Aren't they the people of the Most High? What's going on here?

However, this riddle is not resolved by beginning with the observation, now in the form of a question: "Why didn't Jesus come to call the righteous?" That's the wrong place to start. Instead, we must begin with the statement, now, too, in the form of a question: "Why did Jesus come to call sinners?" What does this particular question reveal about both Jesus and his ministry that the other question apparently does not? The answer to this particular question will bear considerable fruit, for it will reveal new things about what it means to be righteous as well as what it means to be a sinner. In other words, Jesus did not come to call those who were righteous in their own eyes, those who were already very much self-satisfied. Who could help such a people? Who could assist those who had repeatedly refused to see their own very real need precisely because of a mistaken understanding of righteousness? Instead, Jesus came to call those who were mindful of their own sin, who were well aware of falling short of the glory of God, and who were, therefore, painfully conscious of their genuine need for redemption. In fact, that call to sinners, with its reconfiguration of some conceptions of righteousness, is an emblem of the gospel itself. That will become clearer in the days ahead.

The Prayer

Lord, lead me away from self-satisfaction and into a deeper understanding of your grace and mercy. May the good news of your life, death, and resurrection, Jesus Christ, spill over out of my heart and into the world.

The Questions

Why would Jesus call a tax collector to be one of his disciples? Was he trying to make a point about the kingdom of God that he was announcing? What does such a call indicate about the person of Jesus?

Day 13

One of the Teachers of the Law

MARK 12:28–34 *One of the teachers of the law came and heard them debating. Noticing that Jesus had given them a good answer, he asked him, "Of all the commandments, which is the most important?"*

"The most important one," answered Jesus, "is this: 'Hear, O Israel: The Lord our God, the Lord is one. Love the Lord your God with all your heart and with all your soul and with all your mind and with all your strength.' The second is this: 'Love your neighbor as yourself.' There is no commandment greater than these."

"Well said, teacher," the man replied. "You are right in saying that God is one and there is no other but him. To love him with all your heart, with all your understanding and with all your strength, and to love your neighbor as yourself is more important than all burnt offerings and sacrifices."

When Jesus saw that he had answered wisely, he said to him, "You are not far from the kingdom of God." And from then on no one dared ask him any more questions.

Consider This

This conversation between Jesus and a Jewish scribe is a part of a series (the fifth of six) that was taking place in the outer court of the temple. In fact, the scribe noticed that Jesus had already given a good answer in an earlier dialogue, perhaps the one between Jesus and the Sadducees in terms of the promise of the resurrection (Mark 12:18–27). In any case, this teacher of the law approached Jesus apparently with good intentions, that is, with no guile or without any design to entrap him as others, especially the Pharisees and the Herodians, had tried to do (vv. 13–17). Once again, not all of the religious leaders held negative attitudes toward Jesus. That's simply a myth. Some, like this scribe, desired to learn from his engaging wisdom. He was one of the few exceptions in the ongoing religious opposition.

The question posed that day was worthy of any rabbi because it required deep reflection in consideration of all the 613 laws of the Torah (the first five books of the Bible) in order to win the basic, fundamental insight pervading them all: "Of all the commandments, which is the most important?" That's a question that everyone who desires to love God above all should ask. It already indicates a measure of wisdom. As a good Jew, steeped in the traditions of his people, Jesus began his reply by citing the Shema (a confession of faith that is recited by Jews twice a day): "Hear, O Israel: The LORD our God, the LORD is one" (Deut. 6:4).

Jesus continued the quotation from Deuteronomy, though he changed the text slightly, in his declaration that one must, "Love the Lord your God with all your heart and with all your soul and with all *your mind* and with all your strength" (emphasis added). Indeed, the Old Testament passage had simply mentioned loving God in terms of your heart, soul, and strength, and Jesus added "with all *your mind*" as well, highlighting that the love of God requires all of who we are as persons, as embodied souls with both hearts and minds that are energized by the call of God upon them. The addition of Jesus then was welcomed, and evidently well received by the scribe, because it revealed the meaning of the ancient text in its depth and fullness. Precisely because God is one, and no other, devotion to the Most High requires all that we are, whatever faculties, capacities, or talents that we possess.

Jesus, however, was not done. To the passage in Deuteronomy, he added a commandment from Leviticus: "Love your neighbor as yourself" (19:18). That is, he reached for different books of the Bible and put two passages together. Other Jews had made this connection as well—that these two commandments do, indeed, belong together. Such a linkage, for example, can be found in the writings of Philo, a Jewish contemporary of Jesus.[1] Nevertheless, Jesus did do something new here, and in a way much different from the traditional interpretations of the period. His understanding of the Leviticus passage cracked it open to reveal its full, original intent precisely when it was viewed in light of the first commandment to love God above all. The religious leaders of the first century had understood the command to love your neighbor as yourself as directed to "anyone among your people" (Lev. 19:18)—in other words, as restricted, by and large, to a fellow Hebrew or Jew. In short, it hardly applied to Gentiles in their thinking. However, Leviticus 19:33–34 (and in a similar way in Deuteronomy 10:19) did, indeed, open up the circle of love to include "the foreigner residing among you," and Jesus understood that teaching so very clearly and lived accordingly.

To be sure, the ministry of Jesus, especially in terms of his key teachings, underscored that the neighbor does not simply correspond to the favored and limited groups in which first-century Jews often participated. That circle of love was far too small, too restrictive. Its circumference had to be broadened. The neighbor now included such folk as Samaritans, Gentiles, Syrophoenicians, and even one's enemies—in other words, anyone who bore a human face, anyone created in nothing less than the image and likeness of God.

If you doubt any of this, consider what Jesus taught in the parable of the good Samaritan found in Luke 10:25–37 in which an expert in the law, seeking to justify himself, had asked him: "And who is my neighbor?" (v. 29). Jesus replied to this frank question by telling a story in which a priest, a Levite, and a Samaritan all played very surprising and unexpected roles. The point of the parable was to teach a grand truth that had obviously escaped this very pious and educated man—and he was certainly not alone.

Precisely because God is one, the Almighty as Creator not only is over all but loves both Jew and Gentile alike. Put another way, monotheism (belief in one God exclusively) tolls the death knell for the channeling of divine love to a limited, restricted, and exclusive group, one that, due to its own misunderstanding of what the love of God entails, has become in effect one tribe over against all other tribes. More to the point, a tribal understanding of a people always represents a diminishment in the understanding of *who God is*. When this happens, the Holy One is reduced (in the people's minds, at least) to being merely "the god of a tribe," a powerful and exalted defender of the group, perhaps even a nationalistic god who preserves a particular people at all costs in the midst of all its enemies.

In contrast to this deeply troubled approach, Jesus taught in numerous ways throughout his ministry that the two commandments were intricately related in ways that the rabbis had never imagined. Simply put, God could not be loved with all our heart, mind, soul, and strength *unless* we loved our neighbor as ourselves, unless we broke out of the limitations, the restrictions of our self-created tribal ways, in order to see and embrace the "other," someone so very unlike ourselves. Only then would a transcendent God, the one who is above all the petty tribalisms of group life, be rightly adored. To be a true monotheist, then, is an enormous challenge, not only to love God above all but also to love one's neighbor as oneself in which the circle of love is broad, wide, and generous. In short, that circle is great precisely because God is great.

There's one last way, however, in which all of this can go wrong, horribly wrong, even when the love of God and neighbor is just beginning to be properly appreciated. It's the last holdout, if you will, the final obstacle on the way to a generous and inclusive love— the kind of love that Jesus called for, one that once again even embraces our enemies, those whom we judged to be "the other." Precisely because this last holdout is so very near the kingdom of God, yet without entering in, it is, therefore, all the more serious. Remarkably enough, the scribe in his response to Jesus, in noting that he had spoken well, also had a sense of this peril, one that all serious religion faces. This man, given his sincerity and wisdom, must have reflected on this danger much earlier and at great length. What had the teacher of the law replied? Adding commentary to the two great commandments, he pointed out in a very perceptive way: "To love him with all your heart, with all your understanding and with all your strength, and to love your neighbor as yourself is *more important than all burnt offerings and sacrifices*" (emphasis added).

This last judgment of the scribe was both sound and trustworthy. Though burnt offerings and sacrifices as modes of worshiping the Almighty were clearly important in the history of Israel, they were never the most important things of all. They were the means, the instruments, to glorify God; they were never the ends or goals of the faith itself. It took deep wisdom and an abundance of honesty to recognize that. Recall the words from Hosea: "For I desire mercy, not sacrifice, and acknowledgment of God rather than burnt offerings" (Hos. 6:6). Consider also the counsel of Proverbs 21:3: "To do what is right and just is more acceptable to the Lord than sacrifice." In fact, Jesus had considered the response of the teacher of the law so wise that he told the man, "You are not far from the kingdom of God." Simply put, after God, people are most important of all! The glory of God shines through their being (the image of God) in a way that is without parallel in all of creation. It's not about stuff or things; it's about *persons*.

In a similar way, what if we took some of the elements of the Christian faith—matters pertaining to modes of worship, understandings of ministry, and even forms of prayer—and made them decisive, evidently the most important things of all, such that even within the Christian communion of faith believers would now be badly divided, alienated in their many differences? What if such things caused fellowship to be broken, through stated rule and precept, and love was thereby lessened among those who claimed with their lips that they were the ones forever committed to the universal love of God and neighbor, to the two great commandments of which Jesus spoke? If, however, such *religious* folk could not even love those of their own broader household of *faith*, with its various members, how then could they ever love the *other* in the way that the commandment required and as emphasized by Jesus? Even the teacher of the law was beginning to understand that much. Would it be, then, that the Christian faith, so construed, had become just another tribe, just another group, one among many, and thereby, at least in some sense, turned on its head?

The Prayer

Father, would you broaden my gaze and help me to see all people and places with your eyes? Help me to move beyond the boundaries of my comfort and into any corner of creation you lead me.

The Questions

Why do you think Jesus added to the words of Deuteronomy 6:5? What did the inclusion of "with all your mind" in Mark 12:30 suggest in terms of Jesus's understanding of what it means to be a human being? Do we love and worship God with our minds? How could such worship be done more generously, more fully?

Day 14

The Jews

JOHN 8:42–59 *Jesus said to them, "If God were your Father, you would love me, for I have come here from God. I have not come on my own; God sent me. Why is my language not clear to you? Because you are unable to hear what I say. You belong to your father, the devil, and you want to carry out your father's desires. He was a murderer from the beginning, not holding to the truth, for there is no truth in him. When he lies, he speaks his native language, for he is a liar and the father of lies. Yet because I tell the truth, you do not believe me! Can any of you prove me guilty of sin? If I am telling the truth, why don't you believe me? Whoever belongs to God hears what God says. The reason you do not hear is that you do not belong to God."*

The Jews answered him, "Aren't we right in saying that you are a Samaritan and demon-possessed?"

"I am not possessed by a demon," said Jesus, "but I honor my Father and you dishonor me. I am not seeking glory for myself; but there is one who seeks it, and he is the judge. Very truly I tell you, whoever obeys my word will never see death."

At this they exclaimed, "Now we know that you are demon-possessed! Abraham died and so did the prophets, yet you say that whoever obeys my word will never taste death. Are you greater than our father Abraham? He died, and so did the prophets. Who do you think you are?"

Jesus replied, "If I glorify myself, my glory means nothing. My Father, whom you claim as your God, is the one who glorifies me. Though you do not know him, I know him. If I said I did not, I would be a liar like you, but I do know him and obey his word.

Your father Abraham rejoiced at the thought of seeing my day; he saw it and was glad."

"You are not yet fifty years old," they said to him, "and you have seen Abraham!"

"Very truly I tell you," Jesus answered, "before Abraham was born, I am!" At this, they picked up stones to stone him, but Jesus hid himself, slipping away from the temple grounds.

Consider This

Our text is part of a larger conversation concerning whose children the opponents of Jesus were. The Jewish leaders, themselves, had insisted that Abraham was their father (John 8:39), but then they moved their case over to the claim, as they continued to dispute with Jesus, that "the only Father we have is God himself " (v. 41). Now, imagine this: in the outer court of the temple—quite publicly, and following the Feast of Tabernacles, no less, so it was likely an area still crowded—Jesus responded to these claims made by his detractors in the following way: "You belong to your father, the devil." It was only at this point of the dispute that the Jewish leaders shot back: "Aren't we right in saying that you are a Samaritan and demon-possessed?"

We have a difficult time with this exchange today. Many of our social sensibilities predispose us not to see what is actually in the text, or if we do indeed allow ourselves enough freedom and the good sense to see it, then we immediately explain it away. We do all of this because we are trying to hold onto a picture, an image, of Jesus that we have constructed over time, and from various sources by the way, one that however cannot be found in the pages of the gospels, *any* gospel. It's a concocted image of a Jesus who is always soft-spoken, one who never challenges others publicly, one who never makes people feel uncomfortable, and one who in the end is always in tune with whatever the group wants at the particular moment in which he participates. Groups are always more significant than individuals, right? Numbers are always the most important things of all, right?

Getting along, social cooperation, and harmony are all good things, and they are, to be sure, significant and of great value. However, they aren't the most important things of all; they never were. What, then, could possibly be more vital, more weighty, more important, than social acceptance and group harmony? In one word: God. The clash between Jesus, on the one hand, and the Jewish leaders, on the other hand, is no minor dispute, no argument over things that don't really matter. For the sake of upholding the basic, life-affirming *truth* of who God is, Jesus no doubt realized that this dispute would become an unavoidable and titanic struggle, messy at times, precisely because so much was at stake. "If God were your Father," Jesus cautioned these religious leaders, "you would love me, for I have come here from God. I have not come on my own; God sent me." The problem, however, was that these particular Jews (for several Jews did accept Jesus, see John 8:31) did not love Jesus, not at all. In fact, they rejected both him and his words, a solid indication that their profession of knowing God was deeply mistaken and troubled—yes, troubled. To retreat here for the sake of some imaginary, contrived notion of peace at all costs would be ill-advised. Truth is that important.

Badly stung by the claim of Jesus that their father was neither Abraham nor God, the Jewish *leaders* (there is nothing inherently contrasting between Jewishness and Jesus) employed a well-worked defense that was often effective in putting opponents in their place. That is, they went the name-calling, bad-mouthing, social-ostracizing route and contended not only that Jesus was a Samaritan—"he's not one of us"—but also, worse yet, that Jesus was possessed by a demon! In terms of the first charge of being a Samaritan, the Jewish religious leaders had probably heard stories about Jesus being from the north, the Galilee area, and that fact alone (given the history of Samaritans and Jews) would likely be enough to create walls of prejudice and separation in the minds of those Jews who took great pride in living in Judea, not far from the temple where God is rightly worshiped. In terms of the second charge, it was an accusation so strong and dark that it usually meant the conversation was over—but, evidently, not in this particular case, for neither Jesus nor his critics were done.

Ignoring the claim that he was a Samaritan, Jesus declared that he was not possessed by a demon (indeed, he had cast demons out in Matthew 8:28–34; Luke 4:31–41) and then he changed the direction of the conversation. Earlier, the talk had been about who was the father of his Jewish opponents. In that conversation it was all about them. Now it concerned who was the Father of Jesus. Indeed, the very next words that Jesus uttered, after he had denied that he was possessed by a demon, were: "but I honor my Father and you dishonor me. I am not seeking glory for myself; but there is one who seeks it, and he is the judge." After this reply, Jesus said something startling, given the flow of the exchange up to this point: "Very truly I tell you, whoever obeys my word will never see death." The Jews within earshot thought such a claim was evidence of pure insanity and so they now felt confirmed in their earlier judgment by exclaiming, "Now we know that you are demon-possessed!" Interpreting the words of Jesus in the only way they knew how—that is, literally—the Jews failed to distinguish between physical death, spiritual death, and eternal death. Still puzzled by all of this, they continued: "Abraham died and so did the prophets, yet you say that whoever obeys your word will never taste death. Are you greater than our father Abraham? He died, and so did the prophets. Who do you think you are?"

Jesus began to answer this most significant question, "Who do you think you are?" which sets up the climax of our passage by drawing a contrast between his relation to his Father, on the one hand, and the relation of the Jews to their supposed father Abraham, on the other. Thus, Jesus pointed out that his Father, whom the Jews before him claimed as their God, is the one who glorifies him. Why couldn't the Jews then recognize the family resemblance? At any rate, when Jesus turned his attention to Abraham, in particular, he surprisingly enough did not claim him as his father, as we would expect, and as every other Jew undoubtedly would; instead, he observed to those Jews present that

"*Your* father Abraham rejoiced at the thought of seeing my day; he saw it and was glad." What's going on here?

Still puzzled and likely exasperated at this point, the Jews responded to Jesus: "You are not yet fifty years old, . . . and you have seen Abraham!" "Very truly I tell you," Jesus replied, "before Abraham was born, I am!" With this last piece of the puzzle in place, we can now begin to see more clearly the picture that Jesus was painting. Oddly enough, in one sense Abraham was not and could not be the father of Jesus simply because Jesus, as the eternal Word made flesh (John 1:1-4), was ever before him, both temporally speaking and, more important, in terms of rank and being: "before Abraham was born, I am!" In other words, Jesus, given his divine nature, as affirmed in the first chapter of John's gospel, is marked by nothing less than eternity. He is, therefore, ever before Abraham. How, then, could Abraham possibly be his father?

In another sense, however, tracing the lineage of Jesus through Joseph, as the Gospel of Matthew does, Abraham was indeed the ancestor of Jesus and, in that sense, his father. But the larger point of this contentious exchange was to declare publicly that the one who was the Father of Jesus was none other than the I AM WHO I AM who had been revealed to Moses (Ex. 3:14) as the true God, the Holy One of Israel. It is this one who is the Father of Jesus as evidenced by the language of "before Abraham was born, *I AM*" (emphasis added). The Jews recognized this language, of course, made the proper connections, and then finally realized what Jesus was actually claiming. What was their response? "They picked up stones to stone him."

The Prayer

God, I belong to you. Open my spiritual eyes to fully grasp the beauty of your incarnation, in order that your Son, Jesus, would be glorified in me just as you are in him. Conform my life to the pattern of holiness and goodness that you promise to all of your children.

The Questions

How is the issue of *identity* the key to understanding the words of both Jesus and the Jews in the account of John 8:42–59? How do the Jews appeal to God to inform their identity? What about Jesus? Why can't the Jews accept the identity of Jesus?

Day 15

The Jews in the Temple Courts

JOHN 10:22–39 *Then came the Festival of Dedication at Jerusalem. It was winter, and Jesus was in the temple courts walking in Solomon's Colonnade. The Jews who were there gathered around him, saying, "How long will you keep us in suspense? If you are the Messiah, tell us plainly."*

Jesus answered, "I did tell you, but you do not believe. The works I do in my Father's name testify about me, but you do not believe because you are not my sheep. My sheep listen to my voice; I know them, and they follow me. I give them eternal life, and they shall never perish; no one will snatch them out of my hand. My Father, who has given them to me, is greater than all; no one can snatch them out of my Father's hand. I and the Father are one."

Again, his Jewish opponents picked up stones to stone him, but Jesus said to them, "I have shown you many good works from the Father. For which of these do you stone me?"

"We are not stoning you for any good work," they replied, "but for blasphemy, because you, a mere man, claim to be God."

Jesus answered them, "Is it not written in your Law, 'I have said you are "gods"'? If he called them 'gods,' to whom the word of God came—and Scripture cannot be set aside—what about the one whom the Father set apart as his very own and sent into the world? Why then do you accuse me of blasphemy because I said, 'I am God's Son'? Do not believe me unless I do the works of my Father. But if I do them, even though you do not believe me, believe the works, that you may know and understand that the Father is in me, and I in the Father." Again they tried to seize him, but he escaped their grasp.

Consider This

The Festival of Dedication was a joyous event in the Jewish calendar for it commemorated the victory of Judas Maccabaeus against the aggression of the Seleucid Empire with the unstoppable consecration of the temple in Jerusalem in 164 BC. Three years earlier the temple had been desecrated by the Syrian king Antiochus Epiphanes, who had sacrificed a pig on the altar. The festival, which was referred to by Josephus as the Festival of Lights[1] (what we know today as Hanukkah), was celebrated on the twenty-fifth of Kislev (Jewish calendar), which often meant sometime in December.

In terms of location, our text indicates that Jesus was walking in Solomon's Colonnade, which faced the temple in Jerusalem off the court of the Gentiles. The colonnade was made up of impressive pillars about forty feet high, and it was covered over with a roof. Here, rabbis and their students would often gather to discuss matters of Jewish law as well as to escape a wintry wind. A number of Jews gathered around Jesus, which in some circumstances could be perceived as a threatening move, an entrapment, and they questioned him: "If you are the Messiah, tell us plainly." Jesus had not yet made a public statement to this effect in Jerusalem, although he had confessed privately to a Samaritan woman (John 4:25–26), to the man born blind (John 9:35–37), and to Nicodemus (John 3:13) precisely along these lines.

Jesus replied to those Jews surrounding him that he had, in fact, already told them in the sense that the works or miracles he had done in his Father's name testified as to who he is. The problem of the Jews in the colonnade, however, was that they did not believe because, as Jesus put it, "you are not my sheep."

Turning his attention away from the Jews, Jesus began to reflect, interestingly enough, on those not present who did, indeed, believe in him and on what powers undergirded and sustained their ongoing belief: "My sheep listen to my voice; I know them, and they follow me. I give them eternal life, and they shall never perish; no one will snatch them out of my hand. My Father, who has given them to me, is greater than all; no one can snatch them out of my Father's hand." That the sheep listen to the voice of the shepherd is akin to stating that the disciples of Jesus have the narrative of the gospel, the good news of Jesus, ever before them—it's in their hearts, minds, and actions. It penetrates their very being. In a real sense it's a story that has become their own story. It's therefore a constant companion and ever-present friend. Again, the disciples of Jesus are caught up in this grand narrative throughout life's journey from youth to middle age and on to old age. How could it be otherwise? How could they live any other way? In short, the words of Jesus as the good shepherd are the standard, the norm, by which all other stories are judged. That's what perseverance over time looks like.

What, then, holds such faithfulness in place? It is both Jesus as well as the Father who together ensure that these sheep, these loyal ones, cannot be snatched out of their hands. The providential love of God is both mighty and great. Beyond this, the strength and vitality of such persevering grace, marvelously enduring over time, can also be seen, from the human side of things, in the obedient faith of the disciple Peter, for example, who exclaimed on one occasion: "Lord, to whom shall we go? You have the words of eternal life" (John 6:68). In such lasting faith, then, Jesus is multicolored; everything else is gray.

After this brief discourse on the enduring devotion of his sheep, Jesus concluded his observations with a statement that simply infuriated those around him: "I and the Father are one." The word *one* here in Greek is in a form which indicates not only that the Father and Jesus are distinct persons, but also that they are one in essential nature.[2] In other words, this utterance entailed much more than the simple claim that Jesus was a good person, in harmony with the will of God, a condition that any observant Jew could hope for. Instead, Jesus was claiming so much more, that he was of the very nature, the very essence, of God and, therefore, divine. And that's exactly how the Jews interpreted his words, since they "picked up stones to stone him."

How is it, then, that these religious Jews in the temple area, shortly after a feast, so quickly turned from being an inquisitive group, seeking an answer from Jesus, to becoming a mob ready to stone him? Like a school of fish quickly changing direction, the transition of a group into a mob is often sudden, a surprise to some, even though many unnoticed cues are often already in place. In our text, Jesus had clashed with *the ethos* of this group of Jews, which is always a socially dangerous thing to do. He had run up against what this group held dear in terms of its basic assumptions about God, faith, and the Jewish tradition.[3] Indeed, the affirmation of Jesus in terms of his relation to the Father went well beyond what these Jews believed even the Messiah would be: pious and extraordinary, to be sure, yet ever distinct from God.

As such, Jesus quickly became an outsider beyond the circle of affection and care. More than that, he was despised because, in the eyes of these Jews, he had committed nothing less than blasphemy. From their vantage point, Jesus had the audacity to claim far more than any person should ever do. Deeply offended, this group of Jews surrounding Jesus shifted quickly from reason to passion, from thinking to raw emotion and feeling. The animated spirit that had emerged among them as well as the powers that they were now wielding were both heady and exhilarating. Now a mob, much like the lynch mobs in the Deep South in America during the nineteenth century, this group wanted quick, decisive, and irreversible action. No time remained for either courts (religious or otherwise) or due process. Stones in one context would have to do, nooses in another. However, the dynamics were very much the same.

Realizing that the Jews were about to stone him, Jesus deftly deflated the situation by posing a question that simply stymied them. It was, therefore, one that disrupted the attempt at violence: "I have shown you many good works from the Father. For which of these do you stone me?" The Jews countered that it was not due to any work but because Jesus had claimed to be God that they wanted to stone him. Having moved the Jews back from feeling to thinking, at least for the moment, Jesus then dug deep and posed a difficult question that required significant reflection: "Is it not written in your Law, 'I have said you are "gods"'? If he called them 'gods,' to whom the word of God came—and Scripture cannot be set aside—what about the one whom the Father set apart as his very own and sent into the world? Why then do you accuse me of blasphemy because I said, 'I am God's Son'?" This question is actually an entire argument in itself in the form of "from the lesser to the greater."[4] In other words, if the Jews could acknowledge on the basis of their own Law (see Psalm 82:6) that those to whom the word of God came are rightly called "gods" (whether they be prophets, judges, or some other folk), then *how much more* is it fitting to refer to the one whom the Father set apart as the Son of God? Once again, Jesus outthought his critics.

Sensing, however, that those around him neither embraced his words nor his argument, Jesus directed them to his works as a last resort, the many signs of wonder in his ministry that had testified that "the Father is in me, and I in the Father." However—words, works, or person—none of it made any difference. The Jews would simply have none of this. They, therefore, tried to seize Jesus, "but he escaped their grasp." The mob had emerged once more.

The Prayer

Lord, I confess you as the Word of God in whom I have eternal life. May the quality of my life now be measured by this—your eternal kingdom, which you are bringing to earth faithfully, day by day.

The Questions

Why is it that no one can snatch the sheep out of the hands of Jesus and the Father (see John 10:29b)? How does this inform our understanding of both divine and human action with respect to salvation? What does the manifestation of persevering grace look like in a human life?

Day 16

Simon Peter

MARK 8:27–33 *Jesus and his disciples went on to the villages around Caesarea Philippi. On the way he asked them, "Who do people say I am?"*

They replied, "Some say John the Baptist; others say Elijah; and still others, one of the prophets."

"But what about you?" he asked. "Who do you say I am?"

Peter answered, "You are the Messiah."

Jesus warned them not to tell anyone about him.

He then began to teach them that the Son of Man must suffer many things and be rejected by the elders, the chief priests and the teachers of the law, and that he must be killed and after three days rise again. He spoke plainly about this, and Peter took him aside and began to rebuke him.

But when Jesus turned and looked at his disciples, he rebuked Peter. "Get behind me, Satan!" he said. "You do not have in mind the concerns of God, but merely human concerns."

Consider This

Caesarea Philippi was outside Galilee, and the villages around it made up the farthest distance that Jesus would be from Jerusalem. This city, which was northeast of the Sea of Galilee, a part of the Golan Heights today, had a pagan heritage in that much earlier, following Alexander the Great's conquest, the city had been founded and called Paneas after the god Pan.[1] Around 3 BC or so,

Herod Philip rebuilt the city and named it after Tiberias Caesar and himself.

On the way to the villages around this city, away from the noise of Jerusalem, Jesus turned reflective and posed a question to his disciples: "Who do people say I am?" Since Jesus had the disciples consider his own identity through the lens of the people, that is, in terms of common report, the answers could be colored by all sorts of factors. The first reply, that Jesus was John the Baptist who had come to life again, was uttered by Herod Antipas (Mark 6:16) in the wake of having executed the prophet at the request of Herodias, his brother Philip's wife, whom he had unlawfully married. Deep personal and psychological factors, perhaps energized by guilt, prevented Herod from seeing who Jesus actually was.

If the people had known of the proper relationship between John the Baptist and Jesus, that the one pointed beyond himself to the other (John 3:30), then they would have never imagined that Jesus was Elijah, for this Old Testament prophet as well pointed beyond himself and prepared the way for the one who was yet to come: "'I will send my messenger, who will prepare the way before me. Then suddenly the Lord you are seeking will come to his temple; the messenger of the covenant, whom you desire, will come,' says the LORD Almighty" (Mal. 3:1). In fact, Jesus himself would soon make the connection between John the Baptist and Elijah: "But I tell you, Elijah has come, and they have done to him everything they wished, just as it is written about him" (Mark 9:13). The final response, however, was little better than these first two. Though the claim that Jesus was one of the prophets set him apart in the eyes of the people, even from the religious leaders of the day, such a description, given its general nature, didn't say very much.

Having considered what the people thought of him, Jesus now focused his attention on Peter: "Who do you say I am?" Thinking perhaps what his other fellow disciples had considered as well, Peter was the first one to confess: "You are the Messiah." Interestingly enough, Mark's account of Peter's reply is very brief, given the similar though far more lengthy account found in Matthew: "You are the Messiah, the Son of the living God" (16:16), a statement after which Jesus had much to say about Peter himself and the significance of his confession. The Greek word in our text that is translated into English as "Messiah" is Χριστός from which we get our English word, *Christ*. Accordingly, Peter confessed then that Jesus is the Christ, which is actually a title, since its Hebrew translation is always rendered as Messiah, the Anointed One.

Professing that Jesus is the Christ by Peter is undoubtedly a revelatory moment in Mark's gospel, marking a genuine before and after, which makes the response of Jesus all the more curious, for he "warned them not to tell anyone about him." But why did he do that? Shouldn't such a grand truth be celebrated and spread far and wide? As a good teacher, Jesus was well aware of the context in which he labored and how such a truth would likely be received. During the Intertestamental period, from 430–6 BC, some of the literature of this age gave life to the nationalistic hopes of the Jewish people. To illustrate, the *Psalms of Solomon*, an apocryphal book (that is, not a part of the Hebrew Bible), which was written during the second or perhaps the first century BC, anticipated a messiah who would establish David's throne, destroy sinners, and rid Jerusalem of all Gentiles, among other things.[2] Given this history, the popular understanding of the Messiah held by many first-century Jews would likely clash with what Jesus had in mind.

Recall that Peter in our text had used the word Χριστός, which means Christ or Messiah. Jesus, however, preferred a different expression in verse 31. In the first of his three predictions of his passion and death in this gospel (Mark 9:31 and 10:33–34 being the other two), Jesus used the phrase "the Son of Man," but he developed it beyond what the book of Daniel had offered in terms of suffering (7:21) or what Peter had in mind. That is, to the pain of what Daniel had envisioned, Jesus added wretched suffering—agonizing and unwanted anguish: "the Son of Man must suffer many things and be rejected by the elders, the chief priests and the teachers of the law, and that he must be killed and after three days rise again." Beyond this, regarding the phrase, "the Son of Man," Jesus not only embraced the principal meaning of Daniel in terms of a magnificent figure who was given "authority, glory and sovereign power" (Dan. 7:14) at the end of days, but he also invested this phrase with suffering, deep and wide, at the same time. This was new, in terms of its extent, *disturbingly* new. This phrase then was not only informed by the book of Daniel, but also by the book of Isaiah:

> He was despised and rejected by mankind, a man of suffering, and familiar with pain. Like

one from whom people hide their faces he was despised, and we held him in low esteem.

Surely he took up our pain and bore our suffering, yet we considered him punished by God, stricken by him, and afflicted. But he was pierced for our transgressions, he was crushed for our iniquities; the punishment that brought us peace was on him, and by his wounds we are healed. We all, like sheep, have gone astray, each of us has turned to our own way; and the Lord has laid on him the iniquity of us all. (53:3–6)

In light of this teaching, why should suffering be associated with the Messiah, "the Son of Man," and the things of God at all? It doesn't seem to make much sense. When we think of God as the greatest of all, a greater than which cannot be conceived, the one who created the starry heavens, we often have in mind the words, *glory, honor, power, success,* and *triumph*—not "suffering," "rejection," "being despised," "crushed," and "failure." If God is good—the best possible good—how can that goodness, in terms of a messianic figure, be understood by what looks like punishment, pain, and rejection? What's so good about suffering? What's so great about rejection? More important, what does Almighty God have to do with any of this?

If we think like this, then we can take some comfort in recognizing that Peter—great disciple that he was—thought like this as well, even right after his great confession of Jesus as the Messiah. At least at this point in Peter's journey, in his estimate of things, Jesus was to have nothing to do with these very negative things for he was, after all, someone special, God's Anointed One. However, such comfort that we might initially enjoy with Peter quickly fades away once we realize that with these understandings in place, of what the Messiah is and should be, Jesus could only say to us what he did, in fact, say to Peter: "Get behind me, Satan!" It will take the many texts, reflections, and questions in the days ahead to demonstrate just why this is so. This is not a simple matter; it has to do with how God will be revealed in Jesus Christ.

Though his words were surprisingly strong, a full-throttle rebuke, Jesus knew exactly what he was doing. Even though Peter had confessed Jesus as the Christ (as great as this testimony was), nevertheless at this point, Jesus yet remained to Peter something of a stranger.

The Prayer

Heavenly Father, align me to your purposes and help me to see through attempts of darkness to employ me against your kingdom agenda. May my every thought, word, and deed be infused with testimony to the lordship of Jesus and his glory in our world.

The Questions

What kind of Messiah were first-century Jews likely looking for, given their recent history? How would this compare with the Suffering Servant of Isaiah 53?

Day 17

The Sanhedrin

JOHN 11:32–54 *When Mary reached the place where Jesus was and saw him, she fell at his feet and said, "Lord, if you had been here, my brother would not have died."*

When Jesus saw her weeping, and the Jews who had come along with her also weeping, he was deeply moved in spirit and troubled.

"Where have you laid him?" he asked.

"Come and see, Lord," they replied.

Jesus wept.

Then the Jews said, "See how he loved him!"

But some of them said, "Could not he who opened the eyes of the blind man have kept this man from dying?"

Jesus, once more deeply moved, came to the tomb. It was a cave with a stone laid across the entrance. "Take away the stone," he said.

"But, Lord," said Martha, the sister of the dead man, "by this time there is a bad odor, for he has been there four days."

Then Jesus said, "Did I not tell you that if you believe, you will see the glory of God?"

So they took away the stone. Then Jesus looked up and said, "Father, I thank you that you have heard me. I knew that you always hear me, but I said this for the benefit of the people standing here, that they may believe that you sent me."

When he had said this, Jesus called in a loud voice, "Lazarus, come out!" The dead man came out, his hands and feet wrapped with strips of linen, and a cloth around his face.

Jesus said to them, "Take off the grave clothes and let him go."

Therefore many of the Jews who had come to visit Mary, and had seen what Jesus did, believed in him. But some of them went to the Pharisees and told them what Jesus had done. Then the chief priests and the Pharisees called a meeting of the Sanhedrin.

"What are we accomplishing?" they asked. "Here is this man performing many signs. If we let him go on like this, everyone will believe in him, and then the Romans will come and take away both our temple and our nation."

Then one of them, named Caiaphas, who was high priest that year, spoke up, "You know nothing at all! You do not realize that it is better for you that one man die for the people than that the whole nation perish."

He did not say this on his own, but as high priest that year he prophesied that Jesus would die for the Jewish nation, and not only for that nation but also for the scattered children of God, to bring them together and make them one. So from that day on they plotted to take his life.

Therefore Jesus no longer moved about publicly among the people of Judea. Instead he withdrew to a region near the wilderness, to a village called Ephraim, where he stayed with his disciples.

Consider This

The scene portrayed in our text takes place in Bethany, a couple of miles from Jerusalem. Lazarus, the friend of Jesus and the brother of Mary and Martha, has died. In seeing Mary as well as the Jews who accompanied her weeping, Jesus was deeply moved and wept. Even during this time of grief with its painful human emotions, some of the Jews simply could not stop their criticism of Jesus, which in this setting was most inappropriate: "Could not he who opened the eyes of the blind man have kept this man from dying?" This insensitive and unthinking comment may help us to understand the nature of the emotional condition of Jesus as he was deeply moved once more when he approached the tomb. The Greek word which is behind our English translation of "deeply moved" suggests not only emotional depth but also indignation.

Jesus ordered that the stone which sealed the tomb be taken away. Martha objected that there would be a bad odor since her brother had been dead for four days. The body of Lazarus had likely begun to decompose, to rot, to putrefy. It would be awful. Accordingly, as our text clearly indicates, this was not the resuscitation of a body that had simply lost consciousness or had swooned, nor was it the reviving of a body whose several vital functions had waned, giving merely the *appearance* of death. No—Lazarus was flat-out dead, just like all those other human beings centuries before him who had died. Given the severity of the situation, Jesus responded to Martha with words of comfort: "Did I not tell you that if you believe, you will see the glory of God?"

After they took away the stone and before Jesus issued his second command, he prayed to God, the Holy One of Israel: "Father, I thank you that you have heard me. I knew that you always hear me, but I said this for the benefit of the people standing here, that they may believe that you sent me." This heartfelt expression of thanksgiving reveals not only that Jesus had already prayed concerning the matter at hand, and that he had been heard by his Father, but also that his own working was ever a participation in the life of God. Earlier, after

Jesus had healed a man on the Sabbath, who had been an invalid for thirty-eight years, he exclaimed to the Jewish leaders who were then persecuting him: "Very truly I tell you, the Son can do nothing by himself; he can do only what he sees his Father doing, because whatever the Father does the Son also does. For the Father loves the Son and shows him all he does. Yes, and he will show him even greater works than these, so that you will be amazed" (John 5:19–20).

In a loud voice, Jesus cried: "Lazarus, come out!" And so, "The dead man came out," at which point Jesus ordered, "Take off the grave clothes and let him go." Observe that this coming to life again of Lazarus is different from the resurrection at the last day when the faithful will rise with immortal bodies. Clearly, Lazarus did not receive such a glorious body as he came forth from the tomb. That promise yet awaits. Lazarus would, after all, die again, which is an impossibility for those who are resurrected at the last day. Indeed, at that climatic event the dead will be "raised imperishable," as the apostle Paul points out in 1 Corinthians 15:42. Moreover, since the raising of Lazarus was neither the resuscitation of a never-really-dead person nor the resurrection to eternal life promised for the future, then the situation of Lazarus was distinct. Among other things, it was an occasion to reveal not only the power and glory of God but also who Jesus is. Its radiance had shown forth.

As a result of this miracle, many Jews believed in Jesus. Why wouldn't they? What's difficult to understand, however, is that other Jews, who had seen the very same miracle, went to the Pharisees to relate what Jesus had done. In doing so, they probably were not well motivated. Such a response, if it were the case, would demonstrate that not even a stupendous and spectacular sign, taken in by eyewitnesses, would necessarily lead to faith. The human heart and will are remarkably complex and at times very strange things. In any event, the Pharisees and the chief priests soon called a meeting of the Sanhedrin—a body that was supposedly made up of seventy men—which would include both Pharisees and Sadducees, as well as the high priest (in this case, Caiaphas) who presided over them. Evidently concerned about the future of the Sanhedrin, someone complained: "If we let him go on like this, everyone will believe in him, and then the Romans will come and take away both our temple and our nation." Caiaphas, who had been appointed high priest by the Roman governor Valerius Gratus back in AD 18, abruptly countered: "You know nothing at all!"

High priests, in a class by themselves, were not known for being prophetic, but Caiaphas unwittingly took on the mantle of a prophet that day when he declared: "It is better for you that one man die for the people than that the whole nation perish." Jesus would indeed die for the Jewish nation as predicted, but not in the way that Caiaphas had imagined. The death of Jesus would be so rich in meaning that it would burst the bounds of a simple execution, as Caiaphas and others had wanted, and it would even embrace the "scattered children of God," which John's gospel seems to suggest are Gentiles who would be united with the Jewish people. Seeing Jesus only as a threat to themselves, and with that concern intermingled with their fear of Rome, the members of the Sanhedrin "plotted to take his life" from that day forward.

What was the cause of this death sentence for Jesus? What evil had he done? What crime had he committed? In short, he had the audacity to raise a man from the dead. There it is in all its glory. For the good work of bringing a man to life, Jesus was condemned by no one less than the highest religious authority of the Jewish people. Simply put, out of life will come death. The reward for a very good deed will be destruction. But why? What's going on in this topsy-turvy world? This question cannot be answered adequately if the focus is simply on the miracle itself, the raising of Lazarus. Indeed, that's something the members of the Sanhedrin hardly considered at all; their concern was largely directed elsewhere. That is, its members were focused on the *consequences* of this miracle for themselves—their power, their privileges, their very way of life. They saw a good, a great good, that they had enjoyed for years. Jesus would threaten all of this by ushering in something *new* which the old ways, the long-lived traditions, the usual circumstances, could not embrace or, better yet, even tolerate. Here was a fork in the road that the Sanhedrin could only view as a detour.

But there's more. In failing to consider the miracle itself and what it revealed about the identity of Jesus and the work of God among the Jewish people, the religious leaders were taking on a self-imposed blindness that would allow them to participate in greater and greater evil. Accordingly, not only must Jesus be eliminated, but the one associated with this great miracle must be destroyed *as well*. We have already encountered the evil of a double degree of separation (see John 12). Now we have the evil of a double degree of death. As John reveals in his gospel just beyond our text: "So the chief priests made plans to kill Lazarus *as well*, for on account of him many of the Jews were going over to Jesus and believing in him" (12:10–11, emphasis added). Spiritual blindness can actually lead to madness—even for religious people.

The Prayer

Lord of goodness and beauty and truth—may I recognize the work of your hands around me everywhere, cherishing it as gifts for me, your child, and for the world which you affectionately love. Remove from me any blindness to your ways and grant me grace to follow you faithfully.

The Questions

If Jesus knew that he would raise Lazarus from the dead, then why was he deeply moved such that he wept? Explore this matter in terms of the identity of Jesus.

Day 18

Chief Priests, Teachers of the Law, and Elders

MARK 12:1–12 *Jesus then began to speak to them in parables: "A man planted a vineyard. He put a wall around it, dug a pit for the winepress and built a watchtower. Then he rented the vineyard to some farmers and moved to another place. At harvest time he sent a servant to the tenants to collect from them some of the fruit of the vineyard. But they seized him, beat him and sent him away empty-handed. Then he sent another servant to them; they struck this man on the head and treated him shamefully. He sent still another, and that one they killed. He sent many others; some of them they beat, others they killed.*

"He had one left to send, a son, whom he loved. He sent him last of all, saying, 'They will respect my son.'

"But the tenants said to one another, 'This is the heir. Come, let's kill him, and the inheritance will be ours.' So they took him and killed him, and threw him out of the vineyard.

"What then will the owner of the vineyard do? He will come and kill those tenants and give the vineyard to others. Haven't you read this passage of Scripture:

> *"'The stone the builders rejected*
> *has become the cornerstone;*
> *the Lord has done this,*
> *and it is marvelous in our eyes'?"*

Then the chief priests, the teachers of the law and the elders looked for a way to arrest him because they knew he had spoken the parable against them. But they were afraid of the crowd; so they left him and went away.

Consider This

While Jesus was in Jerusalem, walking in the temple courts, the chief priests, teachers of the law, and elders questioned him in terms of his authority. Jesus, in turn, wisely challenged the questioners: "John's baptism—was it from heaven, or of human origin? Tell me!" (Mark 11:30). Since the religious leaders refused to answer this question—probably because their answer would get them into trouble with the people—then Jesus would not answer theirs as well. Nevertheless, in our text, which immediately follows this account, Jesus did answer the question of his authority—but not in a way that the religious leaders would appreciate.

It is exceedingly difficult to communicate painful truths to people who are self-deceived, who are largely unaware of their own participation in evil. A direct approach of calling such people out on their actions rarely works. It's just so much wasted effort and may even be counterproductive. Indeed, many people are masters at verbal self-defense; they quickly accuse the accusers of some fault, throwing back the charge and, thereby, never considering their own shortcomings, or they simply hide behind the pretense of a well-constructed image of the self that is ever beyond accusation, and in their minds at least, beyond evil. To get through to such people, it is best to proceed not directly but indirectly, perhaps through a story or a parable. This is precisely what Jesus did in our account.

If one crafts an engaging story or parable in which listeners will get caught up in the narrative, then they will often be eager to make deeply held judgments about the justice or injustice of particular actions in the story and sometimes, as a consequence, unwittingly condemn themselves. This is what the prophet Nathan did when he told a story about a ewe lamb to King David, who with great passion, and a strong sense of righteousness, ended up convicting himself (2 Sam. 12:1–15). "You are the man!" Nathan cried (v. 7). And while parables in the Gospels are often used to keep some as the outsiders that they are, to use the words of Mark's gospel, "so that, 'they may be ever seeing but never perceiving, and ever hearing but never understanding; otherwise they might turn and be forgiven!'" (4:12), the situation in our text is much different. Jesus actually employs the form of a parable, which in this instance functions in many respects as an extended analogy, in order *to reveal* to these questioning religious leaders not only who they are, beyond the facades of piety, but also who Jesus is and from where his great authority comes.

Employing the images of a vineyard, winepress, and watchtower that are also found in Isaiah's Song of the Vineyard (where, however, they have different meanings, see Isaiah 5:1–7), Jesus told the story of a man who "planted a vineyard. He put a wall around it, dug a pit for the winepress and built a watchtower." The man then "rented the vineyard to some farmers and moved to another place." At harvest time the owner of the vineyard, who is clearly God in this parable, sent a servant (that is, a prophet) to collect some of the fruit of the vineyard, to receive some of the produce of the kingdom of God. We will see toward the end of this parable why the vineyard cannot be Israel, Judea, or the Jewish people but represents nothing less than the kingdom of God, itself, that had been planted by the Almighty at the beginning of the story and that was now tended by tenants (the religious leaders of Israel in the past and of the Jews in this present, first-century setting).

The parable continues and we observe that wave after wave of servants (prophets) were sent by the owner of the vineyard (God) to the tenants (religious leaders) who increased the brutality of their response with each successive wave—first beating, then striking on the head, and then ultimately killing. So great was the patience of the owner in this narrative that even after all this abuse, more servants were sent: "some of them they beat, others they killed." Finally, in the face of repeated failure, the owner of the vineyard (God) sent his son, whom he loved, and who was none other than Jesus: "They will respect my son." As the heir sent by the Father, Jesus should have received the fruit of the kingdom. But the tenants of the story, the religious leaders, had something else in mind.

The key to unraveling the deep meaning embedded in this artfully crafted parable has to do with the proper identification of the vineyard. First of all, we know that the vineyard cannot be the one imagined earlier by Isaiah in the form of Israel, simply because Israel cannot be given to others as our text indicates: "He will come and kill those tenants and give the vineyard to others." Such an identification would simply be absurd. Second, that there are actually two vineyards in our text, and not one, is evident once we recognize that the tenants (the religious leaders) believe that the living God is not really necessary for the ongoing life of the vineyard that they are managing quite well, thank you very much, and that by all accounts they want to own utterly—all by themselves! In fact, they think that God is either dead or is of so little consequence that if they kill his son then the vineyard will be theirs!

So then, the first vineyard in our parable is the one planted by the Most High, the Holy One of Israel, at the beginning, and it represents nothing less than the kingdom of God. This is the vineyard that will be given to others after the wicked tenants are killed. The son, who is Jesus, is utterly identified with this vineyard, this kingdom, and so he quite naturally seeks some of its fruit on behalf of his Father. Accordingly, when the tenants (the religious leaders) cast the son out of the vineyard, it is not the kingdom of God that's intended here, that is, the first sense of the word *vineyard*. Clearly, the religious leaders do not have that kind of power and authority, although in their stubborn pride they think that they do. Simply put, they cannot cast Jesus out of the kingdom of God. That's an impossibility. It's deeply problematic to think otherwise. So then, when the tenants (the religious leaders) throw the son out of the vineyard, it's out of a kingdom very much of their own making.

What is the nature of this second vineyard, this substitute kingdom, that the religious leaders had created? It is an all-too-human kingdom, one that grants the religious leaders enormous privileges of power and authority, as they oversee both the temple and the traditions, and one that places them ever at the center. If we could compare this kingdom to a hymn, it would not be the means whereby the religious leaders worshiped the one who transcended them in holiness, beauty, and glory. Instead, its lyrics would be marked by "the I, me, mine, self, and the like."[1] In other words, it would be characterized by the language of a very horizontal, self-referential religion. Elsewhere, in the Gospel of Matthew, for instance, Jesus cautioned his followers about self-invested religion that was masquerading as the worship of the God of Israel: "Everything they do is done for people to see: They make their phylacteries wide and the tassels on their garments long; they love the place of honor at banquets and the most important seats in the synagogues; they love to be greeted with respect in the marketplaces and to be called 'Rabbi' by others" (Matt. 23:5–7).

Put another way, the religious leaders—the tenants of our text—created a tribe, with sharp in-group and out-group relations, with powerful social forces of popularity and approval, all of which made them the stars of the story. They believed that they were holy and righteous, faithful to the traditions that they had been given, because, among other things, they continually separated themselves from those whom they despised: "'God, I thank you that I am not like other people—robbers, evildoers, adulterers—or even like this tax collector. I fast twice a week and give a tenth of all I get'" (Luke 18:11–12). Moreover, these religious leaders did not like to think that they were merely tenants, common laborers, but that they were or, at least, should be the owners—that the vineyard really did belong to them. Naturally, they appealed to God in all of this, to buttress their power, to legitimize their position, and this worked well in the eyes of so many people, but on some level even these religious leaders realized, in their moments of fleeting honesty, that they were participating in a sham that was chock-full of hypocrisy. How was this so? Because when the son of the vineyard owner came, they did indeed recognize him. They knew precisely who he was. And what did they want to do in order to maintain the pretense? They wanted to kill him! They had bloody murder on their minds.

In sorting out the two different vineyards, with their respective kingdoms, we are in a better position to understand the climax of the passage: "'The stone the builders rejected has become the cornerstone; the Lord has done this, and it is marvelous in our eyes.'" In the past many have interpreted this particular verse in terms of the ignorance of the builders in not recognizing the worth of the stone they had, in fact, rejected. However, that interpretation is not a possibility here. Not only does the parable inform us that the tenants realized who the son of the owner of the vineyard actually was, but Jesus himself also revealed to the religious leaders in real life by means of this parable that his authority came not from below but from above—that he was and is the Son of God. If the religious leaders understood the parable well enough to recognize that it had been spoken against them, then they also realized, on some level, that the Father of Jesus is the rightful owner of the vineyard. Consequently, the rejection of Jesus by the religious leaders—they "looked for a way to arrest him"—arose not out of ignorance, which would imply no fault, but out of genuine knowledge of who Jesus was and what kind of threat—and it was a threat—he posed to *their* kingdom.

The Prayer

Father, may your kingdom come in all of its fullness in my heart and home. Displace any vain attempt to set up my own kingdom, and welcome instead my surrender to your Holy Presence and kindly leading.

The Questions

Consider the two different vineyards in this parable and what they represent. How does this distinction illuminate, in some sense, the relation of the church today to the kingdom of God?

Day 19

Jesus

MATTHEW 10:34–39 *"Do not suppose that I have come to bring peace to the earth. I did not come to bring peace, but a sword. For I have come to turn*

> *"'a man against his father,*
> *a daughter against her mother,*
> *a daughter-in-law against her mother-in-law—*
> *a man's enemies will be the members of his own household.'*

"Anyone who loves their father or mother more than me is not worthy of me; anyone who loves their son or daughter more than me is not worthy of me. Whoever does not take up their cross and follow me is not worthy of me. Whoever finds their life will lose it, and whoever loses their life for my sake will find it."

Consider This

The opening verse of our text may come as a shock to some. That puzzlement can only increase as we call to mind some of the Old Testament prophecies concerning the Messiah. Isaiah, for example, describes a Prince of Peace (see Isaiah 9:6–7) and Zechariah, for his part, depicts a king who is "righteous and victorious, lowly and riding on a donkey" (see Zechariah 9:9–10), a depiction that will be enacted in the life of Jesus later on. The key to solving this present problem, and one that can reconcile the passages just cited with our current text, is found in one of the most beloved and joyous passages of Scripture in which the heavenly host celebrate the birth of Jesus: "Glory to God in the highest heaven, and on earth peace to those on whom his favor rests" (Luke 2:14). This last phrase is very significant, though it is often ignored and passed over quickly, for much meaning is contained in these few words. To illustrate, the NASB translates this phrase as "peace among people with whom He is pleased," and the ESV, in a similar fashion, renders it as "peace among those with whom he is pleased."

Since real peace is associated with those who enjoy the favor of God, now understood as those with whom God is pleased—with such people who do the very will of God in their lives—then the introduction of this moral dimension can now unmask the kind of phony peace that Jesus always rejected. Reflecting upon the ministry of Christ so far in our journey, we realize that he did not promote a peace of exhaustion or laziness, one that surrenders to or indulges evil, and is, therefore, silent when great harm is done to the neighbor. We note also that he spurned the counterfeit peace that refuses to take good and evil into account as those human beings who are under its deceptive power, and in the name of freedom, end up shackled and in deep bondage. Moreover, we observe that Jesus renounced that peace which is not troubled at all with thoughts of God or of the Messiah, is heedless in terms of a coming judgment, and has, therefore, made an individual human life, with its circus of desires, the center. In short, peace at all costs is ever complicit with evil in some fashion, on some level. That's the kind of peace that Jesus always rejected.

Of course, the sword that Jesus mentioned in our text is not a real sword, an instrument of physical violence, but a metaphorical one. In fact, when his enemies later came to arrest him, and one of his followers came to his defense by striking the servant of the high priest and cutting off his ear, Jesus rebuked his defender: "Put your sword back in its place . . . for all who draw the sword will die by the sword" (Matt. 26:52). The meaning of the metaphorical sword of our text is displayed in the verb at the center of the action in verses 35 and 36: "For I have come *to turn* "'a man *against* his father, a daughter *against* her mother, a daughter-in-law *against* her mother-in-law—a man's enemies will be the members of his own household'" (emphasis added). Our English translation of "to turn . . . against" may not be the most helpful choice in displaying the action of the Greek verb διχάζω which is behind our text. The basic idea here is to "divide in two, separate"[1] or even to split, an activity often associated with swords.

If we were to consider our passage as a poem with a one-line introduction (v. 34) and two stanzas (vv. 35–36 and 37–39), then we could easily see that in the midst of the separations of the first stanza between men and fathers, daughters and mothers, and daughters-in-law and mothers-in-law, Jesus is actually the subject, the principal agent, of this dividing action, as if by a sword, for he has come to turn all of these people against one another. In short, Jesus creates division; yes, fosters division. Does this sound like the Jesus we know, the one we have been taught?

Though Jesus is the foremost actor here as verse 35 indicates, nevertheless—and this has often been missed—his action is not direct, as we might initially suppose, but indirect, and it is that distinction that makes all the difference. Christ is an indirect actor here in the sense that he raises up disciples, those who in deep devotion and ongoing obedience put aside evil and do the good as they are enabled, empowered by the vivifying grace of God. In other words, they are real disciples and not hypocrites. These followers, however, are also situated in a network of family relationships where much of the action of our stanza takes place. And though we might think at the outset that those who have not taken on the yoke of discipleship in these families would be marked by freedom, openness, and a live-and-let-live attitude, nevertheless, an odd and unexpected dynamic often occurs. Repeatedly confronted with the innocence and sheer goodness of the lives of their transformed relatives, brothers and sisters, sons and daughters, fathers and mothers, the remaining family members now feel judged, put upon, and anxiously uncomfortable. They, therefore, go on the offensive (see 1 Peter 4:3–5) and the separation, the division, that Jesus indirectly brings about is widening, ever widening. He is the Prince of Peace, to be sure; but again, not of peace at any cost.

The action in our second stanza is somewhat different: it's not about division and separation but about fellowship and communion; it's concerned with loving one another. In this setting, Jesus is working with familial love and affection—the love between sons and daughters and their parents, for example—a great good to be both cherished and enjoyed. The challenge of the teaching of Jesus in this context then comes not with the recognition of the *value* of such love, for everyone can agree on it's important. Rather, the challenge comes in the form of the ranking of many loves in a hierarchy of sorts in which one love is recognized as greater, of more value, than another. Put another way, it's one thing to have values—and we all have them—it's quite another thing to rank them, a process that would prove to be difficult, perhaps even painful, but in the end would be filled with rewards in the form of deeper self-understanding. By teaching that those who love father or mother, son or daughter, more than Jesus are not worthy of him, Jesus, in effect, is claiming an area of devotion and love that transcends all of these significant loves and is, therefore, of much more value. It's a love that belongs to God alone. In short, Jesus is teaching far more in this setting than some have imagined.

The last line of our second stanza, "Whoever does not take up their cross and follow me is not worthy of me," almost seems out of place. Prior to this we have two lines of the positive values of the love of fathers and mothers, sons and daughters, but now we have the negativity of embracing death, that is, of taking up a cross. However, this line can also be expressed in terms of a positive value. It would then read like this: "They who love *their own lives* more than me are not worthy of me." Our own lives are clearly valuable and for some, however, this is as positive or as great as things will ever get. So why then didn't Jesus continue the parallelism, with three positive values in a row, instead of ending up on what looks like a negative note?

In fact, Jesus did continue the parallelism, but it's in the very last line of our stanza: "Whoever finds *their life* will lose it, and whoever loses *their life* for my sake will find it" (emphasis added). By expressing this truth both negatively and positively, Jesus underscored that the focus of this teaching is not on ourselves—that is, the fathers, mothers, sons, and daughters we love—but on the much higher value of Christ. Indeed, the forces of self-love are so strong that even taking up a cross can be filled with a self-preoccupation ("See what a good disciple I am! Oh, how I have suffered!") that can become morbid in its misdirection, in its turn toward self and negativity. This, too, must die. How then can this last vestige of self, bleeding through virtually everything, be laid aside? A first step, but an important one, entails looking in an entirely different direction and recognizing that all the action here in this second stanza is oriented, once again, toward Jesus. He is the goal; we are not. Accordingly, things are done well when they are done, as our text states, "for my [Jesus's] sake."

The Prayer

Jesus, I offer my body to you as a living sacrifice, welcoming any tension or turmoil this may bring in my life. Help me to accept division that originates in faithfulness to you, while honoring and dignifying those who turn against me for your sake.

The Questions

Was Jesus teaching that the love of fathers and mothers, sons and daughters, is not important? What is the larger dimension to which Jesus appealed so that these loves can be properly understood?

Day 20

The Crowd in the Temple Courts

JOHN 7:14–24 *Not until halfway through the festival did Jesus go up to the temple courts and begin to teach. The Jews there were amazed and asked, "How did this man get such learning without having been taught?"*

Jesus answered, "My teaching is not my own. It comes from the one who sent me. Anyone who chooses to do the will of God will find out whether my teaching comes from God or whether I speak on my own. Whoever speaks on their own does so to gain personal glory, but he who seeks the glory of the one who sent him is a man of truth; there is nothing false about him. Has not Moses given you the law? Yet not one of you keeps the law. Why are you trying to kill me?"

"You are demon-possessed," the crowd answered. "Who is trying to kill you?"

Jesus said to them, "I did one miracle, and you are all amazed. Yet, because Moses gave you circumcision (though actually it did not come from Moses, but from the patriarchs), you circumcise a boy on the Sabbath. Now if a boy can be circumcised on the Sabbath so that the law of Moses may not be broken, why are you angry with me for healing a man's whole body on the Sabbath? Stop judging by mere appearances, but instead judge correctly."

Consider This

Jesus had been traveling in Galilee and he didn't "want to go about in Judea because the Jewish leaders there were looking for a way to kill him" (John 7:1). When the Feast of Tabernacles arrived, however, Jesus was urged by his brothers to head to Jerusalem in order to "show yourself to the world" (v. 4). Jesus was reluctant at first, but he eventually headed out for Jerusalem and arrived there around the middle of the feast. He then began to teach in the temple court area.

Though we do not know the content of the teaching of Jesus on that day, the Jews were simply amazed: "How did this man get such learning without having been taught?" We recall that when Jesus went to the synagogue to teach in his hometown of Nazareth, he had to face the prejudices of the local populace in a barrage of six questions that focused on his occupation and family heritage among other things (Mark 6:1–6a). Here, the prejudices are somewhat different but no less annoying. In Jerusalem the Jews, a group that likely included some religious leaders, were in effect saying, "Jesus, you are not connected to any rabbi that we know; moreover, we are not aware of any school that you are a part of; you're not one of us." And those pointed observations would have been the end of the matter for most people, especially when prejudice holds sway—but not for Jesus. He's different.

Granted, Jesus was taught neither the Bible nor the Jewish traditions by a famous rabbi as the apostle Paul had been instructed by Gamaliel (Acts 22:3). The authority of Jesus came not from some other human being, some celebrated teacher, on which Jesus would then be dependent as a disciple. Rather, the source of his magnificent learning was higher, much higher; it was not from humanity, but from God: "My teaching is not my own. It comes from the one who sent me." Notice that Jesus did not make his own learning, his own efforts, the basis of his authority. He didn't claim, for example, that he was self-taught, a claim that would have been immediately rejected by the religious leaders and perhaps would have become even the occasion for ridicule. In the minds of most first-century Jews, no wise person in the things of God could ever be self-taught. Self-authority was no authority at all!

Moreover, Jesus pointed out: "Whoever speaks on their own does so to gain personal glory." And so on some level, Jesus agreed with the general nature of the criticism directed his way. What the Jewish leaders missed, however, was that behind Jesus is the authority of no one less than God: "but he who seeks the glory of the one who sent him is a man of truth; there is nothing false about him." Consequently, not only is the source of the teaching of Jesus Almighty God, but Jesus also ever sought, not his own glory, but that of the Most High. The question of authority, then, has served to illustrate the relation of Jesus, as a true human being, to God, the Father. It is a loving relationship of trust and ongoing dependence that puts aside any hint of self-glorification or idiosyncratic authority. What's more, Jesus maintained that anyone could discover whether his teaching came from God or not—that is, put the claim of Jesus to the test—by seeking to do the will of the Most High.

The second half of our text is difficult to comprehend unless one takes into account an earlier passage, John 5:7–15, which refers to the healing of an invalid at the pool in Bethesda. Though it was the Sabbath, Jesus ordered the man: "Get up! Pick up your mat and walk." Since the man was now carrying his mat on the Sabbath, an action forbidden in the way the Jewish religious leaders had interpreted the law of Moses, these leaders, therefore, questioned the man and later persecuted Jesus who, in their eyes, was the real culprit behind this religious offense. Chapter 7 of John's gospel reveals a simmering murderous intent, and that "the Jewish leaders there were looking for a way to kill him" (v. 1), no doubt because Jesus had violated the Sabbath in their eyes. Beyond this, these leaders had been offended by some of the things Jesus had said in their presence in the past, especially in terms of his relationship with the Father.

The crowd at the temple courts was not aware of any of this history and what effect it had upon the religious leadership who were present in this area as well. And so, when Jesus pointed out, "Yet not one of you keeps the [Mosaic] law," and then asked, "Why are you trying to kill me?" the crowd growled: "You are demon-possessed. Who is trying to kill you?" Observe the social dynamics of the crowd here, for it will pay dividends later on and in other forms. This mass of people was utterly ignorant of the murderous designs of the Jewish leaders among them but that didn't seem to matter at all. The crowd would simply have its say, weigh in, and express its judgment regardless of what it knew or did not know, for, after all, it had the strength of greater numbers on its side. It spoke with a very loud voice. But is truth a function of volume? Again, since the crowd was not aware of any murderous intent on the part of others, then in their minds it simply didn't exist.

Making itself the center of meaning and judgment, in a very narrow and self-referential way, buoyed by its great numbers that it found both intoxicating and invigorating, the crowd—now actually a mob by this point—went all in for the falsehood that the religious leadership did not want to kill Jesus. Furthermore, because the crowd could not be wrong in its judgment (once again, the social dynamics are in play), then Jesus must be delusional and paranoid—in short, demon-possessed. In such cases *the other* is always at fault. But there's more. Unlike the crowd, the religious leaders in the temple court area were not deceived. They had known the score all along. That they remained silent in the face of these lies resulted in their own greater guilt and complicity. Ignorance could not save them.

Jesus was well aware of the poor judgments that had been made by both the crowd and the religious leaders. In order to show these religious leaders their faults, Jesus—once again, as a careful thinker and teacher—invited them to reason clearly about Mosaic law and the will of God, for they did indeed know about the healing recorded in John 5:7–15. If the Sabbath required no work at all, then why was it that a male child must be circumcised on the eighth day even if it's the Sabbath? Simply put, if keeping the Sabbath could embrace the good of ceremonial observance, *how much more* could it embrace the good of healing a man, setting him free, on that same day? Is not this the work of God? Again, what kind of god would refuse to heal a suffering man on the Sabbath day? What kind of god would make him wait? Is such a god to be worshiped and adored? Well aware that a clash of theologies had by now erupted, Jesus concluded his reply in the following helpful manner: "Stop judging by mere appearances, but instead judge correctly."

The Prayer

Divine Judge, before whom all my thoughts are laid bare, draw me to you even as I depend on your grace and mercy. Where I must judge, help me to see past appearances and into the heart of the matter. Give me resolve as well as tenderness as I relate to people bearing your image.

The Questions

Compare and contrast the response to the teaching of Jesus between the hometown folk (Mark 6:1–6a) and the Jews in the temple court area (John 7:14–24). List all the prejudices of each group as to why Jesus shouldn't really have been able to teach in the way that he did. What do these prejudices teach us about each group? Are such prejudices alive and well today?

Day 21

Herod Antipas

LUKE 13:31–35 *At that time some Pharisees came to Jesus and said to him, "Leave this place and go somewhere else. Herod wants to kill you."*

He replied, "Go tell that fox, 'I will keep on driving out demons and healing people today and tomorrow, and on the third day I will reach my goal.' In any case, I must press on today and tomorrow and the next day—for surely no prophet can die outside Jerusalem!

"Jerusalem, Jerusalem, you who kill the prophets and stone those sent to you, how often I have longed to gather your children together, as a hen gathers her chicks under her wings, and you were not willing. Look, your house is left to you desolate. I tell you, you will not see me again until you say, 'Blessed is he who comes in the name of the Lord.'"

Consider This

At this point in his ministry all sorts of people wanted to kill Jesus. The Pharisees let him know that Herod, the tetrarch of Galilee, had designs in this area as well. This was the same Herod who had beheaded John the Baptist at the behest of Salome. Demonstrating once again that not all Pharisees were opposed to Jesus, a familiar truth by now, these religious leaders cautioned him about the death threat and advised him to flee Galilee. Jesus had already determined to make his way to Jerusalem, seemingly out of the domain of Herod, and so death would not come at the hands of the tetrarch. In replying to the Pharisees, Jesus employed frank and direct language: "Go tell that fox," an expression that we find only in the Gospel of Luke. Though in the twenty-first century such language might suggest cunning or cleverness on the part of Herod, in the first century it probably connected shafts of cunning to a larger mine of ineptitude.[1]

As he headed toward Jerusalem, undeterred by threats of any kind, Jesus gave evidence of the meaning of his current actions as being part of a larger goal or purpose. In other words, Jesus saw with eyes wide open, so to speak, what awaited him in the holy city, the city of David, for he observed: "no prophet can die outside Jerusalem." What was it about this city, that should have epitomized the precious faith of Israel, that caused it to descend at times into tirades of stoning and bloodshed? And what was it about prophets, in particular, that provoked such a frenzy of violence? A key to both questions can be seen in how prophets are described by others, that is, by the faithful remnant, once their blood is spilled. These heroes of the faith, many of whom become martyrs, remain faithful in a *suffering witness to the truth of God* even at the cost of their very lives. It is the persistence of prophets—what their detractors often call "stubbornness," or "aggressiveness," or even "madness"—in holding forth a painful truth that the community would rather not acknowledge or even hear, and that religious people find so exasperating. Jesus knew what was coming.

Reflecting upon his relationship to the holy city and all that it represents, Jesus turned surprisingly emotional and spoke in the language of the heart by uttering a lament: "Jerusalem, Jerusalem, you who kill the prophets and stone those sent to you, how often I have longed to gather your children together, as a hen gathers her chicks under her wings, and you were not willing." The repetition of the name of the city as well as the disclosure of a passionate longing for a caring, loving relationship—together, these elements suggest deep affection and, in the end, when such longing is frustrated, considerable emotional pain. Rejection and ostracism, as well as cutting off the numerous graces and comforts of the community, enjoyed by *so many*, are hurtful regardless of who is on the receiving end. As a real flesh-and-blood human being with psychological, emotional, and social needs, Jesus suffered greatly as he was cut off from the affection and care, and at times, even from the goodwill of the community. What so many others enjoyed and what some even took for granted in a rich and engaging communal life would be denied to him. He would be singled out, marked, and isolated. His name and reputation would be disfigured in some circles. And, at last, he would be spurned and rejected.

Why was it, then, that someone of the character of Jesus—who went about doing good through healing, teaching, and proclaiming the kingdom of God—why was it that such a person, whose goodness was and remained far deeper than we are able to fathom, would continue to be rejected by a religious leadership that should have known better? A surface examination of the context of first-century Israel, with the kind of religious leadership it had, will hardly reveal the answer.

Actually, there's a mystery here. On a superficial level, the kind most often embraced by the masses of the first century, religiously speaking, things looked fairly good: the Pharisees, Sadducees, and the chief priests basked in the authority and the legitimacy of Moses, and they did, indeed, do much good. In fact, that was very much a part of their social and religious power, and we would be foolish not to recognize it. These leaders stressed the importance of tradition; they encouraged the education of the young; and they held the right views about Rome given its oppressive rule (although some of the Sadducees might not have even cared), even if they didn't express such views publicly.

Like the tenants of the vineyard in the parable that Jesus had already told (Mark 12:1–12), the religious leadership of first-century Israel was indeed tending the vineyard—that's not the problem here—but they had mistakenly imagined that they were the owners of this vineyard and not the tenants that they actually were. As a consequence, this vineyard had become a kingdom very much of their own making. And so, when the God of Abraham, Isaac, and Jacob sent prophets to them—like John the Baptist, for example, or his very Son, Jesus—the response could only be rejection that might have sounded something like this: "We don't need you here; we have everything under control. Go away!" In other words, the major elements of the Jewish faith at the time—the Torah, the priestly sacrifices at the temple, as well as the sacred traditions—were all in place, but they were bent to serve not the Holy One of Israel, but the interests of the religious leaders themselves. If their focus had been on the Holy One who transcended them both in power and glory, then they would have accepted Jesus.

Again, on the surface all looked well in this world though so much had already been redefined. Beneath the surface, however, things looked remarkably different. Here was a deception foisted upon the simple and naive among the people of an enormous self-love that would simply not tolerate a rival. Even religion and the sacred can be made to do the bidding of self-absorption or the wants of some favored, self-centered group that is intoxicated with its own power and status. Knowing this situation as it was, with its pretense stripped away, and therefore not simply how it appeared to be, Jesus as a good physician had to issue a stark warning: "Look, your house is left to you desolate." Those were very strong words and they confirm our reading of the text. And yet desolation, as dark and as thoroughgoing as it is, would not last; it would not be the final word for this people: "I tell you, you will not see me again until you say, 'Blessed is he who comes in the name of the Lord.'" Blessedness will come; it cannot be stopped. And it will bear the name of Jesus.

The Prayer

Heavenly Father, thank you for the example of your Son, Jesus, who sought your will and served you regardless of the opposition that he faced. Remind me when I feel alone or face opposition that I do not own the vineyard. I serve at your pleasure and for the glory of his name.

The Questions

How can the highest things, such as an appeal to a holy and glorious God or to the sanctity of religion, be employed for much less noble ends? In what ways can the practice of religion become deceptive? What could bring illumination and proper discernment in this area so that God might be rightly worshiped and the people edified?

Day 22

Disciples Then and Now (Part One)

LUKE 6:20–23

Looking at his disciples, he [Jesus] said:
"Blessed are you who are poor,
for yours is the kingdom of God.
Blessed are you who hunger now,
for you will be satisfied.
Blessed are you who weep now,
for you will laugh.
Blessed are you when people hate you,
when they exclude you and insult you
and reject your name as evil,
because of the Son of Man.

"Rejoice in that day and leap for joy, because great is your reward in heaven. For that is how their ancestors treated the prophets."

Consider This

The verses above make up a part of Jesus's Sermon on the Plain and they can be compared to Jesus's Sermon on the Mount as found in Matthew 5–7. Though some of the material in these two gospel accounts is similar, there are important differences to be noted as well. To illustrate, Matthew lists nine beatitudes or blessing statements ("Blessed are . . .") but Luke has only four. Again, Luke has four woe statements ("Woe to you . . ."), which are not a part of our text but follow it, but Matthew has none. We have not included these four woe statements from Luke as a part of our text simply because their theological and ethical *content* reveal very clearly that in this material Jesus had shifted his audience. That is, he was no longer addressing his disciples directly, which is our major concern here, but a much larger population—"a great number of people from all over Judea, from Jerusalem, and from the coastal region around Tyre and Sidon" (Luke 6:17)—that included within it both false prophets as well as the sinfully self-satisfied.

In terms of the first beatitude found in Luke, Jesus looked directly at his disciples and exclaimed, "Blessed are you who are poor, for yours is the kingdom of God." Matthew expresses this beatitude in a different way from Luke's account as follows: "Blessed are the poor in *spirit*, for theirs is the kingdom of heaven" (Matt. 5:3, emphasis added). At first glance, in a comparison of these texts, it may appear that they are teaching different things: Luke is evidently focused on the material, maintenance needs of the poor, while Matthew considers poverty more broadly (and people can be poor in all sorts of ways) in terms of one's spirit. This difference, however, should not be overblown.

It must be borne in mind, once again, the audience that Jesus addressed in Luke's text. He was speaking, after all, to his *disciples* who were poor. These were not just any people; they were indeed special, set apart.

Jesus was not teaching about poverty, broadly speaking, but of the poverty that characterized the lives of those who believed in and were obedient to him. This additional element makes a world of difference. Clearly, in this setting, both physical poverty and a lively faith were in the mix, two things and not just one. When that is the case, Jesus affirmed that such physical want, as difficult as it may be, cannot undo or overthrow the overwhelming reality of being blessed, despite one's poverty. When the most important value of all is in place—when we let God be God in our lives—blessing cannot be stopped. It's simply impossible.

Another implication of this pungent teaching found in Luke is that being a genuine, faithful disciple of Jesus may not lead to the fulfillment of all our material needs. Many believers may yet be lacking in some areas of their lives: "Blessed are you who hunger now, for you will be satisfied. Blessed are you who weep now, for you will laugh." To be sure, being disciplined for many will lead to a better life but, clearly, not for all. Why is this so? It's because the causes of poverty are complex and go far beyond the personal dimensions of life and entail factors that escape individual or even family control. Jesus fully understood this. Think of the great harm, then, that is done to the poor when poverty is viewed simply as the curse of God.

All of the Synoptic Gospels (Matthew, Mark, and Luke) record not only that Jesus was well aware that he would suffer many things at the hand of the elders, the chief priests, and the teachers of the law, and would in the end be killed, but also that he taught his disciples about all of this very clearly. Nothing of this darkness, this evil, was hidden from them. Moreover, the fourth beatitude of our current text in Luke reveals the hatred that would be directed against the disciples of Jesus: "Blessed are you when people hate you . . . because of the Son of Man." Compare this with a different account found in Matthew in which Jesus taught his followers: "You will be hated by everyone because of me" (10:22a). The Gospel of John, however, displays the reason for such hatred directed against both the Master and his disciples: "If the world hates you, keep in mind that it hated me first. If you belonged to the world, it would love you as its own. As it is, you do not belong to the world, but I have chosen you out of the world. That is why the world hates you" (15:18–19).

Granted, the topic of hatred is both an uncomfortable and a difficult one. As a consequence, many of us would like to move on quickly. To hear the voice of hatred, and to consider painfully what it actually means, is like listening to a very loud crying baby. We just want it to stop. However, if we become so inattentive, for fear of discomfort, in terms of reckoning what hatred in fact is, then we will never understand what Jesus had to confront throughout much of his ministry and what *all* of his disciples, past and present, would inevitably face. What's more, if we fail in grappling with hatred forthrightly, then we will not understand the height, breadth, and the depth of the gospel correctly. Indeed, the gospel or the good news is not only the greatest story ever told, or that could ever be told, but it is also the utmost celebration imaginable of the love of God as well as the *universal* love of neighbor. We will make that case in greater detail in the days ahead. For now, however, our focus must be and will remain on the exact opposite of the gospel: hatred.

The word *hate* in our text, in this fourth beatitude, conveys two key ideas. First of all, hatred is made up of a strong dislike or an intense aversion to a person or peoples.[1] For example, there may be people in our own families, communities, or broader society, who because of their values and the way they live their lives, evoke a strong, negative response from us in the form of a deep-seated aversion. Notice it is precisely because we find that our own good values are being threatened by others that a strong dislike to them may arise and possibly take root in our hearts. Odd as this may seem, some people are poised to go down the highway of hatred, not fully aware of the evil that they will eventually embrace, simply because their focus is always on the good they seek to preserve in the face of threats, real or imagined, coming from the *other*. What they neglect to consider, however, in this heedless descent, is the real harm they are willing to do to their neighbor—all to preserve the *values* they hold dear. This is what the beginning of moral and spiritual blindness looks like.

The second element that causes hatred to arise is malice or ill will.[2] Not only do some people have a strong aversion in their hearts toward others, but they also go well beyond this to wish misfortune or outright evil upon them. That's precisely what malice or ill will is. It's a necessary element for hatred to arise. Moral and spiritual blindness is compounded here, and people can actively engage in self-deception with respect to the evil that they will do or intend to do. Since the hated *other* is a threat to the values of the community—perhaps even a religious community (think of the hatred directed at Jesus by religious leaders)—then one is justified, indeed even entitled, to bring great harm to the one so despised. Put another way, hatred always contains elements of lying and self-deception. People may even be so deceived that they believe they are actually doing the very will of God![3]

We are not trying to suggest that some members of the Christian community are not subject to the same kind of misgivings and deceits that have played out among the Jewish religious leadership of the first century. Unfortunately, the Christian faith can be perverted as well. It can go horribly wrong by taking on a much-diminished narrative, a substitute story, one that masquerades as the gospel, championed by false prophets, and that departs in significant ways from the universal love of neighbor. Jesus warned his disciples about this at several points in his ministry.

To get at this unfortunate reality we are compelled, for the sake of truthfulness and honesty, to make a distinction between nominal and even hypocritical Christians and true disciples of Jesus Christ. Let's be clear: the two are neither to be confused nor mistaken for each other. This is where the naive may stumble or be outright misled. In terms of nominal Christians, the Christian faith may become just another tribe. Do we really love Jesus, or do we love "X"? Fill in the blanks here (denomination, economic status, cultural or social power, ethnicity, race, etc.). Take your pick. Such a greatly diminished "faith" may prove to be attractive to some, for it can offer enticing measures of meaning, purpose, and social power as an ongoing reward. And some will take enormous delight in being so distinguished from others as Jesus had warned (see Luke 18:11).

When this corruption of the Christian faith has occurred—when lesser meanings are mistaken for ultimate ones, and empowered by strong social forces, by a heady appeal to numbers—language may be taken up by the self-righteous in public forums as an avenging sword whereby they employ insults, demeaning epithets, and even engage in character assassination for those who are judged to be "the other," those beyond their limited circles of meaning. In doing so, the self-righteous thereby become guilty of the very evil that Jesus warned against in the fourth beatitude: employing insults and rejecting the names of others as evil. And nominal Christians and hypocrites may find themselves in the end railing against the very disciples of Christ—those who have remained faithful to the Master, the Holy One who transcends them in goodness, power, and glory.

All of this troubled public discourse spoken by the less-than-faithful cannot be justified by any appeal to justice. Indeed, such language has no defense. Instead, it has all the markings of deep aversion and animated ill will which is none other than the grammar of hatred. Are we surprised by this? Then let us ask ourselves some very frank questions: How is such language edifying? How does it show our love for God and our neighbor? How does it even reflect the golden rule? Does such language ever seek reconciliation, or does it glory in condemnation and division? In short, what person, Christian or not, would like to be subject to the kind of verbal attacks that have now become the staples on Christian websites or in public forums?

In the eighteenth century, John Wesley, being the good pastoral leader that he was, cautioned the church precisely against this great evil in his pointed sermon, "The Cure of Evil Speaking."[4] We will do well to heed the counsels of this sermon, especially today, given all the many venues for self-expression now available to us. In our own twenty-first century, in the midst of a growing information and data revolution, it must be brought to mind that some people are unfortunately digging their own graves with their keystrokes.

The Prayer

Precious Jesus, I am again reminded that you were hated—not by the world but by those who should have loved you most, yet you did not return that hatred. Help me be your wholehearted disciple whose life is marked by true righteousness and who pursues the purposes that matter to you, even when I am despised, misunderstood, or judged wrongly for it.

The Questions

How can being poor prepare one, in a certain sense, to be open to the gospel? How can being poor prepare one, in another sense, to be closed to the gospel?

Day 23

Disciples Then and Now (Part Two)

LUKE 9:22-26 *And he [Jesus] said, "The Son of Man must suffer many things and be rejected by the elders, the chief priests and the teachers of the law, and he must be killed and on the third day be raised to life."*

Then he said to them all: "Whoever wants to be my disciple must deny themselves and take up their cross daily and follow me. For whoever wants to save their life will lose it, but whoever loses their life for me will save it. What good is it for someone to gain the whole world, and yet lose or forfeit their very self? Whoever is ashamed of me and my words, the Son of Man will be ashamed of them when he comes in his glory and in the glory of the Father and of the holy angels."

Consider This

Given what views of the Messiah the Jews held at the time, Jesus had to take special care, even after Peter's confession at Caesarea Philippi, to instruct his disciples as to just what kind of Messiah he would be. There would be no military victories in his name; no triumphal columns or monuments erected; the yoke of Rome would not be thrown off. Rather, the Son of Man would be rejected by religious leaders, those who claimed the mantle of God, who sat in the chair of Moses, and then Jesus would be murdered, but "on the third day be raised to life."

After expressing this very sobering truth, which was helping to correct some of the mistaken views of the Messiah that lingered even among his own disciples, Jesus then turned his attention to what was entailed in discipleship, the cost of being a serious follower: "Whoever wants to be my disciple must deny themselves and take up their cross daily and follow me." This verse must be understood in terms of the goal or purpose of discipleship itself; in other words, with respect to what course of action or way of life would lead disciples to be just like their Master. Two counsels were offered by Jesus: first, disciples must deny themselves, forsaking any pleasure, any worldly good, that gets in the way (in the sense that it blocks the path) of remaining faithful to the Master. Second, disciples must not only forsake getting-in-the-way pleasures or goods, but they must also take up their cross daily, which indicates something more—they must be willing to embrace suffering, and not seek to avoid it at all costs, when it becomes necessary in order to remain faithful to Jesus.

Christ continued his teaching about discipleship with a puzzling declaration: "For whoever wants to save their life will lose it, but whoever loses their life for me will save it." Notice that in this pithy statement we have two values being turned upside down. It looks like we've just entered an inverted world. Saving will result in loss. Loss will result in saving. What could this possibly mean? The key to unlocking the wisdom of this teaching is found in the two little words, *for me*. Here we have two distinct paths laid out: the first one, which is marked by autonomous self-concern and is alienated from Jesus, will result in loss. The second one, which is marked by surrendering autonomous self-concern and being properly related to Jesus, will result in being saved. In short, Jesus was teaching his disciples that being in a proper relationship with him was the most important thing of all.

If we bring this wisdom of the preceding verses to the next one of our text—"What good is it for someone to gain the whole world, and yet lose or forfeit their very self?"—we realize immediately that by gaining the whole world Jesus was not simply referring to material things or stuff. He was *also* referring once again to *relationships*, a truth that, as we will see, will be borne out in the remainder of our text. The word *world* in this passage means not only "the whole of everything created by God,"[1] which includes material things, but it also embraces a "realm of existence, a way of life,"[2] indeed, a network of persons and relationships that are unfortunately hostile to God. This, too, is what it means to be worldly.

Most Christians in the world today are neither rich nor is the allure of wealth their chief temptation. The rampant consumerism of the West does not play out in the same way in the two-thirds world. One of the major challenges, then, for both rich and poor Christians today is indeed a worldly one, but it comes from another quarter, one that Jesus addressed as well: "Whoever is ashamed of me and my words, the Son of Man will be ashamed of them when he comes in his glory and in the glory of the Father and of the holy angels." Here the worldly challenge comes in the form of relationships, of sustaining networks of associations in terms of acceptance, recognition, belonging, approval, and even honor, which if they are cut off can lead to great and deep suffering, even at times to a loss of livelihood.

The poor, like other people, are situated within communities of family, friends, workers, and other key relationships which, if they are cut off through the loss of social approval, can have greater consequences for them than for the rich since the poor are so heavily dependent upon these connections. Nevertheless, the middle class as well as the rich may feel the power of these same large social and cultural forces, along with pressures to conform, with the result that, like the poor, they, too, may be tempted to deny Christ in order to get along, to fit in, or to preserve some supporting relationships in any number of social environments. So, then, the warning that Jesus gave to those who would be his disciples ("whoever") belongs to all, to both rich and poor. To be sure, being ashamed of Jesus, the threat of selling out, of denying Christ, for the sake of some social good is a universal temptation. After all, who wants to be rejected? Who wants to be left out? Who wants to be shunned?

The dynamics of being ashamed of Jesus within a particular social setting and then ultimately denying Christ or selling out can be expressed in terms of two competing narratives or stories with a number of important transitions. When followers of Jesus first begin to feel shame in the presence of a particular group (family, work, or university setting, for example), the story or identity of that group, which is alien to Christ (that's why they're feeling the shame), is now beginning to take hold in their hearts and minds. This new narrative, which is often defined in terms of politics either from the left or the right, is celebrated and sustained by powerful social and cultural pressures and well-traveled pathways that often lead to conformity. Oh, these believers, at this stage of their descent, will still define the good in terms of Jesus and the gospel story, though they are now increasingly reluctant to share many of their beliefs in this new and challenging setting. They want to be more tactful, more appropriate, as they put it. Most often, they're just simply silent.

As they remain in this by now increasingly threatening environment, they start to define the good not really in terms of the gospel any longer but in terms of the new narrative, often a partisan political one, by convincing themselves, with various levels of self-consciousness and self-deception, that this is what it *really* means to be a follower of Jesus. They may take considerable pride in this transition, and boast of it, since other believers, the common lot in their view, lack such great and profound insight. They may even begin to look down upon some Christian believers, those who remain faithful to Jesus.

At this point, for those who are on this downward spiral, their faithlessness is now complete. How is this so? In short, the gospel story has been displaced by another narrative whether it be a social, cultural, or political one. The gospel has been switched out. This can happen slowly, incrementally over time, with the support of newfound friends along the way, with smiles and affection, or it can occur rapidly almost like a conversion. If such folk remain in the institutional church, and some will not, they will continue to use the language of Christ, grace and salvation, giving evidence of their own self-deception, but it doesn't matter anymore. Everything has been redefined in terms of their new, preferred narrative that now rules the day. When this happens, the words of Jesus can only be foreboding and disturbing: "the Son of Man will be ashamed of them when he comes in his glory and in the glory of the Father and of the holy angels."

The Prayer

Lord, I long to be connected to something bigger and better than myself. Help me not be so devoted to those connections that I lose sight of the relationship that matters the most—the only true and abiding relationship that can sustain and nourish me—the relationship that I have with you.

The Questions

Is there a sense in which the kingdom of God was, is, and is yet-to-come? What makes this kingdom "of God" and how does it differ from the kingdoms of this world?

Day 24

Disciples Then and Now (Part Three)

JOHN 6:52-69 *Then the Jews began to argue sharply among themselves, "How can this man give us his flesh to eat?"*

Jesus said to them, "Very truly I tell you, unless you eat the flesh of the Son of Man and drink his blood, you have no life in you. Whoever eats my flesh and drinks my blood has eternal life, and I will raise them up at the last day. For my flesh is real food and my blood is real drink. Whoever eats my flesh and drinks my blood remains in me, and I in them. Just as the living Father sent me and I live because of the Father, so the one who feeds on me will live because of me. This is the bread that came down from heaven. Your ancestors ate manna and died, but whoever feeds on this bread will live forever." He said this while teaching in the synagogue in Capernaum.

On hearing it, many of his disciples said, "This is a hard teaching. Who can accept it?"

Aware that his disciples were grumbling about this, Jesus said to them, "Does this offend you? Then what if you see the Son of Man ascend to where he was before! The Spirit gives life; the flesh counts for nothing. The words I have spoken to you—they are full of the Spirit and life. Yet there are some of you who do not believe." For Jesus had known from the beginning which of them did not believe and who would betray him. He went on to say, "This is why I told you that no one can come to me unless the Father has enabled them."

From this time many of his disciples turned back and no longer followed him.

"You do not want to leave too, do you?" Jesus asked the Twelve. Simon Peter answered him, "Lord, to whom shall we go? You have the words of eternal life. We have come to believe and to know that you are the Holy One of God."

Consider This

Jesus had already performed the great sign and wonder of feeding five thousand people on "the far shore of the Sea of Galilee" (John 6:1). After this, Jesus and his disciples crossed the lake in order to reach Capernaum. Realizing that Jesus was no longer on the far shore, the crowd who had been fed crossed the lake as well, headed for Capernaum, and looked for Jesus. The scene is now set for the lengthy discourse in which Jesus taught the people: "I am the living bread that came down from heaven. Whoever eats this bread will live forever. This bread is my flesh, which I will give for the life of the world" (v. 51).

This last teaching evoked a sharp response from the Jews who had heard it. Earlier they had been well fed; now they were puzzled. They argued among themselves, "How can this man give us his flesh to eat?" Knowing what they were quarreling about, Jesus responded in a way that only puzzled them further: "Whoever eats my flesh and drinks my blood has eternal life, and I will raise them up at the last day. For my flesh is real food and my blood is real drink. Whoever eats my flesh and drinks my blood remains in me, and I in them." One of the reasons this teaching was so difficult for first-century Jews is that the Torah, the Mosaic law, taught that blood must not be consumed. If we consider the passage, "But you must not eat meat that has its lifeblood still in it. And for your lifeblood I will surely demand an accounting" (Gen. 9:4–5), along with, "I will set my face against any Israelite or any foreigner residing among them who eats blood, and I will cut them off from the people" (see Leviticus 17:10–12), we immediately see the problem.

The response of Jesus to the Jews in Capernaum, however, was not only difficult in its original context, but it also has remained a challenge for the church today in that various theological traditions discover and affirm different meanings in these very same words. How can this be? Part of the difficulty is that Jesus employed large and powerful metaphors in his discourse at Capernaum and disagreement has emerged in terms of their proper referents, then as now. We will not solve all of these interpretive challenges here, for they are simply too great, but what we can do is *describe*, in grace and charity, two key ways (though there are more) our text has been interpreted by different Christian traditions.

One way to decipher the challenging declaration of Jesus in our text that "unless you eat the flesh of the Son of Man and drink his blood, you have no life in you," is to discern its meaning against the backdrop of what Jesus taught earlier: "For the bread of God is the bread that comes down from heaven and gives life to the world" (v. 33) and "I am the living bread that came down from heaven. Whoever eats this bread will live forever. This bread is my flesh, which I will give for the life of the world" (v. 51). And now for the crucial question: Who or what is that bread that must be eaten and that will give life to the world? It is none other than Jesus Christ himself, "the living bread that came down from heaven."

Beyond this, however, our text states: "Whoever eats my flesh and drinks my blood," and so here we have a focus not simply on bread and flesh, taking in the larger context, but also on blood. The addition of the word *blood* in this setting does, indeed, make a significant difference; it adds to the meanings that are already present. How so? Since blood is likely an allusion to Christ's crucified body bleeding on the cross, then the difficulty of our text of eating the flesh of Christ and drinking his blood is not resolved by simply referring to *the person* of Christ, who has come down from heaven, but it must also include *the event* of his crucifixion on the cross when his blood was poured out and spattered. That's what the addition of the word *blood* suggests.

Viewing the eating of bread and the drinking of wine as a deep and rich consumption of the person (Christ) and event (on the cross) that are brought together at Calvary is a powerful metaphorical way to communicate the high standards and requirements of Christian discipleship. All of this is taken into us such that it becomes a part of us. In a certain sense, this is what it means to be a follower of Jesus. This may come as a surprise to some who have never considered this large passage in quite this way. One of the things to marvel about here is that Jesus taught truths of vast importance in very few words.

Accordingly, to be a disciple of Christ is not just the taking up of another path, another way, to some generalized or common goodness. Indeed, there is nothing ordinary or common about this journey. The words that Jesus proclaimed require nothing less than that Christ be *in us*, interpenetrating our very being! The relation between Christ and his followers will be greater, tighter, closer, and more intimate than what we might have initially supposed or imagined. His blood will course through our veins. His life will become our life: "the one who feeds on me will live because of me." This is not any half-hearted following that costs little. The expense is huge, staggering. So then, in this first interpretation, Jesus employed *words*—he made use of powerful rhetorical expressions, to point to both his life and death, to his own person and to the event of his dying. By doing so, he also illuminated the path of discipleship. This journey, then, is marked by the all-consuming nature of personal and communal appropriation, a genuine ingestion. No wonder some people were put off by this teaching.

Another way of interpreting the words of our text— "unless you eat the flesh of the Son of Man and drink his blood, you have no life in you"—is to see them in light of the Lord's Supper which Jesus officiated shortly before his death: "And he took bread, gave thanks and broke it, and gave it to them, saying, 'This is my body given for you; do this in remembrance of me.' In the same way, after the supper he took the cup, saying, 'This cup is the new covenant in my blood, which is poured out for you'" (Luke 22:19–20). This is the sacramental or the liturgical view, and it is championed by several Christian traditions. In fact, many of the early church fathers, both in the East and the West, interpreted our text essentially in this way. To illustrate, Cyril of

Alexandria (AD 378-444), in his "Commentary on the Gospel of John," wrote the following: "Even the body of Christ itself was sanctified by the power of the Word made one with it, and it is thus endowed with living force in the blessed Eucharist so that is it able to implant in us its sanctifying grace."[1]

Since no human being is a pure spirit like the angels in heaven but is composed of body, soul, and spirit, then it is understandable that at the Last Supper Jesus would identify all of the earlier meanings that he sought to communicate at Capernaum with the physical, tangible realities of bread and wine. Jesus, in so many ways, was a great teacher. As earlier there was an economy of words, now there is an economy of things. In this current setting, there are, in fact, only two. We take the bread and eat it, and the life of Christ, the body of Christ, is now in us by faith as we are open to receive all that is truly present. Again, we take the wine and drink it, consume it, and the blood of Christ—its life-giving power—is now in us by faith as we are open to receive all that is truly present. To participate in this sacrament, then, is a rich and overflowing means of grace. It is a fountain of life. It will, of course, be necessary for all disciples, then as now, in light of Jesus's own clear command to "do this in remembrance of me" (Luke 22:19).

Recall that in the first interpretation of the difficult passages of our text Jesus used words, a distinct rhetoric, to point to his own person and to an event: his bleeding death on the cross. In a similar fashion, the second interpretation employs distinct objects—the bread and wine of the Last Supper—once again, to point to the person of Christ and to the event of his bloody death on the cross at Calvary and to view this now in a sacramental way. In each case, metaphors point to realities beyond themselves. That's the whole point in using them. And things like bread and wine do so as well. Consequently, a flat, literal interpretation will hardly work here; it will only baffle or confuse its hearers. And that's why Jesus affirmed, as a good teacher: "The words I have spoken to you—they are full of the Spirit and life." So then, consuming the bleeding, dying body of Christ on the cross, and feeding on all of its profound and life-changing meaning, is the *reality* that Jesus always pointed to whether by word or by object. What an economy of expression; what a path of discipleship!

Some of the larger group of disciples, however, who had witnessed the feeding of the five thousand, and who had followed Jesus to Capernaum, found this teaching to be disturbing: "This is a hard teaching [the Greek word, σκληρός, sklēroˇs, suggests "harsh or severe"[2]]. Who can accept it?" Jesus spoke with them further but then, as our text indicates: "From this time many of his disciples turned back and no longer followed him." This unexpected turn of events may have perplexed us in the past especially if we noted, somewhat painfully, that Jesus did not run after these departing disciples and shout something to the effect: "Wait, don't go; you've misunderstood what I've said. Give me some more time and I will explain it all to you." Instead, Jesus simply let them walk away; he let them go—and they never came back.

To be troubled in this particular matter (if it looks like Jesus is not being a good teacher or an energetic evangelist) is a sure sign that we have misread this passage. These disciples did not leave because they didn't *know* what Jesus was teaching—oh, they got that. They left because they couldn't *accept* it.

After this, Christ turned to his twelve disciples and asked: "You do not want to leave too, do you?" Simon Peter spoke for all when he exclaimed, and in a way similar to his confession at Caesarea Philippi: "Lord, to whom shall we go? You have the words of eternal life. We have come to believe and to know that you are the Holy One of God."

The Prayer

Jesus, thank you for being my example of self-giving sacrifice and love, but help me, Lord, to grasp and cling to the true meaning of Holy Communion—to embrace the truth that you abide in me, and that I abide in you. Your life is my life, your blood, the life-giving power that flows through me. Help me, Lord, to share that life and power with everyone I meet.

The Questions

Does the church today run after those who know the teaching of Christ but refuse to accept it? What would be the likely consequences of such a course of action for the future of the church?

Day 25

The Crowd

JOHN 12:12–19 *The next day the great crowd that had come for the festival heard that Jesus was on his way to Jerusalem. They took palm branches and went out to meet him, shouting,*

> *"Hosanna!"*
> *"Blessed is he who comes in the name of the Lord!"*
> *"Blessed is the king of Israel!"*
>
> *Jesus found a young donkey and sat on it, as it is written:*
>
> *"Do not be afraid, Daughter Zion;*
> *see, your king is coming,*
> *seated on a donkey's colt."*

At first his disciples did not understand all this. Only after Jesus was glorified did they realize that these things had been written about him and that these things had been done to him.

Now the crowd that was with him when he called Lazarus from the tomb and raised him from the dead continued to spread the word. Many people, because they had heard that he had performed this sign, went out to meet him. So the Pharisees said to one another, "See, this is getting us nowhere. Look how the whole world has gone after him!"

Consider This

There had been many celebrations in Jerusalem before leading up to the Passover, but this one was different. Reports of the great miracle of Jesus raising Lazarus from the dead (John 11:32–54) circulated through the crowd and continued to spread the word among the people. After a supper was held at Bethany in his honor (John 12:1–2), Jesus made his way to Jerusalem. This would be a triumphal entry, a grand entrance, and it was so significant that all the Gospels report it. With stories of his death-to-life miracle in the air, Jesus was greeted by a great crowd and the people took palm branches and shouted: "Hosanna! Blessed is he who comes in the name of the Lord! Blessed is the king of Israel!" What an acclamation! What a day this was!

The shout, the praise of the people, was an echo from the book of Psalms: "Lord, save us! Lord, grant us success! Blessed is he who comes in the name of the Lord. From the house of the Lord we bless you" (118:25–26). There are three parts of these two verses from the Psalter that are of interest to us. The first part, "Lord, save us" or as the Aramaic phrase would put it, "Save us now,"[1] corresponds to "Hosanna," a word that, by the way, is used much differently today, often as a general expression of joy without the specific call for redemption. The second part of this praise, "Blessed is he who comes in the name of the Lord," could have been said of any holy man or woman who loved God, the Holy One of Israel. There's nothing unique here.

Third, however, notice that Psalm 118 does not contain the last praise offered by the people: "Blessed is the king of Israel." That tribute or honor is indeed unique, set apart, and it could not have been spoken about just anybody. But what kind of king did the people have in mind: someone who could feed the masses, raise the dead, or throw off the yoke of Rome? Someone who could smooth out the inconveniences and annoyances of life? Would the crowd have been so energetic and lavish in its praise if it had understood just what kind of king Jesus offered himself to be? Aware of it or not, the people who gathered that day for the upcoming festival would see this distinct kingship, which does indeed have roots in Jewish tradition as we will see shortly, displayed right in front of their eyes!

Earlier, after Jesus had fed five thousand people near the Sea of Tiberias (John 6:1), some of the folk had wanted to make him king, but Jesus, rightly understanding their motivation, withdrew from them. Now in Jerusalem, and through his actions of finding and sitting upon a young donkey, Jesus was demonstrably willing to be acknowledged as a king, as a ruler. Indeed, he was well aware that by these actions he was fulfilling a specific prophecy found in Zechariah 9:9: "Rejoice greatly, Daughter Zion! Shout, Daughter Jerusalem! See, your king comes to you, righteous and victorious, lowly and riding on a donkey, on a colt, the foal of a donkey." The language of our text in John, which is reminiscent of this passage from Zechariah, is however slightly different: "Do not be afraid, Daughter Zion; see, your king is coming, seated on a donkey's colt." The elements of Daughter Zion, a king, and the donkey's colt are all there in both passages but only the gospel account mentions, "Do not be afraid," as an added word of encouragement. Such reassurance would be needed.

Though Nathanael had already acknowledged that Jesus is the king of Israel: "Rabbi, you are the Son of

God; you are the king of Israel" (John 1:49b), the disciples struggled to understand the significance of the donkey riding and the proclamation of the crowd. In fact, our text indicates that they "did not understand *all* this" (emphasis added). The meaning, the substance, of all that was happening along the road that day had escaped them. Since Jesus rode atop a donkey's colt and not some sleek, dark stallion, which would be the preference of military leaders, he entered Jerusalem giving yet another hint, another clue, as to just what the kingdom of God is all about. Jesus, like the Jewish prophets before him, demonstrated humility, a value whose celebration would be a puzzle to both Greeks and Romans alike. In fact, neither the Greek nor the Roman pantheon of gods ever praised the worth of being humble, lowly, or meek. These gods, often driven by animated lusts, had nothing to do with such mean things.

Again, from all the gospel accounts, it appears that the disciples, surprisingly enough, were slow learners and at times even remarkably dull especially in terms of grasping what the kingdom of God entailed. Such honesty adds to the trustworthiness of the gospel narratives. To illustrate, after Peter had confessed that Jesus is the Christ, the Son of God, and after Jesus had taught about his upcoming suffering, rejection, and death, Peter then rebuked him. In his thinking at the time, what did suffering, rejection, and death have to do with God and the kingdom? It simply didn't compute. Isn't God the greatest, the highest, the most exalted, and the coming kingdom therefore simply glorious? Aren't better things ahead?

Even in terms of the other two followers who made up the inner circle of the disciples beyond Peter—James and John Zebedee—serious misunderstanding and confusion were evident in terms of the kingdom of God. Thinking about the coming kingdom in a very carnal, worldly way, James and John were preoccupied with their own position within it: "Let one of us sit at your right and the other at your left in your glory" (Mark 10:37)—a veiled request that not surprisingly caused sharp division among the rest of the disciples when they learned of it. In fact, they were indignant. So then, though Peter, James, and John were among the inner three, and though they alone were with Jesus on the Mount of Transfiguration, even *they* grappled, on some levels, with the identity of Jesus and just what kind of kingdom he was offering.

Since the crowd that had been with Jesus when he raised Lazarus from the dead continued to spread the word, many people, who were simply there to attend the festival, went out to meet Jesus. Such a flocking to Christ, caused by the singing of his praises, disturbed the Pharisees. No doubt in a fit of jealousy, which helps to explain their energetic response, the religious leaders cried: "See, this is getting us nowhere. Look how the whole world has gone after him!" The irony here is obvious. These religious leaders had tried to stop Jesus, but they failed miserably. In their zero-sum world, if Jesus advanced, they could only decline. In the days ahead they would have to do something about *that*.

The Prayer

Lord, we all dream. We all have ideas of how things should be or could be. Help me see who you truly are and understand the kingdom you bring to earth through us. As I shout joyfully, "Hosanna!" let me also pray earnestly, "Save us now," in every circumstance.

The Questions

What does riding a donkey's colt symbolize? How does such an action reveal something about both the person and mission of Jesus? How is the kingship of Jesus different from that of all others?

Day 26

Jesus and the Apostles

LUKE 22:14-23 *When the hour came, Jesus and his apostles reclined at the table. And he said to them, "I have eagerly desired to eat this Passover with you before I suffer. For I tell you, I will not eat it again until it finds fulfillment in the kingdom of God."*

After taking the cup, he gave thanks and said, "Take this and divide it among you. For I tell you I will not drink again from the fruit of the vine until the kingdom of God comes."

And he took bread, gave thanks and broke it, and gave it to them, saying, "This is my body given for you; do this in remembrance of me."

In the same way, after the supper he took the cup, saying, "This cup is the new covenant in my blood, which is poured out for you. But the hand of him who is going to betray me is with mine on the table. The Son of Man will go as it has been decreed. But woe to that man who betrays him!" They began to question among themselves which of them it might be who would do this.

Consider This

As good Jews, Jesus and his apostles reclined at the table in order to celebrate the Passover, the commemoration of God's deliverance of the Hebrew people from Egyptian bondage (see Deuteronomy 16:1–8). This Passover, however, took on special meaning because beyond its historic reference to an ancient captivity and a mighty deliverance, Jesus related this meal to the future, to his own upcoming suffering. In fact, he told his apostles that he would not eat this meal again until the kingdom of God came. Put another way, Jesus would not eat another Passover until he was crucified and raised from the dead in glorious power, actions that would bring about a much greater deliverance, even freedom from the captivity of sin and death. Such a fulfillment then could be seen in the post-resurrection meals found in Luke's gospel (24:30–31, 41–42) or perhaps in a much later period after the second coming of Christ.

The author of the Gospel of Luke (and the book of Acts) was likely influenced by the apostle Paul. We can see this influence in terms of how the material of our text is arranged into three parts. The first part, verses 14–18, describes the Passover, which we have just considered. The third part, verses 21–23, explores the betrayal of Jesus by his own disciple Judas, an account that both Mark and Matthew place at the beginning of their narratives and not at the end as Luke does. The second part, our principal interest right now, describes a meal, but this one seems to be somewhat different from the Passover, and it is not exactly clear how this other meal is related to the first. Indeed, its details correspond to what the church referred to as "the Lord's Supper" in 1 Corinthians 11:20. To see this similarity between the two accounts, between a gospel and an epistle, compare verses 19 and 20 of our current text with what Paul wrote in 1 Corinthians 11:23b–25: "The Lord Jesus, on the night he was betrayed, took bread, and when he had given thanks, he broke it and said, 'This is my body, which is for you; do this in remembrance of me.' In the same way, after supper he took the cup, saying, 'This cup is the new covenant in my blood; do this, whenever you drink it, in remembrance of me.'" The similarities between these two accounts are striking.

The way that Luke arranges his material in our passage suggests that the Passover meal, with its bread and many cups of wine, flows into a different meal, the Lord's Supper, with its specific focus on the person and work of Jesus. The bread of verse 19 does not principally derive its meaning from the historic affirmations of the Passover (although there are some similarities) but from its present context that points to the body of Christ, "given for you." Here Jesus was no doubt referring to his upcoming sacrifice on the cross at Calvary. He knew what was coming. In the same way, the cup that Jesus held in verse 20 is best understood not in terms of the cups (plural) of the Passover feast but in terms of the present context, that is, the Lord's Supper and of Christ's upcoming passion on the cross, now specifically with respect to his blood, "which is poured out for you." Notice also that the language of "given for you" and "which is poured out for you" both reveal that what is being offered is a sheer gift to be received. The direction is from Christ to us.

So then, in placing his material in this way, Luke presents the old—the Passover—in terms of the new, the Lord's Supper. Here both similarities and contrasts can be noted. To illustrate, it is only the Lord's Supper that illuminates in a very pointed way the fulfillment of God's purpose that will take place in the death and resurrection of Jesus Christ. That is, the Passover in this account points beyond itself to a greater meal and to a greater deliverance that is remarkably *new*. In fact, only Luke's text refers to the cup of this supper as "the *new* covenant in my blood" (emphasis added). Both Mark and Matthew, for their part, simply refer to "my blood of the covenant" (Mark 14:24a; Matt. 26:28a). Continuity with the past, however, can be seen in terms of the new covenant promised earlier by the prophet Jeremiah:

> "The days are coming," declares the Lord, "when I will make a new covenant with the people of Israel and with the people of Judah. It will not be like the covenant I made with their ancestors when I took them by the hand to lead them out of Egypt, because they broke my covenant, though I was a husband to them," declares the Lord. "This is the covenant I will make with the people of Israel after that time," declares the Lord. "I will put my law in their minds and write it on their hearts. I will be their God, and they will be my people." (31:31–33)

Luke's account then, in our judgment, is far more clear and crisp in its telling of the story. It highlights the contrast between the old and the new while mindful of their similarities. Indeed, God's redemptive activity is not simply a continuation of what is already past, though the past does indeed prepare for it. That's something very helpful to recognize.

The contrast between the old and new in terms of these meals can also be seen in that most of the religious leaders of the Jewish people during the first century would not make this transition from the traditional religious meanings, well more than a thousand years old, to what was new—to what was now being offered as an utter gift. These leaders would continue to embrace the Passover and many other traditions, but they would ultimately reject the Lord's Supper, especially when they finally figured out that it pointed to both the person and work of Christ. The common folk also rejected the new, following along comfortably, hardly disturbed at all, in all of the old ways. Tradition is as settled as the past that holds it in place. It can, in some instances, offer a sense of security that is not fully warranted, especially when God is doing something new. Such is the case here.

At this intimate meal Jesus uttered some of the most precious words ever spoken by anyone at any time: "This is my body *given for you*" and "This cup is the new covenant in my blood, which is *poured out for you*" (emphasis added). The fellowship, love, and affection among those present (with but one exception), reclining at the table, surely must have been sweet, even tender. Given such a thick atmosphere of friendship and devotion, it is all the more disruptive, a breach of the deepest confidence, when the betrayer picked this occasion above all others to set in motion his evil design. Knowing what he was to do, why did he even attend the supper at all?

So deceitful was the faithless one that the other apostles apparently didn't know who it was, as evidenced by their anxious questioning among themselves. Because Luke placed the betrayal at the end of our text, this means that Judas had received both the bread and the cup from Jesus. The offering of these gifts was surely a sign, and it tells us far more about Jesus and his kingdom than it ever does about the betrayer. Though Luke did not record it, both Mark and Matthew revealed what Jesus had declared in terms of this hypocrite: "It would be better for him if he had not been born" (Mark 14:21; Matt. 26:24).

The Prayer

Lord, as I reflect on the Lord's Supper, help me to understand that you gave yourself for us. The gift that you have given was not only for the worthy and worthwhile, but it was offered freely to everyone—even the one you knew would betray you. Help me to live out that self-giving love unconditionally, offering it freely even to those who have hurt me, just as you did.

The Questions

Why did Jesus offer both the bread and wine to Judas, knowing that the disciple would betray him? Does this action on the part of Jesus reveal something about who he is? What does it reveal about the kingdom of God?

Day 27

Sinners

MARK 14:32–42 *They went to a place called Gethsemane, and Jesus said to his disciples, "Sit here while I pray." He took Peter, James and John along with him, and he began to be deeply distressed and troubled. "My soul is overwhelmed with sorrow to the point of death," he said to them. "Stay here and keep watch."*

Going a little farther, he fell to the ground and prayed that if possible the hour might pass from him. "Abba, Father," he said, "everything is possible for you. Take this cup from me. Yet not what I will, but what you will."

Then he returned to his disciples and found them sleeping. "Simon," he said to Peter, "are you asleep? Couldn't you keep watch for one hour? Watch and pray so that you will not fall into temptation. The spirit is willing, but the flesh is weak."

Once more he went away and prayed the same thing. When he came back, he again found them sleeping, because their eyes were heavy. They did not know what to say to him.

Returning the third time, he said to them, "Are you still sleeping and resting? Enough! The hour has come. Look, the Son of Man is delivered into the hands of sinners. Rise! Let us go! Here comes my betrayer!"

Consider This

After the Last Supper, Jesus and his disciples made their way to Gethsemane, an olive orchard or garden across the Kidron Valley from Jerusalem. He told eight of his disciples (Judas was obviously absent) to "Sit here while I pray," and then he took Peter, James, and John, the so-called inner circle, along with him. These three may have been chosen on this occasion because each of them had earlier professed their willingness to suffer for Jesus. For example, in a passage that immediately precedes our text, Peter exclaimed: "Even if I have to die with you, I will never disown you" (Mark 14:31). Earlier, James and John, after requesting for themselves two of the best seats in the kingdom of God, in answer to the follow-up question of Jesus, "Can you drink the cup I drink or be baptized with the baptism I am baptized with?" they shot back, "We can" (Mark 10:38–39), apparently not realizing at the time all that would be entailed.

When many people consider the suffering of Jesus, they immediately think of the cross with its gory blood and torturous physical pain. However, not only did the suffering of Christ, his passion, begin much earlier than this but it also included, judging from the language of our text, some of the most agonizing emotional pain possible well prior to the cross: "he began to be deeply distressed and troubled. 'My soul is overwhelmed with sorrow to the point of death,' he said to them." In terms of this first phrase, "deeply distressed and troubled," scholar James Brooks doesn't believe that our NIV translation does justice to the original Greek in terms of the depth and agony of the suffering entailed. He writes: "The NEB does a better job than the NIV, NASB, and RSV in bringing out their meaning: 'Horror and dismay came over him.'"[1] The English word *horror* is a much better choice and begins to convey something of the very dark, desolate, and excruciating emotions that Jesus as a flesh-and-blood human being was now experiencing. However, in terms of the second phrase, actually a sentence, the NIV does a much better job: "My soul is overwhelmed with sorrow to the point of death." However, what does it mean to be so overwhelmed with sorrow that one is at death's door? This is a reality at the very limits, the boundaries, of human experience. Few people have experienced such pain. It is to fill the cup of emotional anguish to the brim.

Moreover, these distressing emotions cannot be properly assessed simply in terms of the prospect of physical torture. Jesus was no coward at Gethsemane. Knowing all that lay ahead of him—physical pain, to be sure, but also and perhaps more important, deep emotional and even spiritual pain—Jesus was deeply disturbed and moved. Who wouldn't be? In the garden he perhaps had a vision of the alienation that the cross would entail in which so many key relationships would become darkened and forsaken. Many of his own disciples would abandon him. He would become an object of scorn for so many, written off as a person condemned by God and accursed. What's more, he would be in a place in which even the divine love, though still present, would somehow be obscured. Now that's darkness; that's real horror.

Knowing that "with God all things are possible" (Matt. 19:26), Jesus prayed that this hour might somehow pass from him—or to put it in a slightly different way, that this cup might be taken away. Both the words *hour* and *cup* in this context refer to the very same thing: the upcoming sacrifice of Christ on the cross with all of its physical, emotional, and spiritual pain. Moreover, in his petitionary prayer, notice that Jesus uttered the words "*Abba*, Father," an Aramaic expression that suggests intimacy, a closeness of relationship. The Jews, however, rejected such a usage, a rejection that grew out of their fear of even pronouncing the divine name. Instead, they much preferred to use the word *Adonai* or, as it is most often translated, simply *Lord* (God is my Lord). So then, in the judgment of first-century Jews, at least, the word *Abba* was simply too familiar. It didn't keep in place the proper distance between God and humanity. Jesus thought otherwise.

Returning from praying, Jesus addressed Peter with his personal name "Simon," perhaps indicating a measure of disappointment or displeasure, and asked, "Couldn't you keep watch for one hour?" Then Jesus added a word of caution: "Watch and pray so that you will not fall into temptation. The spirit is willing, but the flesh is weak." Just what kind of temptation did Jesus have in mind that was so grave that he warned his disciples to watch—to be wide awake—to be ever aware of their current environment and all that was happening within it or that was soon to occur? It was none other than the temptation, given the darkness of the hour, to sell out, to abandon Christ, to deny him, to be so driven by fear, to become franticly self-preoccupied, that one would grasp at personal security at all costs. The danger, then, was that such a fearful move could prove to be irrevocable, through a tidal wave of shame and despair, in an unending, spiraling loss. One of his own disciples was about to take that very tortuous path. Jesus knew.

Remarkably enough, another time that Mark employed the exact same Greek word that translates as "keep watch" in our text is in the parable that Jesus told earlier to encourage his followers to be wide awake so that they would be fully ready, well prepared, when he comes again. The narrative is as follows:

> "It's like a man going away: He leaves his house and puts his servants in charge, each with their assigned task, and tells the one at the door to keep watch.
> "Therefore keep watch because you do not know when the owner of the house will come back—whether in the evening, or at midnight, or when the rooster crows, or at dawn. If he comes suddenly, do not let him find you sleeping. What I say to you, I say to everyone: 'Watch!'" (Mark 13:34–37)

Jesus had cautioned his disciples to "keep watch." Instead, they did just the opposite; they fell asleep. Jesus called for heightened awareness; the disciples dozed off. This cycle of Jesus going off to pray and then returning to find his own disciples slumbering was repeated two more times. In this, they failed Jesus again and again. It's not that Jesus needed his disciples to offer comforting words during this dark hour or to fix things, to somehow make it all right. His request was much more modest than that. He just wanted his disciples to be present, to be there, at one of the most crucial hours of his life. There is much to be said for a ministry of presence when we just show up, knowing what is happening and who is involved. We don't have to do or say anything; we just have to be there. It's that simple. But Jesus couldn't have even this. It was denied him—and by his friends, no less! Despite all that Jesus had invested in these men over the last three years, the careful toil and labor, the considerable time and the lengthy conversations, he came up empty. In a real sense, Jesus was in the garden of Gethsemane *alone*.

If the disciples had been sleeping and utterly passive, of no account, others in the area at the time were very busy. In fact, in the interim they had organized a party, if you will, and set out to arrest Jesus. Knowing their intentions, Jesus rightly referred to them as sinners, as those who did not love God or their neighbor as they ought, though they themselves obviously thought that their cause was commendable, worth a nighttime effort. Some among them might have even viewed their enterprise as "just" or even more bombastically as the very "will of God." In the darkness of the hour, they may have inadvertently stumbled onto a grand, complex truth of which they were only dimly aware. That truth was Jesus.

The Prayer

Jesus, as you prayed in Gethsemane, you longed for those closest to you to abide with you—not their gifts, service, or witness. Help me remember that I'm not required to have clever words or elaborate gifts. Help me to offer you and others my presence.

The Questions

In hearing the self-centered requests earlier of James and John, in witnessing the failure of his disciples to watch as he had cautioned them, and in knowing that Judas was about to betray him, what kinds of emotions might Jesus have experienced as a human being? Did all of this make his Gethsemane experience more difficult?

Day 28

Judas

LUKE 22:47–53 *While he was still speaking a crowd came up, and the man who was called Judas, one of the Twelve, was leading them. He approached Jesus to kiss him, but Jesus asked him, "Judas, are you betraying the Son of Man with a kiss?"*

When Jesus' followers saw what was going to happen, they said, "Lord, should we strike with our swords?" And one of them struck the servant of the high priest, cutting off his right ear.

But Jesus answered, "No more of this!" And he touched the man's ear and healed him.

Then Jesus said to the chief priests, the officers of the temple guard, and the elders, who had come for him, "Am I leading a rebellion, that you have come with swords and clubs? Every day I was with you in the temple courts, and you did not lay a hand on me. But this is your hour—when darkness reigns."

Consider This

Judas Iscariot, one of the Twelve, had been preparing for this night for quite some time. Upon Satan entering in him, as the Gospel of Luke informs us elsewhere, "Judas went to the chief priests and the officers of the temple guard and discussed with them how he might betray Jesus" (Luke 22:4). Not long afterward the night of betrayal had finally arrived. The moment was just right. Judas would carry out what he had designed to do, whatever his motivation was for doing so. At the head of a crowd, made up of both religious leaders and common folk carrying clubs and swords (the Gospel of John adds Roman soldiers as well), Judas interrupted the third and last conversation that Jesus was having with his drowsy disciples at Gethsemane. As a way of identifying the man to be arrested, Judas approached Jesus to kiss him, but in Luke's account the scene immediately shifts to the question of Jesus: "Judas, are you betraying the Son of Man with a kiss?" That's exactly what he was doing.

All of the other disciples were evidently afraid to be associated with Christ, for after his upcoming arrest they would immediately flee (Mark 14:50). Beyond this, one disciple in particular would outright deny any association with Jesus as we will see shortly. However, the evil entailed in outright betrayal—well, that's an evil that places betrayal in a category all its own. There are a number of elements in this particular wickedness (that's not too strong a word here) that can prove to be painful even to examine. First of all, what is needed for betrayal is the sheer *goodness* of a solid and loving relationship, one that will eventually be perverted and defiled. Evil is always the corruption of a prior good; Augustine got that right. Judging from the gospel accounts, we can surmise that with his call by Jesus to be a disciple, Judas had likely started out well and with good intentions—but they simply did not last. In the meantime, he was known as a thief, that is, as one who helped himself to the money bag for the group (John 12:6).

Second, evil must somehow emerge in the heart of Judas in the form of disloyalty, faithlessness, and treachery. Even at this early stage, the relationship has *already* been tarnished. Indeed, the duplicity and bad faith that have arisen in Judas's heart must be kept secret though they may break out in complaints—"Why wasn't this perfume sold and the money given to the poor?" (v. 5)—or in backstabbing or in going behind Jesus's back (evil speaking) in arranging with the religious leaders the very scene of our current text. At this third stage, notice that the betrayer *pretended* that all was well though, of course, it wasn't. He kept the charade of being a good disciple going so much so that all the other disciples were clueless in this regard. Judas had to work hard to accomplish this; he had to engage in ongoing deception and deceit, forms of lying, so that the contents of his heart would not be exposed. He had fooled everyone, even his own fellow disciples. He was a master of deception. But he did not fool Jesus.

Finally, the secret is revealed; the betrayal is manifested. Once again pretending to be other than he actually was, Judas approached Jesus to kiss him. In this Middle Eastern culture, a kiss signified "friendship and esteem, even love,"[1] and so the irony of such an action is very great, full of significance. In other words, in this setting what was intended and what was being offered were two very different things. In short, a symbol of friendship had now become a sign of betrayal. Now that's evil!

Having slept on and off through much of the night, the disciples finally saw Judas at the head of the crowd. They then assessed the situation as best they could and asked Jesus if they should strike with their swords. One of them, Peter (according to John 18:10), moved quickly and cut off the ear of Malchus, the servant of the high priest. The question posed by the disciples as well as the immediate resort to violence by Peter together demonstrate that, despite all the careful teaching by Jesus of his upcoming suffering and death, the disciples once again, even at this late stage, failed to understand the ministry of Jesus aright and in what sense he was the Messiah. "No more of this!" Jesus commanded. In Matthew's account of this same incident, Jesus ordered the disciple to "Put your sword back in its place . . . for all who draw the sword will die by the sword" (Matt. 26:52). Demonstrating once again that his kingdom was "not of this world" (John 18:36), Jesus then reasoned with Peter: "Do you think I cannot call on my Father, and he will at once put at my disposal more than twelve legions of angels? But how then would the Scriptures be fulfilled that say it must happen in this way?" (Matt. 26:53–54).

So then, what did Jesus do in the midst of a treacherous situation in which he was about to be arrested by the leaders of a crowd that had come with swords and clubs, when he was being betrayed by his erstwhile disciple, and when bloody violence had already occurred? He healed someone! Yes, he healed someone! Indeed, one of the reasons this account from Luke has been chosen as our text is that his is the only one that relates this restoration miracle. Jesus remained, even in this dark hour, what he had always been from the very start of his ministry—a healer, one who announced through both word and action the transformative, restorative power of the kingdom of God. The evil of others did not undermine the goodness and power of Christ in the least. For their part, however, the disciples had another kind of power in mind, one that would only make things worse.

Jesus then turned his attention specifically to the chief priests, the officers of the temple guard, and the elders who were a part of the crowd, and he asked them a question: "Am I leading a rebellion, that you have come with swords and clubs?" The sense of the original Greek behind this verse appears to be rendered better than the NIV does in the following translations: the NRSV, "bandit"; the NASB 1995, "robber"; and the CEB "thief."[2] Jesus was obviously none of these things, and so he reminded these religious leaders that he had been with them in the temple courts, for all to see, and "you did not lay a hand on me." To be sure, in the light of day and in the midst of many worshipers in the temple area, these religious leaders had much to fear if they sought to arrest Jesus then and there. For what they had in mind they would need a far less public place as well as the cover of night. They had been plotting to take the life of Jesus for a long time (John 11:53). They now had their opportunity, for Judas had set the stage. At long last, they would carry out the desire of their hearts. Jesus pulled the cover away and declared to them: "This is your hour—when darkness reigns." Yes, this was their hour, but it would not last. Darkness cannot overcome the light.

The Prayer

Heavenly Father, in this troubled world, it would be easy to lose sight of your purpose, your kingdom, and my part in healing and restoring everything to you. The evil around me can never diminish the light of your Son, Jesus—the light that I bear. Remind me, Lord, that I am salt and light in the world.

The Questions

What does the healing of the servant of the high priest reveal about Jesus? How does this miracle compare with the others that Jesus did throughout his ministry? Does it have any special significance?

Day 29

Caiaphas, the Chief Priests, and the Sanhedrin

MATTHEW 26:57–68 *Those who had arrested Jesus took him to Caiaphas the high priest, where the teachers of the law and the elders had assembled. But Peter followed him at a distance, right up to the courtyard of the high priest. He entered and sat down with the guards to see the outcome.*

The chief priests and the whole Sanhedrin were looking for false evidence against Jesus so that they could put him to death. But they did not find any, though many false witnesses came forward.

Finally two came forward and declared, "This fellow said, 'I am able to destroy the temple of God and rebuild it in three days.'"

Then the high priest stood up and said to Jesus, "Are you not going to answer? What is this testimony that these men are bringing against you?" But Jesus remained silent.

The high priest said to him, "I charge you under oath by the living God: Tell us if you are the Messiah, the Son of God."

"You have said so," Jesus replied. "But I say to all of you: From now on you will see the Son of Man sitting at the right hand of the Mighty One and coming on the clouds of heaven."

Then the high priest tore his clothes and said, "He has spoken blasphemy! Why do we need any more witnesses? Look, now you have heard the blasphemy. What do you think?"

"He is worthy of death," they answered.

Then they spit in his face and struck him with their fists. Others slapped him and said, "Prophesy to us, Messiah. Who hit you?"

Consider This

Demonstrating its connection with the religious authorities, the crowd that had arrested Jesus now took him to the house of Caiaphas, the high priest. According to Josephus (AD 37–100), the reputation of Caiaphas among the people was not very good, for it was known that he "had purchased the high priesthood from Herod for one year only."[1] The Gospel of John differs slightly from our text in Matthew in that Jesus was brought first to Annas, the former high priest who was the father-in-law of Caiaphas. At any rate, Caiaphas was accompanied by the teachers of the law and the elders. These are some of the same religious leaders who had plotted earlier to kill Jesus (Matt. 26:3–5). In short, the men who were about to judge Jesus were some of the ones who had already conspired against him in the first place.

Everything about the trial that was conducted at the house of Caiaphas smacked of irregularity. We don't know exactly what standards should have been applied in this first-century setting, but later Jewish tradition, almost two centuries later as reflected in the Mishnah (a rabbinic commentary), indicated that such a trial should have taken place during the day in the temple courts since it involved the Sanhedrin, and certainly not on the eve of a festival.[2] Indeed, the haphazard nature of this assembly suggests that it was quickly put together due, in part, perhaps to the recent information received from Judas and those in league with him. Here was an opportunity to be exploited. The religious leaders had been frustrated earlier when they couldn't carry out their designs during the day, when crowds were present, for they feared there would be "a riot among the people" (v. 5). The time to strike was *now*.

Another peculiarity of the trial had to do with the basic approach of Caiaphas and the religious leaders, especially in terms of their line of questioning. Our text states that "the chief priests and the whole Sanhedrin [or at least all who were present] were looking for false evidence against Jesus so that they could put him to death." But why look for false evidence at all? Would it not be better to look for true and sound evidence which would be overwhelmingly convincing? Given this difficulty, it appears that the use of the phrase "false evidence" in this context could mean at least one of two things. First of all, from the perspective of the religious leaders, it would seem to indicate that they did not believe any true evidence was available to convict Jesus of a charge worthy of death—so they had to concoct or manufacture, through an interrogation process, whatever evidence they needed. The second possibility here is that the language of "false evidence" is an editorial comment on the part of Matthew, who knew full well that any evidence of a capital offense against Jesus, even if the religious leaders believed it to be true, simply had to be false.

Given its serious nature, an offense worthy of death would require the agreement of at least two witnesses. Many false witnesses did indeed come forward, but as the Gospel of Mark relates: "their statements did not agree" (Mark 14:56). Finally, two people emerged, and they declared: "This fellow said, 'I am able to destroy the temple of God and rebuild it in three days.'" Since temple worship was at the heart of the Jewish faith at this time, then this last charge would indeed be taken very seriously. It could also help the religious leaders with respect to their ultimate goal.

Since the Jews at the time were under the authority of Rome, they were not permitted to carry out executions. The Romans would not be interested in offenses against religious law—the laws of Leviticus, for example—except when such an offense had a consequence for the state. The intent to destroy the temple could, after all, be viewed as a sign of insurrection, a challenge to Roman governance. This could work. No doubt emboldened by this recent line of testimony, Caiaphas questioned Jesus: "Are you not going to answer? What is this testimony that these men are bringing against you?" But Jesus remained silent, a silence reminiscent of the suffering servant of Isaiah 53:7: "He was oppressed and afflicted, yet he did not open his mouth; he was led like a lamb to the slaughter, and as a sheep before its shearers is silent, so he did not open his mouth."

Magnifying the importance of the words that would soon be spoken, Caiaphas turned up the heat, so to speak, and bellowed: "I charge you under oath by the living God: Tell us if you are the Messiah, the Son of God." Recognizing the severity of oaths, in light of his earlier teaching, "But I tell you, do not swear an oath at all" (Matt. 5:34a), Jesus responded very carefully: "You have said so." So Christ replied in the affirmative (How could he not, in light of his person and ministry?), but he did so in an indirect way rather than a direct one. It was one and the other at the same time. Jesus was not making a statement about himself using his own words. Instead, he was making a statement about himself using the very words of the high priest. Given the circumstances, fraught with verbal peril, it was a wise answer, truthful in so many respects. Indeed, in the way that Jesus had formulated his response in Matthew's account, if Caiaphas took exception to it, then he would, on some level, have taken exception to his own words!

Jesus, however, did not leave it at that. He continued to speak: "But I say to all of you: From now on you will see the Son of Man sitting at the right hand of the Mighty One and coming on the clouds of heaven." Knowing the Scriptures as they did, Caiaphas and the religious leaders would have heard in the words of Jesus a clear reference to Daniel 7:13–14, a passage that described the Son of Man as a glorious, triumphant figure who would come, "with the clouds of heaven" (v. 13). They would also have heard in his response echoes of Psalm 110:1 in which "The LORD says to my lord: 'Sit at my right hand until I make your enemies a footstool for your feet.'" They quickly got the message. Being thought of as a footstool, if they had recognized the full extent of what Jesus was actually saying, would not, of course, be well received. Not surprisingly then, the high priest was furious, and so he tore his clothes (something that high priests should never do, by the way[3]) and cried, "He has spoken blasphemy!" This had been a familiar charge, one made earlier (John 10:33) by many of the religious leaders who were now present at this ad hoc assembly and trial. The big difference, of course, was that now they would have the means, the wherewithal, to make the charge matter. It would stick.

Once Caiaphas and the religious leaders had determined, in their minds at least, that what Jesus had spoken was blasphemy, and therefore was worthy of death, they proceeded to degrade and humiliate him. They spat in his face, struck him with their fists, and slapped him. And as if this were not enough degradation, they then began to mock him: "Prophesy to us, Messiah. Who hit you?" Consider, then, this behavior of the high priest and the religious leaders for a moment. Bear in mind that Jesus had clearly taught earlier, in order that his followers would not be deceived by false prophets, that those claiming to represent the Most High would be known not by what they said or how they dressed or what position they held, but simply by what they did: "By their fruit you will recognize them" (Matt. 7:16a). In light of this consideration, who then bore the face of God to the people better, the high priest and his compatriots or Jesus? We cannot avoid asking this question.

The Prayer

Lord, in your Word, I read how you faced unjust men in power with humility and honesty. Remind me that irrespective of whether those in power today rule justly or unjustly, the desires and goals of this world are not mine. Help me to walk and talk respectfully, with humility and honesty, just as Jesus did, so that others may recognize me as your follower.

The Questions

Why is the factor of what people do—their fruits, so to speak—the best evidence of all upon which to make judgments? How do actions, which can be seen, reveal what cannot be seen such as the motivations, intentions, and the desires of the heart?

Day 30

Peter

MATTHEW 26:69–75 *Now Peter was sitting out in the courtyard, and a servant girl came to him. "You also were with Jesus of Galilee," she said.*

But he denied it before them all. "I don't know what you're talking about," he said.

Then he went out to the gateway, where another servant girl saw him and said to the people there, "This fellow was with Jesus of Nazareth."

He denied it again, with an oath: "I don't know the man!"

After a little while, those standing there went up to Peter and said, "Surely you are one of them; your accent gives you away."

Then he began to call down curses, and he swore to them, "I don't know the man!"

Immediately a rooster crowed. Then Peter remembered the word Jesus had spoken: "Before the rooster crows, you will disown me three times." And he went outside and wept bitterly.

Consider This

As Jesus was taken to the house of Caiaphas for trial, Peter followed him at a distance "right up to the courtyard of the high priest" (Matt. 26:58), motivated perhaps by both love and curiosity. Peter would soon face his own trial in the courtyard and its surroundings for which he was ill prepared. Though Jesus had warned him earlier in the garden of Gethsemane to watch and pray, he nevertheless slept away. Subsequent events would reveal that Peter should have heeded the words, the pointed caution, of Jesus.

A servant girl of the high priest approached Peter while he was sitting in the courtyard and declared: "You also were with Jesus of Galilee." The reference to Galilee may be an indication of geographical pride on the part of the girl who evidently was a Judean and well aware of it. In speaking up, the girl had attracted some attention, and the audience by now was larger than simply Peter and herself. Peter denied the claim "before them all." And to be even more forceful and emphatic in this, his first denial of Jesus, Peter added, "I don't know what you're talking about," a statement that was obviously false. Earlier Peter had boasted in a way in which he had compared himself with the other disciples quite favorably: "Even if all fall away on account of you, I never will" (v. 33). Again, to indicate just how confident he was in terms of his own resolve, Peter had also exclaimed: "Even if I have to die with you, I will never disown you" (v. 35). All of this bravado, however, was now gone, revealed to be little more than empty boasts, and Peter's "trial" was just getting started.

After this scene, no doubt shaken, Peter got up and headed toward the gateway which was a vestibule between the courtyard and the door that led to the street. Perhaps he was thinking about leaving the area, then another servant girl spoke up. But unlike the first one, she didn't address Peter, but the people milling about in the vestibule: "This fellow was with Jesus of Nazareth." Once again, for the second time, Peter would deny any association with Jesus. But this time around he did something different, an action that Jesus had warned against earlier, had even forbidden, but none of this mattered anymore. Peter was gripped by fear. What did he do? He attempted to underscore the truthfulness of his own denial of Jesus by confirming it with an oath. In short, he would swear to the truth of his own lie! He should have kept watch as Jesus had cautioned.

This whole area was filled with so much potential mischief, with many ways to go very wrong, and that's probably why Jesus had warned Peter and others earlier: "But I tell you, do not swear an oath at all: either by heaven, for it is God's throne; or by the earth, for it is his footstool; or by Jerusalem, for it is the city of the Great King. And do not swear by your head, for you cannot make even one hair white or black. All you need to say is simply 'Yes' or 'No'; anything beyond this comes from the evil one" (5:34–37). Again, what had Peter done? He had invoked nothing less than a solemn oath as a cover for his own lying.[1] Fear can make people do strange things.

Though Peter wanted to be near the mouth of the courtyard, perhaps for a quick exit, he nevertheless did not flee but remained in that area. After a little while, Peter was accosted by those standing there who claimed: "Surely you are one of them; your accent gives you away." Peter responded to such a claim in yet a third denial of Christ, and this was his most grave and forceful disavowal of all. Peter not only swore to these people in the vestibule that he did not know the man, as he had stated earlier to the servant girl, but he also began to call down curses. The difficult question here, of course, is upon whom did Peter begin to call down curses? Though our text, itself, does not clearly answer this question, there is more than enough room for ambiguity; nevertheless, there are at least two possibilities that should be considered.

First of all, as in his second denial, Peter may have called down a curse upon himself if he were lying. The logic here would be that he would never do such a thing, that is, take such drastic, self-defeating action of cursing himself unless his statement was true. Simply put, this was yet another round of the liar's game: add strength and force to the pretended truthfulness of what is actually a lie. The problem, however, with this view is that the verb used in our text may not be reflexive. In other words, there is no mention of Peter doing something specifically to *himself.* Nevertheless, this interpretation remains a possibility given the ambiguity of the text.

The second option would be that, in his third denial, Peter actually called down curses upon Jesus himself. This option, however, seems less likely given Peter's earlier confession that Jesus is "the Son of the living God" (16:16) as well as his two earlier boasts about his deep and unwavering commitment to Christ (see 26:33, 35). To be sure, Peter's problem, his predicament, in his third denial was that he needed to add weight to the supposed truth of his grandiose lie. Cursing himself in a harsh and damning way would surely accomplish all of that. It would get the job done. There was no need at all to curse Christ. Why do it? That kind of strength and force was simply unnecessary.

Whether Peter cursed himself or Christ, although it was probably the former, one thing remains abundantly clear. Peter, unlike Judas, was later restored to the sweet graces of fellowship. He didn't despair even after committing a very grave sin. Indeed, upon hearing the rooster crow, Peter remembered the prophecy of Jesus (and recall that the religious leaders in the house of Caiaphas had mocked that Jesus was a prophet) and he began to repent almost immediately as he "wept bitterly." Beyond this, the Gospel of John presents the later encounter of Peter with the risen Christ in an incident that not only demonstrates a hearty restoration of Peter, but one that also prepared him for his generous leadership role in the church at Pentecost (and beyond) when the Holy Spirit was given in fullness. This reconciling text, which offers three affirmations of Peter in the face of his earlier three denials, is worth quoting at length:

> When they had finished eating, Jesus said to Simon Peter, "Simon son of John, do you love me more than these?"
>
> "Yes, Lord," he said, "you know that I love you."
>
> Jesus said, "Feed my lambs."
>
> Again Jesus said, "Simon son of John, do you love me?"
>
> He answered, "Yes, Lord, you know that I love you."
>
> Jesus said, "Take care of my sheep."
>
> The third time he said to him, "Simon son of John, do you love me?"
>
> Peter was hurt because Jesus asked him the third time, "Do you love me?" He said, "Lord, you know all things; you know that I love you."
>
> Jesus said, "Feed my sheep." (John 21:15–17)

Another important issue here calls for our attention. Jesus had taught earlier that, "Anyone who speaks a word against the Son of Man will be forgiven" (Matt. 12:32). So then, whether people call down curses upon themselves in the attempt to solidify a lie or whether they curse Christ out of ignorance (Who could ever curse Christ out of knowledge of who he is?) or out of fear or darkness or abject pain, they can yet and wonderfully be forgiven. The grace of God manifested in Jesus Christ can shine forth and bring joyous cleansing and renewal. The light that has come into the world knows no equal. He offers the luster of refreshing forgiveness, one that gives hope to all. Peter was restored.

The Prayer

Lord, as I examine my life I may sometimes ask, "How could I have done that?" or "What was I thinking?" Fear drives me away from you and deeper into sin until I cannot recognize the difference between the truth and a lie. Thank you, Lord, for your amazing grace and boundless love that casts away all fear.

The Questions

Compare and contrast the betrayal of Jesus by Judas and the denial of Jesus by Peter. In what ways were their actions similar? In what ways were they different? Why was Peter restored and not Judas?

Day 31

Pilate

JOHN 18:28-38 *Then the Jewish leaders took Jesus from Caiaphas to the palace of the Roman governor. By now it was early morning, and to avoid ceremonial uncleanness they did not enter the palace, because they wanted to be able to eat the Passover. So Pilate came out to them and asked, "What charges are you bringing against this man?"*

"If he were not a criminal," they replied, "we would not have handed him over to you."

Pilate said, "Take him yourselves and judge him by your own law."

"But we have no right to execute anyone," they objected. This took place to fulfill what Jesus had said about the kind of death he was going to die.

Pilate then went back inside the palace, summoned Jesus and asked him, "Are you the king of the Jews?"

"Is that your own idea," Jesus asked, "or did others talk to you about me?"

"Am I a Jew?" Pilate replied. "Your own people and chief priests handed you over to me. What is it you have done?"

Jesus said, "My kingdom is not of this world. If it were, my servants would fight to prevent my arrest by the Jewish leaders. But now my kingdom is from another place."

"You are a king, then!" said Pilate.

Jesus answered, "You say that I am a king. In fact, the reason I was born and came into the world is to testify to the truth. Everyone on the side of truth listens to me."

"What is truth?" retorted Pilate. With this he went out again to the Jews gathered there and said, "I find no basis for a charge against him."

Consider This

After a belabored interrogation at night, Jesus was taken from the house of Caiaphas to the palace of the Roman governor in the morning. The fifth of the procurators of Judea, Pontius Pilate was initially installed in AD 26 during the reign of Tiberius. Normally the Roman governor would reside in Caesarea Maritima, but since a Jewish feast was approaching, Pilate made his way, along with his troops, to the praetorium, or palace, that was likely located north of the temple area. The Jewish historian Flavius Josephus (AD 37–100) noted the troubled relationship between Pilate and the Jewish nation in three separate incidents.[1] By now, with Jesus soon to appear before him, and with the Jewish leaders so upset, Pilate knew he had to tread carefully.

Because the Passover feast was approaching, and the Jews did not want to be defiled by entering the home of a Gentile (and thereby become unable to celebrate the feast), they refused to enter the praetorium. The Mishnah, a commentary on various oral traditions going back to the time of Ezra (around 458 BC), took its final form in the third century AD. It expressed this concern of defilement in terms of the Pentateuch (the first five books of Moses), the book of Numbers in particular: "But some of them could not celebrate the Passover on that day because they were ceremonially unclean on account of a dead body" (9:6a). The specific issue in terms of this Roman setting had to do with the belief, likely held by first-century Jews, that the homes of Gentiles were unclean because its members "throw abortions down the drains."[2] The solidified violence as well as the sheer unholiness of this practice were simply nonstarters.

Another significant issue here has to do with the timing of the celebration of the upcoming feast. Since Jesus had already eaten a Passover meal with his disciples, where Judas had been poised to betray him, then this fact raises the question of proper sequencing. This matter can be resolved by the observation on verse 28 of our text that Chrysostom, a Greek church father, made in the late fourth century:

> But what does it mean, "that they might eat the Passover"? He had already done this on the first day of unleavened bread. Either he calls the whole feast "the Passover" or means that they were then keeping the Passover, while Jesus had done so one day sooner, reserving his own sacrifice for the preparation day, when the Passover was celebrated of old.[3]

In terms of the temporal reckoning of the Gospel of John, then, Jesus would be on the cross at the same time that the Passover lambs were being slain.[4] He, therefore, had to celebrate the feast earlier.

Respectful of Jewish sensibilities with regard to matters of ceremonial cleanliness, Pilate went out to the Jewish leaders, leaving Jesus inside the praetorium. In the conversations that followed, Pilate went back and forth between Jesus and the Jewish leaders and he, therefore, at least in some sense, functioned as an intermediary. In addressing the crowd in front of the Roman headquarters Pilate, no doubt, raised his voice in order to be heard: "What charges are you bringing against this man?" The reply the Jewish leadership offered: "If he were not a criminal . . . we would not have handed him over to you," actually evaded Pilate's frank and specific question. That is, it was a reply that was not an answer at all, for no specific crime was mentioned. There was nothing here that warranted the attention of Rome. Likely sensing then that this was a matter of Jewish, not Roman, law Pilate responded: "Take him yourselves and judge him by your own law."

When the Jewish leaders objected to Pilate that they "have no right to execute anyone," in one sense this statement was true; but in another sense, it was false. Granted the *ius gladii,* or the right of the sword, was zealously guarded by Rome in terms of conquered peoples; as the Roman governor, Pilate, and he alone, held the imperium or the supreme power. That much was clear. Nevertheless, there were some notable exceptions to this policy as, for example, later on when Stephen, the first martyr of the church, was stoned to death by Jews (Acts 7:54–60) or when King Herod had James Zebedee, the brother of John, put to death by the sword (12:1–2).

Moreover, if Gentiles had ever dared to enter certain parts of the temple (the Court of Women and the Court of Israel, for example), then the Jews themselves could execute for this capital offense.[5] That also was clear. So then, there appears to be much more going on here. Our text is fraught with subtext. Not only did the Jewish leaders likely fear the people, given the growing popularity of Jesus (and they, therefore, refused to take matters into their own hands), but they also evidently were not satisfied with the usual method of Jewish executions—stoning, strangling, beheading, and the like. Given the hatred they had *already* expressed toward Jesus on several occasions, the Jewish religious leadership might have preferred the Roman manner of execution as well—nearly naked and nailed to a tree. Having already judged Jesus guilty of the worst religious offense of all—blasphemy—they likely favored this method of execution because it was especially degrading and humiliating, far more than stoning or beheading, which were neither as public nor as long.

Earlier Caiaphas, as the chief priest, had asked Jesus a religious question: "Tell us if you are the Messiah, the Son of God" (Matt. 26:63b). Now Pilate, as the Roman governor, posed a political one: "Are you the king of the Jews?" Jesus evidently recognized this shift, and so he questioned Pilate himself: "Is that your own idea . . . or did others talk to you about me?" Pilate would, of course, be concerned about any claim to dominion over areas or over a people that Rome considered under its own authority. But Rome would care nothing about a religious charge, one of blasphemy. This dialogue, then, suggests that the religious leaders possibly had already spoken to Pilate and had translated their original religious concerns into more manageable political ones that would draw the attention of any Roman leader. At any rate, Pilate questioned Jesus further, expressing some frustration with the direction of the conversation: "Am I a Jew? . . . Your own people and chief priests handed you over to me." Then he added in order to get things back on track: "What is it you have done?"

The response of Jesus to this last question of Pilate—"What is it you have done?"—is remarkable in that he ignored it. Instead, Jesus went back to the earlier question of the governor: "Are you the king of the Jews?" Even here, however, there was a twist. In his reply, Jesus did not directly address the issue of kingship, Pilate's chief concern, but of *kingdom*: "My kingdom is not of this world." Then Jesus added, no doubt for emphasis, "my kingdom is from another place." What does that mean? Showing little interest in this manner of reply, of otherworldly kingdoms and the like, Pilate directed the conversation once more back to his original concern: not of kingdoms but of kingship—that is, here-and-now rule that could possibly cause him trouble: "You are a king, then!"

Earlier, Caiaphas had demanded, under the power of an oath, that Jesus tell him if he were "the Messiah, the Son of God" (Matt. 26:63). Jesus responded very carefully, given this difficult context, and stated a clear fact: "You have said so" (v. 64a). In a similar fashion, Jesus answered the implied question of Pilate: "You are a king, then!" once again by being both careful and descriptively accurate: "You say that I am a king." Such a cautious reply, with its measure of affirmation, suggested that what Jesus and Pilate had in mind about kingship were very different things. After this foray, Jesus turned the conversation toward the reason he had been born and why he had come into the world (see also John 1:9–13) in the first place. Simply put, it was to "testify to the truth."

In a much different context earlier, that is, among his own disciples, Jesus had claimed: "I am the way and the truth and the life" (John 14:6a). However, Pilate would have little appreciation of how a person, with an emphasis on a proper *relationship* with him, could possibly be the truth. Relationships and their careful ordering were things unseen, nebulous—and therefore, for many people, largely out of mind. What really mattered, in the mind of someone like Pilate, what held weight, was not the invisible but the visible: in other words, what could be counted (like money and taxes), what could be commanded (like troops), and what could be ordered (like executions). The years of political machinations, of power struggles and compromise, of seeing some of the worst sides of people, of selling out any number of values for the sake of political or administrative expediency or to be in harmony with the will of Caesar himself—all of this had likely taken its toll upon the outlook of Pilate. Indeed, his reply to Jesus was hardly above the level of cynicism: "What is truth?" One can almost hear the dismissive tone of Pilate's voice.

Afterward, the governor went outside once more and addressed the Jewish leaders: "I find no basis for a charge against him." In Pilate's eyes, then, Jesus was likely judged to be some misguided visionary, a fanciful, idealistic leader, one who had little understanding of what actually mattered. Dreams and kingdoms from another place were no threat to Rome.

The Prayer

Jesus, I acknowledge you as king of both the seen and unseen worlds. Help me to move through your kingdom with the heart and character of your holy ambassadors, representing you faithfully to those looking in from the outside.

The Questions

How did Pilate and Jesus understand kingship differently, judging from their own words in the account in John 18:28–38? How did the religious leaders and Jesus understand kingship differently?

Day 32

Herod Antipas

LUKE 23:4–12 *Then Pilate announced to the chief priests and the crowd, "I find no basis for a charge against this man."*

But they insisted, "He stirs up the people all over Judea by his teaching. He started in Galilee and has come all the way here."

On hearing this, Pilate asked if the man was a Galilean. When he learned that Jesus was under Herod's jurisdiction, he sent him to Herod, who was also in Jerusalem at that time.

When Herod saw Jesus, he was greatly pleased, because for a long time he had been wanting to see him. From what he had heard about him, he hoped to see him perform a sign of some sort. He plied him with many questions, but Jesus gave him no answer. The chief priests and the teachers of the law were standing there, vehemently accusing him. Then Herod and his soldiers ridiculed and mocked him. Dressing him in an elegant robe, they sent him back to Pilate. That day Herod and Pilate became friends—before this they had been enemies.

Consider This

Our text in Luke picks up where our last one in John 18:28–38 left off: Pilate was convinced, after his own questioning, that Jesus was innocent, and he told the religious leaders as much. However, these same leaders then objected to Pilate that Jesus "stirs up the people all over Judea by his teaching. He started in Galilee and has come all the way here." At the head of this current chapter, Luke laid out the specific charges drummed up against Jesus in a way that John had not: "And they began to accuse him, saying, 'We have found this man subverting our nation. He opposes payment of taxes to Caesar and claims to be Messiah, a king'" (Luke 23:2). Observe once again that what had originally begun as a religious matter, that is, the charge of blasphemy, had now become a political offense, a full-blown crime against the state. In short, Jesus, so it was argued, was challenging the authority of no one less than Caesar. So then, if his enemies were to be believed, Jesus was a traveling crime show, an insurrectionist against the state, making his way from Galilee to Judea and on to Jerusalem itself only to cause trouble. Where would he go next? What would he say? What would he do? He simply must be stopped.

Upon learning that Jesus had a connection with Galilee, Pilate came up with an ingenious plan that would free him from this predicament. He would turn Jesus over to Herod Antipas, tetrarch of Galilee and Peraea, who was also in Jerusalem at the time to celebrate the Passover feast. Exactly what motivated Pilate to do this, beyond an attempt to pass the buck so to speak, is difficult to determine. Perhaps Pilate realized that Herod would be much more acquainted with Jewish affairs and, therefore, the tetrarch would be the obvious choice to make such a difficult judgment. Or perhaps Pilate simply wanted to extend a political courtesy to Herod, especially since their past relationship had been rocky. Who knows? In any event, Herod was delighted to see Jesus since his reputation as a miracle worker had undoubtedly preceded him. And, of course,

Herod wanted to see a fabulous sign, something special. Indeed, the emphasis in our text on "seeing"[1] suggests that Herod hoped to witness a genuine spectacle, to see a wonderful show—in other words, to be entertained by Jesus. He would, however, be very disappointed in this. Jesus was no performer.

The encounter between Jesus and Herod Antipas was downright odd, even eerie. Recall that this is the same Herod who had wanted to kill Jesus earlier (13:31) and upon learning of this dark intention, Jesus at the time had referred to the tetrarch as "that fox" (v. 32). Interestingly enough, Luke is the only gospel that records this face-to-face incident between the two men now before us. It can hardly be called a conversation or dialogue, because Jesus said nothing, absolutely *nothing*. And so here we have this awkward scene in which Herod, who was now driven more by curiosity than murderous intent, plied Jesus with question after question—and the response just never came. Herod's many questions were met with not a single answer, unless silence itself was the answer.

Herod was the only figure in the Gospels to whom Jesus replied not a word when addressed. But why did Jesus act in this manner? It's puzzling. Perhaps he was tired of being badgered with question after question. Who wouldn't be? Maybe Jesus realized that Herod was not actually interested in what he would have to say. Or perhaps Jesus didn't want to give any credibility to this interrogation since he rejected the charges, and the insinuations associated with them, as simply preposterous. But maybe Jesus was being very intentional, after all, in his silence, thinking of his mission, and of the earlier prophecies that had witnessed to it: "He was oppressed and afflicted, yet he did not open his mouth; he was led like a lamb to the slaughter, and as a sheep before its shearers is silent, so he did not open his mouth" (Isa. 53:7).

When Pilate sent Jesus to Herod, the chief priests and the teachers of the law tagged along, perhaps fearful that Jesus might be acquitted by the tetrarch from all their trumped-up charges. And so, when Jesus wasn't being pestered by Herod with his round of questions, these religious leaders vehemently accused Jesus, giving evidence of their very strong aversion to him in a display of powerful passions and emotions. Though our text only gives these religious leaders one line, nevertheless, they played an important role in this setting. With their harangue in the form of vehement accusations, they had, in effect, become the prosecutors before judge Herod. But where was the defense attorney for Jesus?

The chief priests and scribes had added to the degradation entailed in this interrogation with their verbal assaults on Jesus such that the accused was by now greatly diminished in the eyes of both Herod and his soldiers. The dynamic that played out in this setting, in this ancient kangaroo court, if you will, is a very familiar one even today. That is, when several people, in a show of strength of numbers, begin to criticize, rebuke, or verbally attack another person, putting them on the spot, then many other people who would have otherwise remained silent in the absence of such an emotionally charged atmosphere now feel free, even entitled, to join in—and they do. That's exactly what happened here.

Caught up in this emotional frenzy, Herod failed to realize that, in adding his voice to the mocking and ridicule of Jesus by his soldiers, he had actually debased himself. Indeed, a ruler of the people like Herod should have carried himself in such a way that demonstrated both deep wisdom and a steady judgment, attributes that together would have held in place the basic humanity of the accused as well as the dignity of his own office. Instead, Herod took up the contemptuous speech of his soldiers and joined them in their descent, in their sputtering hateful and demeaning speech. Making sport of Jesus (not the show that Herod had originally wanted, but now a parody), they dressed Christ in an elegant robe in the pretense, in the mockery, that they believed Jesus to be someone important, perhaps a king.

For those people, then and now, who are ever swayed by the strength of numbers, for those who can't get beyond the small world of particular tribes—loud, boisterous, and intimidating at times—and for those who readily take up and participate in charged emotional, social atmospheres, almost like putting on a garment whether it fits or not, Jesus will likely be diminished in their eyes as well. So then, our text, though remarkably brief, is actually packed with much wisdom. Such insight entails distinguishing reality from perception or appearance. That's a tough lesson to learn, especially in human affairs in which celebrated social forces can play such a distorting, disfiguring role.

Though Jesus had indeed been humiliated in the eyes of so many others, people from both high stations in life and in low, such that to them his identity was degraded, he nevertheless remained the *very same person* that he had always been, marked by both abundant goodness and holy love. Mocking could not change that. Ridicule could not undermine it. Hatred could not destroy it. The actual identity of Jesus, his distinctiveness, endured through all the abuse that was thrown at him, no matter how ill-spirited or angry it was, and in a way that can give us all refreshing and lasting hope: "Jesus Christ is the same yesterday and today and forever" (Heb. 13:8).

The Prayer

Heavenly Father, though many in this world fail to acknowledge your Son as the Christ, empower me to worship him and glorify him along with you and the Holy Spirit. May my every thought, word, and deed honor him as the eternal begotten Son, now and forever.

The Questions

Did the identity of Jesus remain the same despite the humiliation he suffered at the hands of Herod and his soldiers? How was that possible? How can the suffering of Jesus in this context give people tremendous hope today?

Day 33

Barabbas

LUKE 23:13–22 *Pilate called together the chief priests, the rulers and the people, and said to them, "You brought me this man as one who was inciting the people to rebellion. I have examined him in your presence and have found no basis for your charges against him. Neither has Herod, for he sent him back to us; as you can see, he has done nothing to deserve death. Therefore, I will punish him and then release him." [Now he was obliged to release to them at the feast one prisoner.]¹*

But the whole crowd shouted, "Away with this man! Release Barabbas to us!" (Barabbas had been thrown into prison for an insurrection in the city, and for murder.)

Wanting to release Jesus, Pilate appealed to them again. But they kept shouting, "Crucify him! Crucify him!"

For the third time he spoke to them: "Why? What crime has this man committed? I have found in him no grounds for the death penalty. Therefore I will have him punished and then release him."

Consider This

Pilate addressed the chief priests, the rulers, and the people once more and repeated their fabricated charge that Jesus was a political revolutionary who had incited the people to rebellion against Caesar. Pilate had conducted an examination of Jesus earlier, and then he had tried to hand off his responsibility to Herod, but the tetrarch simply could find nothing of capital concern, or what was morally or politically troubling in Jesus, and so he sent him back. After all of this, Pilate reported to this mass of people now before him that he had examined Jesus and could discover nothing, absolutely nothing, to substantiate any charge that should warrant death. It was déjà vu, and it was getting old by now, and repetition here resulted in an unmistakable and ongoing posture—at least as far as Pilate was concerned: Jesus was innocent.

After this, the Roman governor declared that he would punish Jesus, through scourging as it turned out, and then he would release him. The problem with this last pronouncement, however, is that if Jesus was indeed innocent, as Pilate believed him to be, then why should he be punished at all? It is likely that this chief Roman official offered this course of action in order to satisfy, at least on some level, the bloodlust of the people. Seeing the gore and the open wounds of Jesus might evoke some measure of sympathy or even compassion among the Jews that could dissuade them from their intended course of action. At this point, Pilate still believed that Jesus would be ultimately released, and so he began to make preparations precisely for that with a suggestion, actually an offer.[2]

It is rare in a journey of this kind that we have to take up a textual consideration, what scholars call lower criticism (we have tried to keep such matters in the background), in order to figure out what's going on. However, we are compelled to do so here. In most popular English translations of the Bible today, such as the NIV, NRSV, NJB, ESV, and CEB, there is no Luke 23:17! This verse, which helps us to understand the current context better in which Pilate will make an offer to the Jews for the release of Jesus, is simply missing. The reason for this omission is that this verse is not found in the most ancient manuscripts that we have. Scholars believe that a later copyist basically imported the substance of Mark 15:6 ("Now it was the custom at the festival to release a prisoner whom the people requested") into our Lucan text.[3] The KJV and the NASB are virtually alone, then, in including this verse, and we have reproduced the NASB translation as a part of our text in order to help readers come to greater understanding.

At any rate, Pilate believed he had finally found a way out of his distressing predicament; he could get off the hook. A custom had emerged among the Jews, although this is not attested beyond the Gospels,[4] that during the Passover celebration a prisoner would be set free. What the later scribe or copyist had inserted into our text as Luke: 23:17 stated: "Now he [meaning Pilate] was obliged to release to them at the feast one prisoner" (NASB). Convinced of the innocence of Jesus, Pilate perhaps believed that the crowd, during this celebratory feast of deliverance, would call out none other than the name of Jesus for release. Instead, they shouted: "Away with this man! Release Barabbas to us!" Luke informs us that Barabbas had been imprisoned for the crimes of both insurrection and murder—hardly a likely choice for clemency. Pilate was probably stunned.

Though there were chief priests and rulers (the Sanhedrin) among them, "the whole crowd" had shouted: "Away with this man! Release Barabbas to us!" It's possible that among this multitude were some of the very same people who had earlier lined the path in

Jerusalem in the midst of shouts of "Blessed is the king who comes in the name of the Lord! Peace in heaven and glory in the highest!" (Luke 19:38). Recall that the religious leaders and a contingent of Roman soldiers had arrested Jesus at night (22:53), perhaps because they wanted to avoid any interference with their efforts that a crowd of support for Jesus during the day might bring. Why, then, has this reversal of the crowd—from shouting "Hosanna!" (John 12:13a) to screaming "Crucify!"—occurred at all and in so little time?

Though our text in Luke offers no clue to solving this puzzle, the three remaining Gospels do so in a very helpful manner. Matthew is typical of this material: "But the chief priests and the elders persuaded the crowd to ask for Barabbas and to have Jesus executed" (Matt. 27:20). The religious leaders, once again, were the principal actors here. Their powers of persuasion—working the crowd, if you will—have illuminated for us some uncomfortable truths playing out here, not only how easily the masses can be swayed to the ill will of a few, an unfortunate fact of life, but also how fickle in general human beings can be. Heedless self-interest can deflect virtually anything. Think of it: in just a few short days, Judas had betrayed Christ; Peter had denied him; and some of the people who had once celebrated Jesus—"Blessed is he who comes in the name of the Lord!" (John 12:13b)—now abandoned him. Then to top it all, they went on to actually accuse him!

But it gets worse. The insurrectionist and murderer that the whole crowd preferred over the humble, donkey-riding Jesus had a very interesting name, one that calls for comment: Barabbas. What's in a name? Well, this particular name is composed of two key Hebrew words (transliterated): *bar*, meaning "son," and *abbas*, meaning "father." And so, if we add these two together we come up with "son of the father," as the name of this rebel. Ambrose, a fourth-century church father, explored the significance of this distinct name in his *Exposition of the Gospel of Luke* as follows: "The interpretation of the name gives the likeness of the image, because Barabbas means 'son of the father.' He belongs to those to whom it is said, 'You are of your father the devil.' They [the religious leaders and the crowd] were about to choose the Antichrist as son of their father, rather than the Son of God."[5] To be sure, we believe that Ambrose was onto something here in pointing out how the crowd chose darkness over light, how they preferred evil over the good. Let's make a brief comparison then between Barabbas, the people's choice, and Jesus, the one who was despised and rejected.

Barabbas and Jesus Compared

Barabbas the sinner is set free	Jesus the Holy One is arrested
Barabbas the guilty is shown favor	Jesus the Innocent is shown ruthlessness and cruelty
Barabbas the rebel is offered mercy	Jesus the Obedient One is offered condemnation
Barabbas the criminal is chosen	Jesus the Wonder Worker is rejected
Barabbas the murderer is offered life	Jesus the Word of Life is sentenced to death

Even after the crowd had cried, "Release Barabbas," Pilate was still intent on setting Jesus free and so he "appealed to them again." But the crowd wouldn't hear of it; they were determined by now to achieve their design and so "they kept shouting, 'Crucify him! Crucify him!'"

Now, of all the dastardly ways of executing people, in which wickedness and cruelty are on full display, crucifixion has to be one of the most dreadful of all. The prescribed course of action in bringing about the death of the victim would be roughly as follows: first of all, a condemnation, along with a sentence, would be pronounced by the Roman authorities. Second, a flogging might take place at this point (as in the case of Jesus, see Matthew 27:26b–31) or it might occur at the place of execution itself, an execution, however, that would always happen outside the city.[6] Third, the condemned would then be forced to carry a crossbeam behind the execution squad, usually made up of four soldiers,[7] one of whom who would hold forth a sign announcing the reason for the execution (usually treason or desertion), so that onlookers would be warned of the terrible consequences of challenging Roman power and might. At the place of execution—as in the case of Jesus, Golgotha (the place of the skull)—the arms of the victim would either be nailed or tied to the crossbeam. This beam would then be attached to a perpendicular pole and the entire structure would be raised, set in the ground, so that the condemned would be forced to face onlookers, that is, whoever wanted to witness this public spectacle, friend or foe alike. And, finally, in attaching the crossbeam to the pole, the executioner might have done it in such a way that the victim's knees would be bent so that breathing would become all the more difficult.[8]

Hanging on a cross in the heat of the day, let's say from noon to three in the afternoon, subjected the condemned to so many kinds of torture: to exposure, to the sun beating down mercilessly with no chance for cover or shade; to the annoyances of biting insects that could not be shooed away, of itches that could not be scratched, and of sweat that could not be wiped; to deprivations of food and drink (some crucifixions lasted days) leading to agonizing hunger and thirst; to blood loss, weakness, and lightheadedness, even fainting, that resulted from both the prior flogging (with sharp pieces of stone on the ends of the whip) and from the nailing to the crossbeam with piercing spikes; and, finally, as a culminating effect of all of this gruesome punishment, the crucified would succumb to exhaustion in which the entire body was spent, worn out, in its ongoing struggle to move the diaphragm just a little (very difficult to do in these circumstances) simply in order to breathe.

Many of those crucified by Rome died of exhaustion, aggravated by blood loss, that together resulted in asphyxiation. The heroic battle to breathe would ultimately be lost. Death followed almost as a mercy but a mercy of a very strange sort. All of this, however, as horrific as it is, especially in the case of Jesus, constitutes simply one dimension (the physical) of the awful realities of crucifixion. We shall consider two more dimensions of this vicious practice in the chapters ahead, which will entail even more suffering. But for now, we have to turn back to the religious leaders, who had been busy working the crowd, for one final observation.

When the religious leaders had first brought Jesus to Pilate from the house of Caiaphas, the high priest, they seemed especially concerned about putting Jesus to death. Noting their powerlessness in this area, they even told the governor: "we have no right to execute anyone" (John 18:31).

Another, even more dark, motivation might have been present as well. Thinking through our text does seem to imply it. It's something hidden in plain sight, so to speak. Consider this: the crowd that was continually calling out, "Crucify him! Crucify him!" was obviously made up of chief priests and religious leaders (the Sanhedrin) as well. Now these same leaders were well acquainted with the manner of Roman crucifixion that entailed affixing the victim to a pole for public display as noted earlier. Add to this piece of information that these same religious leaders surely knew their Bible very well, the Torah (the first five books of the Bible) in particular, especially those passages, as found in Deuteronomy, for example, that related to the curses of God. Do we see the picture that is now beginning to emerge once we bring these two facts together: the Roman practice of execution and Jewish scriptural knowledge? Just what did the Torah declare in a verse that those religious leaders shouting, "Crucify him! Crucify him!" before Pilate surely knew? Wait for it: "Anyone who is hung on a pole is under God's curse" (Deut. 21:23b). There may have been far more here than we have imagined.

The Prayer

Lord Jesus, I receive your innocence for my guilt and your obedience in place of my rebellion. I cherish your standing in my place—indeed hanging on a cross, though you yourself knew no sin. Help me this day and always to choose light over darkness, good over evil, the way of your kingdom over the ways of this world.

The Questions

If we can define a genuine friend as someone who is trustworthy, honest, truthful, and loyal, did Jesus have any friends left as he stood before Pilate?

Day 34

The Governor's Soldiers

MATTHEW 27:27–31A *Then the governor's soldiers took Jesus into the Praetorium and gathered the whole company of soldiers around him. They stripped him and put a scarlet robe on him, and then twisted together a crown of thorns and set it on his head. They put a staff in his right hand. Then they knelt in front of him and mocked him. "Hail, king of the Jews!" they said. They spit on him, and took the staff and struck him on the head again and again. After they had mocked him, they took off the robe and put his own clothes on him.*

Consider This

The chief priests and the religious rulers were closer to their goal. Pilate had been reluctant at every step along the way to pass judgment on the matter at hand, but by now the governor had at least agreed that Jesus should be punished, and so he turned him over to his soldiers. Since the time of his appointment by Emperor Tiberius in AD 26, Pilate resided in the praetorium when he was in Jerusalem. This official residence may have been the old palace of Herod or possibly the fortress of Antonia that was just beyond the Jewish temple.[1] In any event, the whole company of Pilate's soldiers, numbering anywhere from two hundred to six hundred men, gathered around Jesus in the yard of these quarters for they, no doubt, sensed that a spectacle was about to occur.

We should recall that the high priest and the Sanhedrin had already made sport of Jesus (see Matthew 26:67–68). Many of the religious leaders had assembled earlier for the special, quickly called interrogation of the suspect: "Tell us if you are the Messiah, the Son of God" (v. 63b). After the questioning, and after Jesus had spoken the truth plainly about what was to come, clearly affirming a messianic role, they spat in his face and struck him as they mocked: "Prophesy to us, Messiah. Who hit you?" (v. 68).

As the Jewish legislative and judicial court in Jerusalem, the Sanhedrin naturally passed judgment on many matters relating to Jewish law. This body was made up of rabbis who had spent years in training reflecting on the things of God as well as on the traditions of the people. How is it, then, that this august, religious body, which would likely be made up of many pious and devout souls, would be reduced to the crudity and vulgarity of spitting? In other words, how did they so quickly make the transition from reciting the Word of God on their lips one day to using those very same lips to heave a wad of spittle in the face of Jesus on the next?

The governor's soldiers, for their part, would be made up entirely of Gentiles since the Jews, among all the peoples the Romans had conquered by the first century, were excused from military service. These soldiers, then, would look down upon the Jews as a peculiar people, as the "other," and yet, oddly enough, they shared something remarkably in common with them. Both groups, whether Jew or Gentile, whether religious or not, whether pious or profane, were united in their contempt for Jesus. In some respects, the religious leaders outdid their pagan counterparts, especially with their mouths. However, without any religious sensibility or pious desires holding them in check, the governor's soldiers energetically derided Jesus by setting up a mock coronation, and they thereby exceeded the derision even of the religious leaders, at least for the time being.

If a king is to be enthroned, then he must have a suitable robe, a crown (as the symbol of authority), and a staff or scepter. The mockery that played out in the actions of the soldiers consisted chiefly in the deceit that was held in place by a bottomless insincerity. In this travesty, the soldiers pretended to honor Jesus with the giving of a robe, with placing a crown upon his head, and with putting a staff in his hand. But it's all a sham. By these actions the soldiers intended exactly the opposite of what a coronation should entail; not honor but dishonor, not elevation but degradation, not celebration but scorn. The humiliation of the fake ceremony, supported by the legs of insincerity, was magnified in physical violence, in the brutality of repeated blows to the head. And after all the accoutrements of the feigned enthronement were in place, the soldiers then completed the charade, in this honor-and-shame culture, in a spasm of ridicule by kneeling in front of Jesus and shouting: "Hail, king of the Jews!" What a spectacle! What an exhibition! The hundreds of soldiers assembled were not disappointed.

One of the odd things about evil is its very instability as well as its contradictory nature, elements that together, at times, can lead to downright chaos or to very unexpected consequences. To illustrate, the soldiers obviously wanted to demean Jesus through hateful mockery and derision, but in their animated pronouncement, in their contemptuous accolade, they actually and unwittingly spoke the truth. Yes, Jesus is the king of the Jews, but he is a king in a way that the soldiers in their darkness and mockery could not understand. They ignorantly proclaimed a truth that they would likely never know, one that was well beyond them in their current hateful and wretched state. The cry of "Hail, king" would have likely called up visions of Caesar in his pomp and power, but Jesus as a king, standing before Pilate's soldiers, was so unlike Caesar.

How do we imagine that Jesus felt as all of this was happening to him in the face of at least two hundred soldiers, likely more? Have we ever thought about *that*? Did he wonder why such bad things were happening to him? Did he think about the genuine shame, coming in the form of the very diminished views of him, now present among the soldiers—and earlier among the Jews? Shame in this context was something that was done to Jesus; he suffered it. It was nothing less than a social brickbat that had been hurled at him to do him enormous harm. Did that very palpable devaluation of his person and character through concrete actions cause Jesus psychological, emotional, social, and even spiritual pain?

We must recognize that shame and guilt are two very different things—the one necessarily has a social context; the other most often simply an internal, very personal one. Also be aware (and this will be difficult for some, given the usual definitions of shame) that one can be shamed publicly without any guilt at all simply because, as is the case here, the person involved is innocent. But innocence does not prevent real harm or considerable social damage. Again, observe that even though Jesus was without fault he was genuinely harmed, injured in the very diminished views of others bandied about and held in place by both Jews and Gentiles alike. So understood, on this level shame is a public, social product, the debasement of a person in the eyes of others, whether that person is innocent or not, whether that shame, in some fashion, is internalized or not.

Oddly enough, in some people's minds, that is, among those who lack the ability to think critically or who fail to be ever oriented to truth, to be publicly shamed necessarily entails the fault of the object of such shame and censure. In their minds, at least, no individual could ever be right or just in the face of the group's judgment. Swayed by powerful social pressures in the form of raw numbers, many will participate in the amassed powers of the group, finding it heady, and subsequently close their hearts and minds with respect to the victim. "He's getting what he deserves," comes the quick, almost unthinking, cry. "He's a troublemaker." "Crucify him!" This social dynamic, in which groups are transformed into tribes and, in the worse instances, into outright mobs, helps us to understand how both soldiers and rabbis—the latter steeped in the learning of the ancients—could yet find common cause. Together, they were both empowered and strongly motivated, feeling even entitled, to spit in the face of Jesus. For them, Jesus was and remained a stranger.

The Prayer

Heavenly Father, I know my guilt and shame was transferred to Jesus when he willingly went to the cross. Though he was King of the universe, for our sake he was crucified. He experienced the worst reception—that of a criminal—but was received to glory by you. Help me receive him like you did, Father, in my heart with love.

The Questions

What is the difference between guilt and shame? Did Jesus ever suffer the effects of guilt? Did he ever suffer the effects of shame? Is it possible for the innocent to be shamed? Can shame ever be transformed into sympathy or compassion?

Day 35

The Chief Priests and Their Officials

JOHN 19:4–16 *Once more Pilate came out and said to the Jews gathered there, "Look, I am bringing him out to you to let you know that I find no basis for a charge against him." When Jesus came out wearing the crown of thorns and the purple robe, Pilate said to them, "Here is the man!"*

As soon as the chief priests and their officials saw him, they shouted, "Crucify! Crucify!"

But Pilate answered, "You take him and crucify him. As for me, I find no basis for a charge against him."

The Jewish leaders insisted, "We have a law, and according to that law he must die, because he claimed to be the Son of God."

When Pilate heard this, he was even more afraid, and he went back inside the palace. "Where do you come from?" he asked Jesus, but Jesus gave him no answer. "Do you refuse to speak to me?" Pilate said. "Don't you realize I have power either to free you or to crucify you?"

Jesus answered, "You would have no power over me if it were not given to you from above. Therefore the one who handed me over to you is guilty of a greater sin."

From then on, Pilate tried to set Jesus free, but the Jewish leaders kept shouting, "If you let this man go, you are no friend of Caesar. Anyone who claims to be a king opposes Caesar."

When Pilate heard this, he brought Jesus out and sat down on the judge's seat at a place known as the Stone Pavement (which in Aramaic is Gabbatha). It was the day of Preparation of the Passover; it was about noon.

> *"Here is your king," Pilate said to the Jews.*
>
> *But they shouted, "Take him away! Take him away! Crucify him!"*
>
> *"Shall I crucify your king?" Pilate asked.*
>
> *"We have no king but Caesar," the chief priests answered.*
>
> *Finally Pilate handed him over to them to be crucified.*

Consider This

After having been beaten, mocked, and ridiculed by Pilate's soldiers, Jesus was presented before the chief priests and their officials: "Here is the man!" (The Latin is "*Ecce Homo*" as in the Vulgate translation.) Having given repeated indications already of his reluctance to condemn Jesus, Pilate likely had hoped that the appearance of Jesus, degraded in his blood and bruises from the beating, along with the ongoing mockery of his attire, would together evoke the first glimmers of mercy from the religious leaders. Perhaps Jesus had suffered enough. Instead, the Jewish leaders shouted, "Crucify, crucify!" Pilate then repeated once more, "I find no basis for a charge against him." In his frustration, Pilate then began to make sport of the religious leaders by taunting them with his reply: "You take him and crucify him." The Roman governor knew full well that the Jewish leaders had no power either to execute Jesus or to do it in the manner that they so obviously desired, that is, by crucifixion, a point noted earlier (see Day 31). Pilate's reply, then, was a rhetorical insult; it was offered to remind the religious leaders of their place, their subservient position in relation to Rome.

The problem with lying or with being deceptive in terms of one's true motivation is that you have to have a very good memory in order to keep the story straight. This is precisely what the religious leaders, in their exchange with Pilate, failed to do. Although earlier they had offered the pretense that Jesus was a criminal, a threat to the Roman state—"If he were not a criminal," they replied, "we would not have handed him over to you" (John 18:30)—by now the charge was not political or criminal at all, but simply religious: "We have a law, and according to that law he must die, because he claimed to be the Son of God." This shift of frameworks disturbed Pilate, for when he heard the specific claim that Jesus was the Son of God, no longer offered in the political language of "the king of the Jews" (John 18:33), but in specifically religious language, "he was even more afraid." Who was this man?

Fearful, Pilate went back inside for another major interrogation of Jesus. "Where do you come from?" he asked. Observe that Pilate's question was not a geographical one (he had already sent Jesus to Herod), but one far more important. Superstitious as he was, with a belief in a pantheon of gods, Pilate was likely inquiring in terms of the nature of Jesus, exactly what kind of *being* he was. So then, the question, "Where do you come from?" might have suggested that Jesus had come down from heaven and that reality, in and of itself, could pose significant problems for Pilate. In Jesus a greater authority, one from a different realm, so to speak, might be standing right before the procurator. Pilate had good reason to fear.

To Pilate's question, "Where do you come from?" Jesus gave no answer this time around, although he had spoken freely earlier. This silence baffled the governor because issues of life and death were at stake: "Don't you realize I have power either to free you or to crucify you?" In his reply to this further question, Jesus himself actually addressed the major contentious issue that would preoccupy and perplex subsequent generations up until this present day: Who bore the greater burden of responsibility for the death of Christ, was it Rome or Jerusalem?

Speaking carefully, Jesus reminded Pilate of his place as a Roman governor in the larger scheme of things: "You would have no power over me if it were not given to you from above." In other words, not only is God higher than Pilate's office, but also that very office had been established by God (in the general sense of the goodness of rule and governance) in order to be a blessing to the people. Holding the office that he did, one that entailed important and unavoidable duties, and pressed to make a judgment in this case in accordance with the obligations of that office, Pilate would bear less responsibility for the outcome of this than those religious leaders, Caiaphas in particular, who had handed Jesus over to Pilate in the first place.

In light of what he had just learned in this subsequent interrogation, Pilate wanted to set Jesus free. However, given the array of circumstances then in play, he would be unable to do this. Indeed, Pilate was far less free than he had imagined. For one thing, he had the religious leaders to consider and they were now changing the framework once more by reverting back to political arguments that criticized not only Jesus as a threat to the state—"Anyone who claims to be a king opposes Caesar"—but now also Pilate himself: "If you let this man go, you are no friend of Caesar." These leaders were so bold in their actions and determined to have Jesus crucified, that they were willing to threaten even the Roman governor himself. They were willing to complain to Tiberius about what a bad job his procurator Pilate was doing, as if they had been such great Roman subjects all along. Now that move took both nerve and hypocrisy!

Recognizing the difficult position in which he had been placed, Pilate brought Jesus out before the people and sat down on the judge's seat in order to render his verdict. It was the day of Preparation of the Passover, and so the Passover lambs would soon be slain. With the threat of the Jewish leaders likely still in his mind, Pilate nevertheless demonstrated his authority and power as the Roman governor by continuing to make fun of the Jewish leaders by announcing what he knew they would loathe to hear: "Here is your king." In reply, the Jewish leaders shouted, "Take him away! Take him away! Crucify him!" Pilate then continued to mock the chief priests and their officials with great irony: "Shall I crucify your king?" The answer to that question would be decisive for everyone—for Jesus, Pilate, and the Jewish leaders themselves. Now there are some passages in the Bible which, because they are so brief, not even a full verse, we may quickly pass over them and, thereby, fail to appreciate their full significance. Such is the case here, in our current setting, as the Jewish leaders were about to reply to Pilate's taunting question: "Shall I crucify your king?"

Among other things, the response of the Jewish leaders to this question would reflect their long and belabored attempt to eliminate Jesus, to put him to death: "If we let him go on like this, everyone will believe in him, and then the Romans will come and take away both our temple and our nation" (John 11:48). The Sadducees clearly had an interest here. Moreover, such an effort would receive renewed interest, this time from the Pharisees, with the triumphal entry of Jesus into Jerusalem: "See, this is getting us nowhere. Look how the whole world has gone after him!" (12:19). Beyond this, the intentions and passions of the religious leaders would be raised to fever pitch as Jesus was brought before Caiaphas, the teachers of the law, and the elders: "Look, now you have heard the blasphemy. What do you think?" "He is worthy of death" (Matt. 26:65b–66). In short, there were so many elements, and so much prior history, along with troubling motivations along the way, that would feed into the reply of the religious leaders to Pilate. Their obsessive focus on Jesus, manifested in angry shouting and threats, would invariably lead the leadership down a path that should have shocked them, but it didn't, for it would undermine nothing less than their very identity as Jews.

What are those few words full of meaning and rich in implications, what is that brief verse that constitutes the reply of the chief priests to Pilate's question: "Shall I crucify your king?" It is none other than the shouting of what is a grand apostasy, a full sellout, one that undercut all the religious values that these Jewish leaders were supposed to hold dear. Ironically, during the Passover season the cry rang out in Jerusalem: "We have no king but Caesar." Really? *Really?* Was there no room then for the reception of the Messiah, the Anointed One, the one who would usher in the kingdom of God? Or would the claim by anyone to be the Messiah be met with both disbelief and rejection simply because it detracted from the prerogatives and self-driven concerns of the current religious class, the chief priests in particular (see John 11:48)? They had already worked out their accommodation with Rome. What would be next?

In rejecting Jesus, in turning aside any right to kingship other than that of Caesar, the chief priests had abandoned not only the hope of the Messiah, but also no one less than the Holy One of Israel, the one who had set their ancestors free from Egyptian bondage with a mighty outstretched arm. That king was no longer recognized; rather a Gentile potentate, and a Roman one at that, had taken the place of the Most High. Moreover, in their full-blown apostasy this religious leadership, so full of their own present interests and driven by murderous intent, had also betrayed their own people, the Jewish people, who were genuine victims here as well. What then remained of such beautiful psalms that had earlier proclaimed the Holy One of Israel as king: "Hear my cry for help, my King and my God, for to you I pray" (Ps. 5:2) or "The Lord is King for ever and ever; the nations [or heathen] will perish from his land" (Ps. 10:16)? These psalms, as was with so much else, were vacated, emptied out of virtually all meaning.

Now they were simply words once written a very long time ago. The religious leaders had said it themselves so clearly and so undeniably. We must therefore take them at their word: "We have no king but Caesar."

The Prayer

Lord, I know that your authority challenges any other claims to rule, whether they be political leaders or the inner claims of my heart. Send your Spirit to remove any idols vying for reign, and to enthrone you, King Jesus, as the rightful ruler of my life.

The Questions

Is there any significance to Jesus's condemnation occurring on the day of Preparation of the Passover? In other words, does the Jewish religious calendar cast any light on the meaning of the trial and condemnation of Jesus?

Day 36

The Chief Priests, Teachers of the Law, and Elders (Part One)

MATTHEW 27:32–44 *As they were going out, they met a man from Cyrene, named Simon, and they forced him to carry the cross. They came to a place called Golgotha (which means "the place of the skull"). There they offered Jesus wine to drink, mixed with gall; but after tasting it, he refused to drink it. When they had crucified him, they divided up his clothes by casting lots. And sitting down, they kept watch over him there. Above his head they placed the written charge against him:* THIS IS JESUS, THE KING OF THE JEWS.

Two rebels were crucified with him, one on his right and one on his left. Those who passed by hurled insults at him, shaking their heads and saying, "You who are going to destroy the temple and build it in three days, save yourself! Come down from the cross, if you are the Son of God!" In the same way the chief priests, the teachers of the law and the elders mocked him. "He saved others," they said, "but he can't save himself! He's the king of Israel! Let him come down now from the cross, and we will believe in him. He trusts in God. Let God rescue him now if he wants him, for he said, 'I am the Son of God.'" In the same way the rebels who were crucified with him also heaped insults on him.

Consider This

Having been beaten severely by Roman soldiers, Jesus was probably too weak to carry the patibulum (the crossbeam) that could weigh anywhere between thirty to forty pounds.¹ Realizing, perhaps, that Jesus would be unable to complete the death march, the four soldiers who accompanied him forced a man who hailed from a town in North Africa, Simon of Cyrene, to take up the cross. Though little is known about this man from Africa, the Gospel of Mark does reveal that he was the father of Alexander and Rufus (Mark 15:21), two men who were likely known within the church. At any rate, though Simon remains a mysterious figure, he nevertheless is an important one in that what he did on that Friday, as Jesus made his way along the Via Dolorosa, was a wonderful symbol of what all real Christians should do: that is, take up the cross.

Arriving at Golgotha, the place of the skull, an area that some believe corresponds to the site where the Church of the Holy Sepulchre is situated today,² Jesus was offered a drink of wine mixed with gall, a bitter herb. With the addition of the gall, the wine that normally would have been a refreshment was now a concoction of mockery, one that was teasingly undrinkable. However, with or without the herb, Jesus would not have drunk the wine anyway. He only tasted it to see what kind of liquid it was, for he had exclaimed earlier at the Last Supper, surrounded by his disciples: "I tell you, I will not drink from this fruit of the vine from now on until that day when I drink it new with you in my Father's kingdom" (Matt. 26:29).

At the place of execution, Jesus was affixed to the crossbeam with nails (see John 20:25), and then he was attached to a lengthy vertical pole³ that had been placed on the spot earlier. In order to add greater misery to the practice of crucifixion, Rome heightened the emotional and psychological pain of its victims—in other words, the shame—by crucifying them naked or nearly so. Having stripped Jesus of his clothes, the soldiers then made sport of all of this by casting lots for his garments. The Gospel of John informs us that the soldiers divided the clothing of Jesus into four shares, corresponding to the number of soldiers, but even then a seamless undergarment remained. It was for this piece of cloth, "woven in one piece from top to bottom" (John 19:23b), that lots were cast. John also reveals the larger significance of all of this, that the Scripture might be fulfilled, in quoting the substance[4] of Psalm 22:18: "They divide my clothes among them and cast lots for my garment." Many of the events that took place on this day had been prophesized earlier. No one before and no one after could have ever fulfilled such prophecies but Jesus.

As we have already seen, the Jewish religious leaders had gone back and forth in terms of what charges they brought before Pilate: first, there was a political one in the accusation that Jesus was a criminal against the Roman state (John 18:30), but then they slipped up and revealed their true motivation, which was actually a religious one, in the claim that Jesus was the Son of God (19:7). Which charge, then, the political or religious one, would be written on the titulus or placard that would be placed above the head of Jesus on the cross? On this matter the Gospels differ not as to the substance of the charge, but as to its length. To illustrate, the Gospel of Mark, the briefest of all, simply has:

"THE KING OF THE JEWS" (15:26b). The Gospel of John, the longest of all, has "JESUS OF NAZARETH, THE KING OF THE JEWS" (19:19b). However, John alone offers insight into the ongoing struggle between the Jewish religious leaders and Pilate as to the wording of the titulus, as evidenced in the following: "The chief priests of the Jews protested to Pilate, 'Do not write "The King of the Jews," but that this man claimed to be king of the Jews.' Pilate answered, 'What I have written, I have written'" (John 19:21–22). The irony here is unmistakable. The very title of Jesus that the religious leaders had refused to acknowledge was now displayed on the cross itself for all to see, and there was nothing that they could do about it. Jesus would begin his reign right here nailed to a tree as the King of the Jews.

Though all but one of his disciples had deserted him (John 19:26–27), Jesus was not alone. He was crucified between two robbers, though *rebel* might be a better term for them, one of whom, according to the Gospel of Luke, actually conversed with Jesus (see Luke 23:39–43). It is possible that Barabbas was supposed to be crucified in the very spot where Jesus now was. If so, then Jesus took his place. Think about that for a while. But how did Christ get there? He had started out so very well. We saw in Day 1, for instance, that: "The true light that gives light to everyone was coming into the world" (John 1:9). His origin was glorious, for as Jesus had exclaimed: "before Abraham was born, I am!" (8:58). Indeed, he was "with God, and . . . was God" (1:1), and yet he humbled himself even among men and women and took on the form of a servant. It was a humble descent for the sake of a generous identification with others and for love. Oh, the inestimable worth of humility! It's the gateway to the richest and broadest love imaginable. But Jesus did not stop there. He descended further, through the hatred, mocking, and rejection, through the onslaught of shame, even to the depths of a dark and wretched cross, so that there would not be a man nor woman whom Jesus could not touch. He had covered the gamut in terms of all who needed him. There never has been a movement of compassion and empathy so thorough nor the identification with others, the very least of all, so strong and powerful—and just as holy love would have it. Indeed, one of his conversation partners on his dying day was an abject criminal. Divine love shows up in the strangest of places.

Jesus had done his work well, though in the fogged-over eyes of some, with conceptions of God not even worthy of being mentioned, he had been a regrettable failure. The cross had proven it; it was over; he was finished. However, those who turned away in disgust on that dark day just couldn't see it. The kingdom of God was indeed being revealed, and its luster was right in front of their eyes. Sinful pride, however, had obscured their vision. Being blinded by so many other considerations as to who God is, or better yet, who they had imagined the Almighty to be, they were and remained baffled. They just couldn't understand what actually is the nature, the essence, of the Most High *especially in relation to the least of all*. That's a place they rarely wanted to look, perhaps only for a moment, but then to quickly turn away. This, however, was the very best place of all to get a glimpse, a vision, of what the kingdom of God is all about.

In the midst of this deep darkness, a shining, glimmering, and enduring light would emerge. It was the light not of sinful human qualities ascribed to God, mined out of the mountains of all-too-human desires, informed by self-love and sinful pride, and then packaged in an array of superlatives. No! It was the light of nothing less than love, not just any love, of course, but holy love, a love that is simply divine—sublime and incomprehensibly beautiful! Much later, the apostle Paul expressed the humble descent of Jesus, the lowest reaches of the incarnation (the Word becoming flesh), in his following observation:

> Who, being in very nature God,
>   did not consider equality with God something to be used to his own advantage;
> rather, he made himself nothing
>   by taking the very nature of a servant,
>   being made in human likeness.
> And being found in appearance as a man,
>   he humbled himself
>   by becoming obedient to death—
>   even death on a cross! (Phil. 2:6–8)

At the cross, then, the ostracizing, excluding, and rejecting movement that Jesus had suffered under for so long, throughout much of his ministry, had now reached its climax. The religious leaders had been determined to put Jesus to death for a long time by now and with renewed energy along the way. Accusing

Jesus of the worst of all possible sins, that is, of being a blasphemer, the religious leaders had wanted to drive Christ out of this world and, thereby, end his ministry. No place would be left for Jesus to go; he would be utterly restricted once he was nailed to a tree. His enemies had evidently succeeded. They had driven Christ out, pushed him onto a cross that occupied about one square foot of the earth, that's all—a very small footprint, indeed—the amount of space taken up by that infamous, accursed pole. Earlier, Christ had driven the money changers out of the temple (see Matthew 21:12–13). If those folks were present on this dark Friday, they now had their revenge.

But there is rich irony in the midst of all of this, for the way Rome crucified its condemned was to have them displayed along a prominent stretch of road for all to see. It was a spectacle, to be sure, but not the kind Herod had hoped for earlier. The doomed faced the public and all passersby. And since the patibulum (the crossbeam) opened up the arms of Jesus, as he hung on the cross, he faced the world with arms outstretched, offering the widest embrace possible. It was a message of God to the world. And what did Jesus utter? "Father, forgive them, for they do not know what they are doing" (Luke 23:34a).

The Prayer

Heavenly Father, I see divine love on display in the cross. The descent of your Son shows me the true nature of your power—that of humility and self-emptying. May my life be marked by such love, with a deep commitment to you and my neighbors, even when they be found in what seems to me to be the strangest of places.

The Questions

How does the way that Christ was crucified—whom he faced, how he was positioned on the cross, along with what he said—offer clues as to what the kingdom of God is about?

Day 37

The Chief Priests, Teachers of the Law, and Elders (Part Two)

MATTHEW 27:32–44 *As they were going out, they met a man from Cyrene, named Simon, and they forced him to carry the cross. They came to a place called Golgotha (which means "the place of the skull"). There they offered Jesus wine to drink, mixed with gall; but after tasting it, he refused to drink it. When they had crucified him, they divided up his clothes by casting lots. And sitting down, they kept watch over him there. Above his head they placed the written charge against him:* THIS IS JESUS, THE KING OF THE JEWS.

Two rebels were crucified with him, one on his right and one on his left. Those who passed by hurled insults at him, shaking their heads and saying, "You who are going to destroy the temple and build it in three days, save yourself! Come down from the cross, if you are the Son of God!" In the same way the chief priests, the teachers of the law and the elders mocked him. "He saved others," they said, "but he can't save himself! He's the king of Israel! Let him come down now from the cross, and we will believe in him. He trusts in God. Let God rescue him now if he wants him, for he said, 'I am the Son of God.'" In the same way the rebels who were crucified with him also heaped insults on him.

Consider This

As we envision the next part of our text, verses 39–44, we can be guided in our reflections, to some extent, by the Italian artist Tintoretto, whose painting, *The Crucifixion*, was produced in 1565. This masterful work currently hangs in the Scuola Grande di San Rocco in Venice. It was chosen above all because it is a very broad and sweeping canvas, a panorama, and it therefore ably displays the little battalions or squads of people who railed against Jesus. It also invites the use of our imagination which, in this setting, will be very helpful to appreciate the "thickness" of the scene.

The first group, which our text simply identifies as "Those who passed by," hurled insults at Christ while shaking their heads in disdain. Employing an artistic technique that entails the movement of vertical lines, Tintoretto directs the attention of the viewer, with one set of lines, to the center of the painting, where Christ hangs elevated above the chaotic activities taking place below. In another set of diagonal lines, however, evident in the illuminated ground beneath the cross, the artist directs attention to the foreground of the painting, where the passersby should be clearly evident, but they are nowhere to be seen. This may have been intentional or else this first group could be identified with a number of people to the right of the cross, that is, those who will eventually make their way before it.[1] In any event, though this little squad likely thought that they were merely a part of a small drama, of a Jew being put to death by the Romans, it was actually a grand tragedy much larger in meaning than they had imagined. Centuries earlier, Psalm 22 had depicted the very role that these insulters would play: "But I am a worm and not a man, scorned by everyone, despised by the people. All who see me mock me; they hurl insults, shaking their heads" (vv. 6–7).

Not content with the verbal abuse and the wagging of their heads, these passersby then hurled a couple of challenges at Jesus: "You who are going to destroy the temple and build it in three days, save yourself! Come down from the cross, if you are the Son of God!" Misconstruing the words of Jesus in terms of the destruction of the temple (see John 2:19), whether intentional or not, we then hear a familiar refrain in their voices, one that we encountered earlier in the mouth of none other than the Devil: "If you are the Son of God . . ." (see Matthew 4:1–11). How might Jesus have heard these words? Was he being tempted by the Prince of Darkness once more, even here in this dark place and at this very moment, to use powers that would extract him from the torment and agony of the cross, but in a way that would depart from the will of his Father? Was the aggravation and danger of temptation now upon him? Did Jesus suffer this as well?

The second squad—the chief priests, the teachers of the law, and the elders—are off to the left side of the cross in Tintoretto's work, and they are identified by their rich attire and headdress. As our text indicates, they too joined in the mocking of Christ and they taunted him with three affirmations which they, as the religious elite of Israel, found to be preposterous. We can almost hear the cynical and wry tone of their voices: "'He saved others,' they said, 'but he can't save himself!'" But if these religious leaders were willing to admit that Jesus did, after all, save others, then why did they doubt who he is or what his signs of power had shown him to be? Could Jesus have done any of these things unless God was with him? In other words, why hadn't the religious leaders' acknowledgment of "saving others" led to their own faith in Christ? The second taunt of the religious elite—"He's the king of Israel! Let him come down now from the cross, and we will believe in him"—hardly sounds sincere. Signs of wonder, as great as they can be, don't necessarily result in faith. We already know that. Recall the raising of Lazarus from the dead once more. The Gospel of John chronicles the reaction among the religious leaders in the wake of this astonishing event:

> Therefore many of the Jews who had come to visit Mary, and had seen what Jesus did, believed in him. But some of them went to the Pharisees and told them what Jesus had done. Then the chief priests and the Pharisees called a meeting of the Sanhedrin.
>
> "What are we accomplishing?" they asked. "Here is this man performing many signs. If we let him go on like this, everyone will believe in him, and then the Romans will come and take away both our temple and our nation." (11:45–48)

In a similar fashion, Jerome, a Christian scholar who died in AD 420, doubted the sincerity of these same religious leaders in their claim that they would, after all, believe in Jesus if only he would come down from the cross. In making his case, however, Jerome went beyond our text and made a connection to a future event, one that these same religious leaders would later learn about as well. Jerome reasoned in this way: "'Let him come down from the cross, and we will believe in him.' What a deceitful promise! Which is greater: to come down from the cross while still alive or to rise from the tomb while dead? He rose, and you do not believe. Therefore, even if he came down from the cross, you would not believe."[2]

Like the passersby of the cross, the second little platoon—the chief priests, the teachers of the law, and the elders—were hardly aware of the larger drama in which they dutifully played their roles, doing exactly what had been prophesized about them so long ago. And so, they sallied forth with yet another cry: "He trusts in God. Let God rescue him now if he wants him, for he said, 'I am the Son of God.'" As they spoke these words, the religious leaders were oblivious to the reality that they were actually quoting the very similar words of Psalm 22:8: "'He trusts in the LORD,' they say, 'let the LORD rescue him. Let him deliver him, since he delights in him.'"

The last group of revilers, composed of only two, corresponds to the rebels who were crucified with Jesus. In Tintoretto's painting, these two men are still being affixed to the cross with nails and ropes. The one is looking toward Christ, in what appears to be a sympathetic gaze, the other is looking away. The Italian artist suggests a touching scene in his composition between Jesus and one of these rebels who evidently found his way to faith after his earlier harsh words. Perhaps he had witnessed the humble resolve of Christ, who patiently endured his suffering with a remarkable spirit, or perhaps he was moved by the gracious forgiveness of Christ offered for all to hear, himself included. This account, which is only found in the Gospel of Luke, is as follows:

> One of the criminals who hung there hurled insults at him:
> "Aren't you the Messiah? Save yourself and us!"
> But the other criminal rebuked him. "Don't you fear God," he said, "since you are under the same sentence? We are punished justly, for we are getting what our deeds deserve. But this man has done nothing wrong."
> Then he said, "Jesus, remember me when you come into your kingdom."
> Jesus answered him, "Truly I tell you, today you will be with me in paradise." (23:39–43)

Though Jesus knew that paradise awaited him and the erstwhile rebel, his current condition was anything but that. Earlier the criminals had insulted Jesus in a manner similar to the passersby and the religious elite. The very lowest dregs in this first-century society, whom their enemies probably referred to as the scum of the earth—it was precisely these abject and despised offenders who thought that even they had something on Jesus, that even they had grounds for their animated complaints and insults. This was a low point to be sure. The darkness was palpable.

If we consider the horizontal dimension of life, that is, the various relationships with family, friends, and acquaintances, then this last scene at Golgotha looks like desolation. However, it was not actually so.

The cross was a region, so to speak, near the horror of desolation—close to the neighborhood, but not within it. It was *near* desolation.

Though perhaps all of the apostles (see Mark 14:27) had abandoned Jesus, clearly Peter and James of the inner circle were nowhere to be seen. The beloved disciple (see John 13:23–24), whom tradition has identified as the apostle John[3] (though many scholars today disagree[4]), was at the cross, along with Mary, the mother of Jesus. The problem here, of course, is that we don't know just who this beloved disciple was.[5] The answers from an earlier tradition are hardly satisfying. What we do know, however, is that there were several other people present, some women in particular, those for instance who had remained faithful, and who had likely accompanied Jesus from the time that he began his death journey outside the praetorium and on to the site of his crucifixion at Calvary. This little flock remained at Golgotha through it all: faithful, supportive, and loving. Their very presence surely meant so much to Jesus.

So then, the women at the cross were especially prominent, and undoubtedly played an important role, in that some of them are specifically named in the Gospels with the notable exception of the Gospel of Luke, in which they are referred to only in a very general way as "the women who had followed him from Galilee, stood at a distance, watching these things" (23:49b). Consider then, for a moment, the more detailed account found in the Gospel of John: "Near the cross of Jesus stood his mother, his mother's sister, Mary the wife of Clopas, and Mary Magdalene. When Jesus saw his mother there, and the disciple whom he loved standing nearby, he said to her, 'Woman, here is your son,' and to the disciple, 'Here is your mother.' From that time on, this disciple took her into his home" (19:25–27). Add to this testimony the witness found in the Gospel of Mark: "Some women were watching from a distance. Among them were Mary Magdalene, Mary the mother of James the younger and of Joseph, and Salome. In Galilee these women had followed him and cared for his needs. Many other women who had come up with him to Jerusalem were also there" (15:40–41).

A clear picture has now emerged. Jesus was not utterly alone at Golgotha. He had not been abandoned after all. That's a myth. The light of love was standing right in front of his eyes in the form of a band of courageous women and of a mysterious and beloved disciple. It was not all darkness.

The Prayer

Beloved Jesus, your resolve through the taunts and torture on Good Friday were a demonstration of your perfect love and divine holiness. May the courage and faith of the women and beloved disciple be the kind that characterizes my heart today.

The Questions

How might the cry of the passersby, "Come down from the cross, if you are the Son of God!" (Matt. 27:40b), have posed a temptation to Christ? Since the devil tempted

Jesus at the beginning of his public ministry, and he was apparently tempted at the end of his ministry in a similar fashion, is there a larger significance to these bookend temptations that may have structured the ministry of Jesus?

Day 38

Jesus (Part One)

MARK 15:33–39 *At noon, darkness came over the whole land until three in the afternoon. And at three in the afternoon Jesus cried out in a loud voice, "Eloi, Eloi, lema sabachthani?" (which means "My God, my God, why have you forsaken me?").*

When some of those standing near heard this, they said, "Listen, he's calling Elijah."

Someone ran, filled a sponge with wine vinegar, put it on a staff, and offered it to Jesus to drink. "Now leave him alone. Let's see if Elijah comes to take him down," he said.

With a loud cry, Jesus breathed his last.

The curtain of the temple was torn in two from top to bottom. And when the centurion, who stood there in front of Jesus, saw how he died, he said, "Surely this man was the Son of God!"

Consider This

Crucifixions are slow torture. Its victims languish as they struggle to move the body ever so slightly so that the diaphragm can be released from the weight of the chest momentarily. The lungs are then free to expand in order to breathe. Each breath is both a struggle and an achievement. Weakened by this ordeal, already, Jesus would have to face another round of this torture. His arms, pinned to the cross, were useless to help him in any way. Though it was noon, and the sun would be high in the sky, a darkness descended over the whole land—inexplicably so. All three Synoptic Gospels record this eerie event. The darkness may be reminiscent of the plague of darkness that preceded the first Passover in Egypt, displaying the wrath of God upon the enemies of the Israelites, or it may have been prophesized in the eighth century BC by Amos, who declared: "'In that day,' declares the Sovereign LORD, 'I will make the sun go down at noon and darken the earth in broad daylight'" (Amos 8:9). This darkness, however it is understood, may actually have been, at least on some level, a blessing in disguise to Jesus. In the midst of his many torments, he would at least now be spared the agony of the glaring noonday sun beating down upon him.

Three struggling and exhausting hours later, Jesus, who had been silent up to this point, gathered his strength *and timed his breathing so that he could cry out in a loud voice:* "'*Eloi, Eloi, lema sabachthani*'? (which means 'My God, my God, why have you forsaken me?')." This was an echo from Psalm 22, a poetic expression of deep lament, a psalm that ended, however, on a ray of hope. Even at this hour, in the midst of his great passion, Jesus was still quoting Scripture. But what did it mean? Had God the Father forsaken his Son at the cross? Or were the very words, "My God, my God," an expression of a relationship still very much in place, though admittedly obscured by the tragic elements of the cross?

In our text, the Gospel of Mark has posed a question for us that it, itself, does not answer. This, however, should not surprise us. Indeed, all four Gospels have posed several questions, some more difficult than others, that have taken the church literally centuries to reflect upon and answer, especially in terms of two key issues:

(1) Who is Jesus Christ, especially in terms of his person and nature? and (2) In what way has Jesus revealed God the Father to us in the power of the Holy Spirit? Indeed, the proper doctrine of Christ (Christology) and of God (the Trinity) would require centuries of the church's best reflections as it considered not simply the Gospels but the entirety of the witness of Scripture that would include, of course, the writings of the apostle Paul and of others as well.

It is precisely in terms of this perplexing issue—the forsakenness of Christ at the cross—that we must reflect not simply in terms of the small pieces of this puzzle, so to speak, a handful of verses found in our text, but also in terms of the larger picture of this engrossing narrative whereby we can begin to see the connections and the themes that endure. We know, for example, that Jesus was faithful throughout his ordeal—he was and remained an *innocent* lamb of God being slain. And so, when the apostle Paul wrote in 2 Corinthians 5:21, "For our sake he made the sinless one a victim for sin, so that in him we might become the uprightness of God,"[1] we understand this verse to mean that Christ became a victim *for* sin but not as a participant *in* sin.

Second, the elements of the larger picture, displayed in the entire New Testament, in which the narrative of Jesus is interpreted through the apostolic witness, indicate that when Jesus cried out the words of Psalm 22, "My God, my God . . ." this was actually solid evidence that the relationship between the Father and the Son of God yet remained. The Father was after all his God, the God of Jesus of Nazareth, even in this wretched place.

Jesus clearly affirmed this in his cry, and we must, of course, take note of it. If this were not the case, then how could the Gospel of Luke express the dying words of Jesus later on as: "Father, into your hands I commit my spirit" (23:46)? The relationship did, indeed, endure.

Though some may conjecture that forsakenness must mean that the relationship between the Father and the Son of God was broken, disrupted, at Calvary, two key considerations indicate just why such a conjecture, offered as an interpretation of our Marcan passage, is false. Please note that we have, by and large, avoided at-length theologizing in our journey so far, but we can do so no longer. The matter before us is simply too important and, therefore, we must reflect more deeply. Indeed, it concerns nothing less than the relationship of Jesus Christ to God the Father. It's hard to get more important, more weighty, or even more serious than that.

First of all, given the nature of the being of God, and the relations of the Christian Godhead between Father, Son, and Holy Spirit as revealed in Scripture, these very relations are eternal just as God is eternal. In other words, there never was a time when the Son of God, the Word made flesh, was not the Son of God. Arius, an early heretic, had gotten this wrong (there was a time when the Son was not[2]) and the church fathers, especially Alexander of Alexandria (died AD 326), refuted his erroneous teaching. Moreover, there never would be a time in the future in which the Son of God would not be the Son of God, as if the relation with the Father could somehow or other be interrupted or broken. It cannot. To be sure, if such a relation could be severed—if it was only a *temporary* relation—then we would not have God in mind (whose essence is to exist) in any of our reflections. We would simply have some figment of our own imaginations in view. Eternity is an essential attribute of God, not an arbitrary or optional one, as the Cappadocian fathers of the fourth century argued so carefully and so convincingly. Simply put, the relations between Father, Son, and Spirit are *eternal* and, therefore, remain unbroken. Golgotha never changed that. Forsakenness, then, must mean something else here.

Second, if the relationship between the Father and the Son was broken at the cross, if that's what forsakenness means, then how is Jesus the Son of God any longer—that is, divine—and how, then, is God *in this place* reconciling the world unto himself as the apostle Paul so clearly revealed in his observation: "All this is from God, who reconciled us to himself through Christ and gave us the ministry of reconciliation: that God was reconciling the world to himself in Christ, not counting people's sins against them" (2 Cor. 5:18–19a)?

At the end of the eleventh century, in 1094, Anselm, the Archbishop of Canterbury, wrote his very helpful book on the death of Christ entitled *Cur Deus Homo*, or translated into English, *Why God Became Human*. In this work, he argued that if the alienation and separation between God and humanity due to sin were to be overcome, then the God/Human would have to come. There could be no other way. He reasoned in the following manner: human beings ought to make atonement for sin but cannot since they are sinners; God, however, can make atonement for sin but ought not since God is not a sinner at all. Anselm then added these two basic truths together and concluded that only the God/Human both can and ought to make atonement for sin.[3] This is precisely the work of the Messiah.

According to Anselm, then, no other human being could possibly reconcile humanity to God—not Moses, not King David, not Jeremiah—simply because, as sinners, they were all a part of the problem. As great as these religious leaders were (and they were, indeed, great), they could not do this *particular* work. It was beyond them all. Jesus Christ, however, could undertake this labor precisely because he was divine and remained innocent. He and he alone was not a part of the problem. As the Word who was made flesh (see John 1:1), Jesus could do what no other human being could ever do: make atonement for sin. Moreover, as a true human being, Jesus ought to make atonement for sin. That is, he could represent the entire race of humanity. Jesus, then, was and remains the only mediator possible between God and humanity, given who he is as attested by Scripture.

Now watch this: strike at the divinity of Christ, eliminate or interrupt or break the relation of Jesus to the Father, even for a moment at the cross, and atonement—the reconciliation of God and humanity—simply cannot happen. God must be in this horrible place, at this lowest depth, for reconciliation to occur. The crucified body of Christ, this torn and mutilated flesh, is exactly the place where both God and humanity meet. Jesus Christ, as truly divine and truly human, has descended to the depths such that "God made him who had no sin to be sin for us, so that in him we might become the righteousness of God" (2 Cor. 5:21). His union with both God and humanity remained at the cross, precisely at the cross. This is the distinct work of the mediator, the Messiah, the one who reconciles both God and humanity, as Anselm had understood so well.

In what sense, then, was Christ forsaken by God the Father at the cross? In the sense that he was abandoned to all the evil (physical, emotional, psychological, social, and spiritual) that the Roman soldiers, the religious leaders, and others would do to him on that tragic day. God the Father did not come to his rescue. The Father could have sent twelve legions of angels to deliver Jesus from his troubles, but they never came—for they were never sent. As Thomas McCall, a contemporary theologian, put it: "Jesus, as our high priest, stands in our place, on our behalf, facing our sin and our death while unprotected by his Father."[4] Shorn of protection against the wiles of evil men and women at Golgotha, left to sink into this chasm, this abyss, Jesus remained steadfast. But even here, precisely here, in this darkest of places imaginable, "God was reconciling the world to himself in Christ" (2 Cor. 5:19a).

The Prayer

Jesus Christ, you who are truly divine and truly human, thank you that in your body you reconciled heaven to earth, God to people, people to one another, and all of us to creation. Though you were abandoned to suffer the worst humanity conceived of, you offered me your best gift—eternal life. May that life overflow in and through me right here and now.

The Questions

How is it that only someone who is both divine and human can bring about redemption? What does it mean to be redeemed?

Day 39

Jesus (Part Two)

MARK 15:33–39 *At noon, darkness came over the whole land until three in the afternoon. And at three in the afternoon Jesus cried out in a loud voice, "Eloi, Eloi, lema sabachthani?" (which means "My God, my God, why have you forsaken me?").*

When some of those standing near heard this, they said, "Listen, he's calling Elijah."

Someone ran, filled a sponge with wine vinegar, put it on a staff, and offered it to Jesus to drink. "Now leave him alone. Let's see if Elijah comes to take him down," he said.

With a loud cry, Jesus breathed his last.

The curtain of the temple was torn in two from top to bottom. And when the centurion, who stood there in front of Jesus, saw how he died, he said, "Surely this man was the Son of God!"

Consider This

The Aramaic word that Jesus cried out, *"Eloi,"* sounds like the Hebrew word for Elijah, which is *"Elija."*[1] Someone near the cross, likely a Jew and not a Roman soldier, in hearing this word, thought that Jesus was calling for the great prophet to appear, perhaps in order to deliver him. Whether it was a sign of mockery or not, the offer of a sponge of wine vinegar was then made to Jesus, and although our text does not tell us one way or the other, we already know why he wouldn't drink it. "Now leave him alone," someone said, "Let's see if Elijah comes to take him down." No prophet came.

Though many of Rome's crucified lingered for days before they succumbed to exhaustion and asphyxiation, in the account of our Marcan text, the death of Jesus came suddenly, abruptly: "With a loud cry, Jesus breathed his last." Done! That's it. It was over. What did Christ say when he cried? Mark doesn't tell us. He doesn't even offer us a clue. It's left as an indistinguishable cry almost as if it were simply an emotional utterance, a groan, in the face of great suffering now ended. The Gospel of John, for its part, does give us a bit more information (in a way, similar to what we have previously noted in the Gospel of Luke) and it reveals that Jesus, in his final words, cried: "It is finished" (John 19:30). Jesus had taught earlier, as he was envisioning his impending death, that "I lay down my life—only to take it up again. No one takes it from me, but I lay it down of my own accord. I have authority to lay it down and authority to take it up again" (10:17b–18a). That moment had come.

The identification of Jesus with sinners was complete. The descending movement had now run its course. The Word made flesh, transitioning from the form of glory to the form of a humble servant, had died the death of a common criminal, judged and condemned by Gentiles and religious leaders, by Romans and Jews alike. What did it mean, then, that the one who was before Abraham (see John 8:58) had expired on a pole, despised and rejected? For one thing, it revealed that from the heights of glory to the abyss of the cross, there was not a man or woman whom Jesus could not touch. His experience was broad and embracing; his compassion, wide and generous. God had been in this place—here, precisely here. The Highest was in the lowest; the chasm had been crossed.

Was the exact moment of the death of Jesus a critical one, unique in its significance, one that changed the course of humanity forever? Yes! Jerusalem, the city of King David, with its sacred temple for the worship of the Holy One of Israel, could not be silent. That was impossible. Indeed, the temple, the religious heart of the city, spoke loudly; in fact, it shouted. It spoke, however, not in human words, but in the words of a momentous, erupting, and everlasting action: the temple curtain was torn in two from top to bottom! What a message! But who would have the ears to hear it?

If this curtain rent asunder, from top to bottom, was the one separating the Holy Place from the Holy of Holies, as some interpreters believe,[2] then this meant that the way to God was now open. The alienation and estrangement of sinners had finally been overcome, in rich forgiveness, by no one less than God. Provision had been made, through the suffering death of the Messiah, the Anointed One, by which all people, Jews and Gentiles, males and females, rich and poor, could later cry, "*Abba*, Father" (see Romans 8:15). And they would do this no longer as walled-off tribes, not even sitting at the same table with each other, but together, in unison, as the children of God. Ever since the fall of Adam and Eve, the communion of all humanity worshiping the Holy One in spirit and in truth was ever the goal, the point of it all. There never was a moment quite like this one when Jesus died. Something *new* had taken place.

The very last verse of our text is something of a puzzle. Once again, Mark does not give us much help but simply states: "And when the centurion, who stood there in front of Jesus, saw how he died, he said, 'Surely this man was the Son of God!'" How did this Roman soldier, this Gentile, how did he of all people, have the experience, the knowledge, the very wherewithal to make such a statement—and a religious one, at that? As a centurion he was likely the leader of this execution troop. He, therefore, probably had witnessed this entire event. If so, he saw Jesus languish on the cross for six long hours. He heard the mocking of the religious leaders as they wagged their heads. He witnessed the care and the faithfulness of the women and a beloved disciple. He likely had experienced all of this, but none of it is Mark's focus. Instead, he tells us that what moved the centurion was *seeing* how Jesus died—gazing upon the dying Christ, this Roman leader was transformed rapidly, in a flash, as if things had suddenly and unexpectedly come together. He saw what humble, sacrificial love looked like, displayed right before his eyes in the bleeding, suffering, nearly disfigured body of Jesus soon to be a corpse! Yes, soon to be a corpse! Such a love would go all the way even to death's door and beyond. It was unafraid, serene, and incredibly strong. It split temple curtains in two, from top to bottom, from a distance!

These two things of humble, sacrificial love, on the one hand, and of death, on the other hand, had never been brought together, not like this, not quite in this way, placed side by side. The centurion's training as a military man had not prepared him for what he saw, not for any of it. Such a love on the threshold of death, in the least likely of places, was not weak and shameful, or driven by fear, as one might suppose, but confident and radiantly beautiful. It was so sublime and awe-evoking, seen with the eyes of faith, that the soldier didn't have the words for it, and so he spoke with the idiom of divinity, with the borrowed language of the Jews themselves, on his lips: "Surely this man was the Son of God!"

On that day, with the proclamation of this obscure Roman soldier that echoed an important part of the earlier testimony of Peter (see Matthew 16:16), humanity would never again think about God and the things of God in the same way. It was over; it was finished. Such a change would flow through the centuries to reach the world with a new fountain of grace, wisdom, and life. Gone were the attributes, drawn from sinful pride, that were maximized, made superlatives, and then ascribed to the living God. Gone were the abstractions drawn from the things that have been made, from social life and culture or even from family life or a distorted religious vision, all of which were then projected onto God and, thereby, given ultimate value.

In this earlier gross and malformed conception, "god" was but a reflection of an all-too-human creation and, not surprisingly, appeared to be incredibly self-centered, always concerned about conquering enemies—our enemies—and destroying things—their things. This god was powerful, almighty, and in exactly the way that we had wanted it—and needed it. It was always on our side, partisan and useful. It hated what we hated and loved what we loved. Our walls were holy;

our divisions were sanctified; our separations were discrete. Our tribe was simply *the best*. We knew how to intone curses upon the ungodly; those who had fallen short, those so unlike us, and after a while the curses simply rolled off our lips, unthinkingly so, though sometimes they took the form of our fervent "prayers." At other times we were simply indifferent. We kept our distance, to be sure, to protect ourselves and our own very good values—of course. We had all the good ones. We were saved, praise god! It had all worked out so well. Heaven awaited. The "other," however, was and remained a stranger.

But then Jesus came along, and he ruined everything. It was a mess. He hung out with the wrong kind of people, you know the unpopular ones, the ones who cause our heads to turn away quickly, the ones immediately forgotten, and then there were the trouble-makers, the prostitutes, the rabble-rousers, the sinners and the thieves, even the irreligious people who don't think like we do. Imagine that. He sat down at the same table with the riffraff of life, those annoying folks our parents had taught us to dutifully avoid. And they were his friends! His friends! And to top it all, he had a conversation with a couple of rebels as his body was splayed on a tree. He even made a promise to one of them, gave him his word.

In seeing Jesus die, the passion of it all, the Roman centurion saw so much more. Oh, did he see! We must come back to that. What was it? He even called Jesus "the Son of God." What could that language possibly mean here—and spoken by a Gentile, no less? What did this soldier see at Golgotha that the Jewish religious leaders so obviously had not? And what did any of this have to do with *who God is*? Why was that question preeminent here, precisely at this time and in this very dark place? Or was it dark? Yes, things would never be the same again.

The Prayer

Son of God, your resolute love for us shined through the darkest hour of your crucifixion. May I, like the Roman centurion, have eyes to see you for who you are: the promised Messiah, our Savior and friend, my Lord and God. Send your Holy Spirit that my life may always be oriented around the beauty of who you are.

The Questions

How does God revealed in Jesus Christ in the power of the Holy Spirit at the cross—amid blood, suffering, and shame—change the way we think about both God and humanity?

What does such a revelation do to our values and our understanding of who God is?

Day 40

Joseph of Arimathea and Nicodemus

JOHN 19:38–42 *Later, Joseph of Arimathea asked Pilate for the body of Jesus. Now Joseph was a disciple of Jesus, but secretly because he feared the Jewish leaders. With Pilate's permission, he came and took the body away. He was accompanied by Nicodemus, the man who earlier had visited Jesus at night. Nicodemus brought a mixture of myrrh and aloes, about seventy-five pounds. Taking Jesus' body, the two of them wrapped it, with the spices, in strips of linen. This was in accordance with Jewish burial customs. At the place where Jesus was crucified, there was a garden, and in the garden a new tomb, in which no one had ever been laid. Because it was the Jewish day of Preparation and since the tomb was nearby, they laid Jesus there.*

Consider This

So many horrible things had happened to Jesus and in a very short period of time. His disciples were likely shocked that such a person—a gentle and gifted teacher, a caring miracle worker and friend, and one who loved the Holy One of Israel so deeply and in an exemplary way—would meet such a tragic and abrupt end. And yet it was so. All his disciples were gone by now, even the beloved disciple who earlier had been with Mary, his mother, at the cross. A couple of days later, by the first day of the week, the disciples were hiding together behind closed doors "for fear of the Jewish leaders" (John 20:19). *Who would be next?* they probably wondered.

When those convicted of crimes against Rome—such as sedition, insurrection, or treason—were crucified, their bodies were normally left to rot on the pole, to be swarmed by flies and other insects and to be picked apart by ravenous birds of prey. By this practice, Rome intended to magnify both the degradation and the shame for the ones so condemned. After this, the body would be removed and dumped in a common grave for criminals. But that would not be the case here. Enough! By the grace of God, Joseph of Arimathea, who was able to overcome his fear of the Jewish leaders, and in a way that the disciples of Jesus, themselves, obviously had not, stepped forward and asked Pilate if he could take the body away for a proper burial. Probably not thinking very much of the contrived charges leveled against Jesus by the Jerusalem leadership, Pilate agreed.

Joseph of Arimathea was a rich man (Matt. 27:57), a member of the Council, the Sanhedrin (Luke 23:50), as well as a secret disciple of Jesus. But can one really be a secret disciple of Jesus? How does that work? At any rate, although all four Gospels take note of him, he was nevertheless a mysterious figure who is suddenly introduced in our text to play his specific role, and then he just as quickly vanishes from the scene. In his work, however, of caring for the body of Christ, he was joined by a far less mysterious figure who surfaced three times in the Gospel of John, but not at all in the Synoptic Gospels. Who was this man? It was none other than Nicodemus, a Pharisee, who had come to Jesus much earlier at night and who had exclaimed: "Rabbi, we know that you are a teacher who has come from God. For no one could perform the signs you are doing if God were not with him" (John 3:2). Nicodemus and Jesus had gone back and forth in terms of the important question, especially for a religious leader like Nicodemus: Just what does it mean to be born again?

A person of means, Nicodemus brought with him a considerable amount of spices, lavish in some respects, so that he and Joseph could wrap the body, interlacing strips of linen with the myrrh and aloes. This was a Jewish custom in preparation for burial. In contrast, the Egyptians disemboweled the body and placed the organs in separate canisters before they mummified the corpse. Joseph and Nicodemus didn't have these additional tasks in preparing the body, but they nevertheless had to work quickly because the Sabbath was approaching, when no work could be done at all.

The courage of both Joseph and Nicodemus, as they performed the Jewish burial customs, was remarkable, but their actions also came at an additional cost as well: that is, by coming into contact with a dead body, this would render them both unclean, ritually unfit, to celebrate the upcoming Passover meal. Jewish law was very clear and strict on this point. However, basic human decency, making sure that a good person such as Jesus would have a proper burial, overcame any considerations of fear or concerns about ritual purity. If Joseph and Nicodemus had been secret disciples of Jesus in the past out of fear, then they were clearly secret disciples no longer, but this time out of love. The cross had a couple of its earliest converts, beyond the thief on the cross. Together Joseph and Nicodemus made it known publicly that Jesus, the crucified, would not be subject to the usual after-death arrangements of Rome's crucified. The body of Jesus would be treated with respect.

If we examine a map of Jerusalem during the first century, we can see not only the place where Jesus was crucified at Golgotha, just outside the city walls of Jerusalem, and west of the temple, but we can also see the supposed garden of Joseph of Arimathea just slightly northwest of the crucifixion site. In that garden was a fresh tomb, owned by Joseph himself (Matt. 27:60), in which no one had ever been laid. Joseph and Nicodemus, therefore, hurried and placed the body of Jesus in that tomb, one that was actually fit for a king, for the day of Preparation was almost over.

In the many details of the burial of Jesus—such as avoiding the Roman dump for criminals, having the body prepared in accordance with Jewish burial customs with an extravagant amount of spices used, and by being placed in the fresh tomb of a wealthy man—all of these elements together pointed in the direction that the slander, the mocking, the insults, the character assassination, and the hateful designs directed at Jesus would finally be over. At last! If we thought this, however, we would be wrong, dead wrong. Indeed, the kind of strong aversion and animus harbored by the religious leaders against Jesus throughout his ministry didn't just go away after his death. It lingered. To be sure, even after Jesus was dead and buried, some of the religious leaders, the chief priests, and Pharisees, in particular, just couldn't stop the slander or the bad mouthing—and all of this bad behavior was driven not only by fear, the usual culprit, but also by an enormous concern for their own situation and prerogatives. The Gospel of Matthew provides us with the sorry details:

> The next day, the one after Preparation Day, the chief priests and the Pharisees went to Pilate. "Sir," they said, "we remember that while he was still alive *that deceiver* said, 'After three days I will rise again.' So give the order for the tomb to be made secure until the third day. Otherwise, his disciples may come and steal the body and tell the people that he has been raised from the dead. *This last deception* will be worse than the first."
>
> "Take a guard," Pilate answered. "Go, make the tomb as secure as you know how." So they went and made the tomb secure by putting a seal on the stone and posting the guard. (27:62–66, emphasis added)

After all that Jesus had suffered at the hand of the religious leadership, and after what he had uttered on the cross in a generous and gracious spirit, "Father, forgive them, for they do not know what they are doing" (Luke 23:34), what did the religious leaders themselves do? They turned around and called Jesus a "deceiver," even after he was dead, as the one who probably along with his disciples had helped to plan the "last deception." Attributing such intentions to Jesus (and others) actually says something about the chief priests and the Pharisees, those who had concocted such things out of their own imagination and fears, but it tells us nothing—absolutely nothing—about Jesus. Christ was no deceiver. The ministry of the Lord had been open, public, and full of light. To fail to recognize that simple truth would entail measures of spiritual darkness, a darkness that could be felt.

The Prayer

Father, may we be counted among those who faithfully glorify the name of your Son among the earth. Save us from the deception of the enemy and align us to the truth of your gospel. Fill us with your Spirit that we might be your ambassadors in all places.

The Questions

What does it mean to be a secret disciple of Jesus? Is this the form that belief in Jesus takes in the face of severe persecution, or does being a disciple in secret suggest something else?

Day 41

Mary Magdalene

JOHN 20:1–18 *Early on the first day of the week, while it was still dark, Mary Magdalene went to the tomb and saw that the stone had been removed from the entrance. So she came running to Simon Peter and the other disciple, the one Jesus loved, and said, "They have taken the Lord out of the tomb, and we don't know where they have put him!"*

So Peter and the other disciple started for the tomb. Both were running, but the other disciple outran Peter and reached the tomb first. He bent over and looked in at the strips of linen lying there but did not go in. Then Simon Peter came along behind him and went straight into the tomb. He saw the strips of linen lying there, as well as the cloth that had been wrapped around Jesus' head. The cloth was still lying in its place, separate from the linen. Finally the other disciple, who had reached the tomb first, also went inside. He saw and believed. (They still did not understand from Scripture that Jesus had to rise from the dead.) Then the disciples went back to where they were staying.

Now Mary stood outside the tomb crying. As she wept, she bent over to look into the tomb and saw two angels in white, seated where Jesus' body had been, one at the head and the other at the foot.

They asked her, "Woman, why are you crying?"

"They have taken my Lord away," she said, "and I don't know where they have put him." At this, she turned around and saw Jesus standing there, but she did not realize that it was Jesus.

He asked her, "Woman, why are you crying? Who is it you are looking for?"

Thinking he was the gardener, she said, "Sir, if you have carried him away, tell me where you have put him, and I will get him."

Jesus said to her, "Mary."

She turned toward him and cried out in Aramaic, "Rabboni!" (which means "Teacher").

Jesus said, "Do not hold on to me, for I have not yet ascended to the Father. Go instead to my brothers and tell them, 'I am ascending to my Father and your Father, to my God and your God.'"

Mary Magdalene went to the disciples with the news: "I have seen the Lord!" And she told them that he had said these things to her.

Consider This

Mary had been to the tomb early on Sunday morning while it was still dark. The Gospel of Mark (16:1) as well as the Gospel of Luke (24:1) both suggest that Mary was not alone (our text also uses "we" in John 20:2) but was with other women who intended to anoint the body of Jesus with spices. Mary saw that the heavy stone had been removed from the entrance to the tomb, and she realized that the body of Jesus was not there. Where could it be? Running to Simon Peter and to the disciple whom Jesus loved, Mary exclaimed: "They have taken the Lord out of the tomb, and we don't know where they have put him!" Peter and the other disciple then raced to the tomb; the latter got there first, but he didn't go in. Peter finally reached the tomb and entered immediately.

He saw the strips of linen lying there "as well as the cloth that had been wrapped around Jesus' head." The other disciple now entered the tomb. Assessing matters quickly, "He saw and believed." An empty tomb for him apparently meant a risen Christ. The two disciples then went back to where they were staying, leaving Mary, and presumably other women, at the tomb.

Hailing from Magdala, a fishing town on the western shore of the Sea of Galilee, Mary had been a faithful follower of Jesus. According to the Gospel of Luke, Mary, along with some other women, contributed to Jesus out of their own resources. She was likely, then, a woman of some means. Faithful to the end, in a way that others had not been, Mary was even present at the cross, along with the mother of Jesus and Mary the wife of Clopas (John 19:25). The Gospel of Luke also reveals that this was the same Mary "from who seven demons had come out" (8:2b). Jesus had taught earlier in his ministry that those who are forgiven much love much (see Luke 7:47). Mary did, indeed, love greatly.

In a way unlike Peter and the beloved disciple, Mary peered into the tomb for a second time, and she saw not simply the burial cloths but also "two angels in white, seated where Jesus' body had been, one at the head and the other at the foot." Luke refers to this same incident in terms of "two men in clothes that gleamed like lightning" (24:4a). The angels then asked her, "Woman, why are you crying?" Mary's response is noteworthy. She replied, "They have taken my Lord away . . . and I don't know where they have put him." Observe that Mary did not refer to the body of Jesus, a corpse, but to the person of Jesus, a "him." In this atmosphere of love and tender mourning, in the midst of several tears, Mary thought in a way that only love could do.

Turning around, Mary saw Jesus right there, standing before her, "but she did not realize that it was Jesus." This phenomenon of not initially recognizing Jesus after his resurrection from the dead was repeated in the incident after a miraculous catch of fish by the disciples when "Jesus stood on the shore" (John 21:4). It also was duplicated on the road to Emmaus (see Luke 24:15). Jesus then repeated the same question to Mary that the angels had posed earlier: "Woman, why are you crying?" to which he added another query, perhaps to ease the way for Mary's gradual recognition of himself, and in a manner that would not startle her: "Who is it you are looking for?" Mary saw the same empty tomb that the beloved disciple had seen, and even a couple of angels, but she did not yet believe. She was still thinking about recovering the body, and she mistakenly thought that Jesus was the gardener.

In one of the most memorable and tersely described awakenings ever recorded in literature, Jesus spoke but a single word: "Mary." And in turning toward Jesus, the woman simply replied, "Rabboni!" She had now become a woman of great faith. Jesus had taught earlier about the special connection between him and his followers. He compared their relationship to the attentiveness of sheep to the voice of the shepherd: "The gatekeeper opens the gate for him, and the sheep listen to his voice. He calls his own sheep by name and leads them out. When he has brought out all his own, he goes on ahead of them, and his sheep follow him because they know his voice" (John 10:3–4). Mary knew the voice of Jesus well; she had served him. In an instant, she was awakened and transformed. She was looking for a body no longer.

Jesus then issued a command: "Do not hold on to me, for I have not yet ascended to the Father." Some of the early church fathers immediately recognized the nature of what was to some others a very puzzling directive. To illustrate, in commenting on this verse, Chrysostom, a Greek father who died in AD 407, observed: "Do not approach me as you did before, *for matters are not in the same state*, nor shall I any longer be with you in the same way."[1] For his part, Leo the Great, who lived in the fifth century, noted: "I would not have you come to me as to a human body or recognize me by fleshly perceptions."[2] In other words, the resurrected Jesus was different. Perhaps that's why Mary had difficulty recognizing him in the first place. Jesus now had a resurrected body, a spiritual body, one that in some sense was like his old body (so there is continuity here) but in another sense it was different from his old body, that is, it was discontinuous. With Mary, Jesus stressed the difference; with his disciple Thomas later on (vv. 24–29), Jesus would stress the continuity by inviting the doubter to touch the very wounds of his body. So then, in clinging to Christ, Mary was grasping at an old form, in her mind at least, that was now gone. Jesus was teaching her the difference.

Accordingly, the raising of Jesus from the dead was distinct, unique, unlike the raising of Lazarus who with his mortal body would die once more. Jesus, however, would never die again. He had an immortal body. There are such things in the universe. Our world is more glorious and far more exciting than we have imagined.

Jesus is proof. Later on, the apostle Paul pointed out that Christ "has indeed been raised from the dead, the firstfruits of those who have fallen asleep. For since death came through a man, the resurrection of the dead comes also through a man. For as in Adam all die, so in Christ all will be made alive" (1 Cor. 15:20–22). What does such a declaration mean? As the new Adam, Christ will raise up a new humanity. And he will give them eternal life. Here is the *new* that will never grow old; it will last forever.

The raising of Jesus from the dead was such a stupendous event, a new beginning with consequences for all of humanity, that the Father, the Son, and the Holy Spirit in one harmonious voice, in a resounding clarion call, raised the Son out of the shackles of death which could not hold him. To illustrate, on the day of Pentecost, Peter proclaimed for all to hear: "God has raised this Jesus to life, and we are all witnesses of it" (Acts 2:32). The Father said "rise." During his ministry Jesus had proclaimed: "The reason my Father loves me is that I lay down my life—only to take it up again. No one takes it from me, but I lay it down of my own accord. I have authority to lay it down and authority to take it up again" (John 10:17–18a). The Son said, "take it up again." And the apostle Paul taught in a way so full of promise: "And if the Spirit of him who raised Jesus from the dead is living in you, he who raised Christ from the dead will also give life to your mortal bodies because of his Spirit who lives in you" (Rom. 8:11). The Holy Spirit said "rise." Almighty God, then, not sinful humanity, would have the last word on the life, death, and ministry of Jesus Christ: "Rise, rise, rise!" Such was the shout of heaven.

Jesus gave Mary Magdalene one last command: "Go instead to my brothers and tell them, 'I am ascending to my Father and your Father, to my God and your God.'" By speaking in this way, Jesus affirmed, on the one hand, his distinct relationship with the Father, with God, as the Son of God, the eternal Word made flesh. That relationship was and remained unique. On the other hand, however, Jesus announced the intimate relationship ("*Abba*, Father") that was now possible between his Father and his God and the people of God—those who believed in his name and embraced his atoning work. Reconciliation and fellowship, forgiveness and peace, the overcoming of separation, alienation, and division were the principal chords struck here. Simply put, the way was now open for nothing less than *communion*. What's more, Jesus Christ, the divine and human, was ascending to the Father. Humanity would forevermore be at the right hand of God. And that's precisely where humanity belongs; that's what ascension entails.

Mary went to the disciples with this earth-shattering news: "I have seen the Lord!" Yes, she had seen the Lord! In fact, she had touched him!

The Prayer

Father, just as your Son ascended to your right hand in heaven, may I also be raised up to new life and have my heart raised with him. As you gather up to Christ all things in heaven and on earth, unite my heart to serve you and others in my home, church, and community.

The Questions

How does the earlier suffering of Jesus, especially at the hands of the religious leaders—the evil speaking against him, his rejection, the ostracism, his passion, and crucifixion—look from the perspective of the empty tomb brought about by the Father, the Son, and the Holy Spirit?

Day 42

A Couple of Disciples

LUKE 24:13–35 *Now that same day two of them were going to a village called Emmaus, about seven miles from Jerusalem. They were talking with each other about everything that had happened. As they talked and discussed these things with each other, Jesus himself came up and walked along with them; but they were kept from recognizing him.*

He asked them, "What are you discussing together as you walk along?"

They stood still, their faces downcast. One of them, named Cleopas, asked him, "Are you the only one visiting Jerusalem who does not know the things that have happened there in these days?"

"What things?" he asked.

"About Jesus of Nazareth," they replied. "He was a prophet, powerful in word and deed before God and all the people. The chief priests and our rulers handed him over to be sentenced to death, and they crucified him; but we had hoped that he was the one who was going to redeem Israel. And what is more, it is the third day since all this took place. In addition, some of our women amazed us. They went to the tomb early this morning but didn't find his body. They came and told us that they had seen a vision of angels, who said he was alive. Then some of our companions went to the tomb and found it just as the women had said, but they did not see Jesus."

He said to them, "How foolish you are, and how slow to believe all that the prophets have spoken! Did not the Messiah have to suffer these things and then enter his glory?" And beginning with Moses and all the Prophets, he explained to them what was said in all the Scriptures concerning himself.

As they approached the village to which they were going, Jesus continued on as if he were going farther. But they urged him strongly, "Stay with us, for it is nearly evening; the day is almost over." So he went in to stay with them.

When he was at the table with them, he took bread, gave thanks, broke it and began to give it to them. Then their eyes were opened and they recognized him, and he disappeared from their sight. They asked each other, "Were not our hearts burning within us while he talked with us on the road and opened the Scriptures to us?"

They got up and returned at once to Jerusalem. There they found the Eleven and those with them, assembled together and saying, "It is true! The Lord has risen and has appeared to Simon." Then the two told what had happened on the way, and how Jesus was recognized by them when he broke the bread.

Consider This

On Sunday two disciples, one named Cleopas, the other not named at all, were traveling away from Jerusalem toward Emmaus, a village about seven miles away. Today we are not certain just where this village might be located on a map, given the results of archeological findings.[1] At any rate, in light of all that had happened in Jerusalem during the last few days, the direction of the travel is intriguing. Why leave the city, especially since there had been reports from some women, Mary Magdalene in particular (as recorded somewhat differently in the Gospel of Luke), who had encountered "two men in clothes that gleamed like lightning" who affirmed that "he has risen!" (see Luke 24:4–10)? The problem was—and it was a huge one at the time, and one that especially perplexes us today—Mary and the other women, in relating these events, were simply not believed! Think about that for a while. Even the word "nonsense" was in the air and was heard, or perhaps even spoken, by one of the eleven disciples, no less (Luke 24:11). So then, these two disciples were likely leaving Jerusalem because, in their minds at least, there was nothing more to hear. There would be no news worth waiting for. Why stay? They were heading out to Emmaus, then, perhaps to get away from it all: saddened, dejected, and evidently in unbelief.

While they were on the road conversing about all that had occurred in the last few days, Jesus came up alongside the two disciples and asked about what they were discussing. Not recognizing Jesus, Cleopas questioned him: "Are you the only one visiting Jerusalem who does not know the things that have happened there in these days?" "What things?" Jesus asked. "About Jesus of Nazareth," came the reply. "He was a prophet, powerful in word and deed before God and all the people." Rich irony is evident in this dialogue. Consider this: these two disciples, who didn't even recognize that they were talking with Jesus, now marveled at *his* supposed ignorance of "the things that have happened there in these days." So then, in their attempt to enlighten their fellow traveler, they recounted the drama of how Jesus of Nazareth was handed over (to the Romans, of course) by the religious leaders in order to be sentenced to death and then crucified. Expressing their heartfelt disappointment, the two then confessed: "we had hoped that he was the one who was going to redeem Israel." But what sort of redemption was it that they had in mind? Was an empty tomb not enough?

Aware of their unbelief and dejection, Jesus remarkably enough did not comfort these two disciples in their low spirits, and in the suffering that went along with it, but he actually upbraided them: "How foolish you are, and how slow to believe all that the prophets have spoken!" The word *foolish* in this context is best understood not as rash or reckless action, heedless of what is good, but as a dullness, a slowness of understanding, a difficulty in seeing things aright. Though they should have known better—and they really should have—they didn't. Jesus then offered the following illumination: "Did not the Messiah have to suffer these things and then enter his glory?" As we have just seen, Cleopas and the other disciple had already acknowledged that Jesus was a prophet "powerful in word and deed before God and all the people." But could they see the connection between being a prophet and being the Messiah? If so, that would go a long way in clearing up ongoing misunderstanding.

The Jews in the first century, both religious leaders and common folk, would have little difficulty in recognizing that prophets suffer. The names of Elijah as well as Jeremiah, who was himself thrown down a well for his troubles, would quickly come to mind. Beyond this, Jesus "pointed out that a prophet has no honor in his own country" (John 4:44). Accordingly, suffering, persecution, and rejection would be the lay of the land, so to speak, for those people who had both the courage and the boldness to speak the Word of the Lord, to declare the truth, to a sinful and rebellious people. What, then, if one of the roles of the Messiah during much of his earthly ministry would be that of a prophet? Such an understanding would be a hard sell, especially for the Jewish religious leadership during the first century. When they envisioned what the Messiah would be like, they probably had in mind the kingly role, that is, a powerful leader sent by God, someone who could throw off the Roman yoke. So understood, the Messiah would wage war on behalf of the Jewish people and its religious leadership and destroy the despised "other." Perhaps that's what even these two disciples of Jesus had in mind along the road to Emmaus when they said to him, "we had hoped that he was the one who was going to redeem Israel."

If one of the major roles of the Messiah, however, was that of a prophet, at least during the phase of ministry that led up to the death of Jesus (without denying the importance of the other two roles of priest or king), then things would look very different. So understood, the Messiah would not be waging war on behalf of the people or the religious leadership, thereby destroying the hated "other" in which evil would be deemed to be utterly external to the people. No! The Messiah, as a prophet, would be calling the Jews, themselves, as well as their religious leadership, to repent of their own evil! And suffering, wide and deep, would be the cost of such ministry. "Repent, for the kingdom of heaven has come near" (Matt. 4:17), Jesus had warned. Indeed, suffering is the price that sinners demand for speaking the truth of God. In the end, evil would no longer be neatly packaged in an externalized other, an enemy, but it would also be understood as lying within. That's a far tougher enemy to conquer.

Such an honest and humble realization was at the heart of Isaiah's own self-understanding: "'Woe to me!' I cried. 'I am ruined! For I am a man of unclean lips, and I live among a people of unclean lips . . .'" (Isa. 6:5a). Jesus, then, was trying to get Cleopas and the other disciple to see something sparkling new: "Did not the Messiah have to *suffer* these things . . ." (emphasis added). Not only was Jesus a prophet, which the two had already recognized, but he was also the Messiah, the Anointed One of God, and as such he was a *suffering* prophet, a *suffering* Messiah. That was, indeed, new. To be sure, for some people to put the words "Messiah" and "suffering prophet" in the same sentence would be an oxymoron;[2] it would not make any sense at all. But Jesus was the Messiah precisely in this way! Unlike John the Baptist, Jesus was both a prophet and the Messiah, the two offices were embodied, united, in his own person and ministry. And Messiahs do indeed suffer. That's the whole point of Jesus going through the Scriptures from "Moses and all the Prophets," to explain "what was said in all the Scriptures concerning himself."

After teaching the two disciples from the Bible, Jesus "continued on as if he were going farther." They urged him to stay with them since it was almost evening. He agreed. While they were all sitting at the table, Jesus "took bread, gave thanks, broke it and began to give it to them." Their eyes were now open and "they recognized him." Revelation had occurred—finally! The two now saw Jesus, but he quickly disappeared. Why had this recognition happened now, and what was it about the actions of Jesus that had precipitated it? For one thing, the language of "took bread, gave thanks, broke it and began to give it to them," according to some interpreters, such as Augustine (AD 354–430), is reminiscent of the Lord's Supper, the sacrament of Communion. To illustrate, this Latin church father maintained: "And no one should doubt that his being recognized in the breaking of bread is the sacrament, which brings us together in recognizing him."[3]

Other interpreters, however, some from the twenty-first century, disagree. Joel Green, for example, points out that the verbs of the pithy statement drawn from our text in Luke may be "reminiscent of his [Jesus] similar actions in 9:16 in the account of the miraculous feeding,"[4] when he fed the five thousand. This view is supported to some extent by the recognition that in our current text, though bread is indeed present, wine is not mentioned at all. How, then, is this the sacrament of the Lord's Supper without any wine? We obviously will not resolve this issue here. Perhaps then it is best left open, suggesting a number of possible meanings. The chief point is that revelation had occurred, illumination had taken place, by means of these actions either as the culmination of the prior activity of instruction in Moses and the Prophets, or as a consequence of the precipitating actions of taking bread, giving thanks, breaking it, and giving it. The point is that Cleopas and the other disciple now recognized Jesus. Simply put, they believed. And that was marvelous.

The two disciples then reflected upon their prior conversation with Jesus: "Were not our hearts burning within us while he talked with us on the road and opened the Scriptures to us?" With their hearts aglow from the earlier encounter, in the flames of holy love, the two simply had to change direction, turn around, and head for Jerusalem. It was a conversion of sorts—and a powerful one at that. They were no longer sad, dejected, or in unbelief. They had a gospel to proclaim! When they arrived in Jerusalem, they found the Eleven, but quickly realized that the good news had already been received by them from another source: "It is true! The Lord has risen and has appeared to Simon." That truth had been burned into the hearts of Cleopas and his companion. It was the gentle flame of the Holy Spirit, the beauty of holy love that burned within. May that divine love ever glow in our hearts as well, and may it be richly manifested to all others. Yes, it is true. The Lord has risen. The Lord has risen, indeed!

The Prayer

Flame of God, Eternal Spirit, make your home in my heart today. Fill me that I might perfectly enjoy communion with Jesus Christ and so be conformed to his image. May holy love be the measure of my life, to the flourishing of my neighbors and the glory of God the Father.

The Questions

In what ways can the transformation of the two disciples on the road to Emmaus be suitably described as a conversion? Were they not already followers of Jesus? What can this teach us today about our own discipleship journey?

Notes

INTRODUCTION

1. An enormous amount of time was spent selecting the passages in accordance with the chosen theme. I would be embarrassed to admit just how much time was entailed in this lengthy process. At any rate, once a passage was identified, then a judgment had to be made in terms of which of the four gospel accounts (if there were even this many accounts available) would be used. In this thematic approach, which represents an unswerving focus, there are, of course, some beloved stories of the Gospels that are not represented in this collection of passages. For example, the parable of the good Samaritan does not appear as a text, though it is mentioned in passing. In a similar fashion, the account of Jesus washing the feet of his disciples is nowhere to be found. Readers are, of course, encouraged to read the full gospel accounts later.
2. This book, though in a popular form, has been carefully researched as the notes demonstrate. Indeed, I am well aware of the higher critical questions (matters concerning date, authorship, and historical setting, etc.) raised by scholars, but I will rarely bring such information into the reflections simply because that approach, though important, is not the focus of this work. My concern largely has to do with the factual story, its givenness, how it is read

and heard—in other words, how the images and characters that constitute the story are *received* (this is the right word in so many ways) by average, non-scholarly readers.

3. Imagination is engaged, for example, when in reading a text we ask the question how Jesus might have felt or thought as such and such was happening to him. That's a fair question and should be examined to avoid what I am calling a flat reading of the text, one that forgets we are ever dealing with a number of dimensions in our focus on flesh-and-blood *persons*. Second, imagination also comes richly into play when we reflect upon the lives of the people in the gospel accounts, whether saints or sinners, and then compare these lives to our own, either positively or negatively. Such an approach is, after all, how many people will read a story, any story, with its larger-than-life characters.

Day 2: SIMEON

1. Arthur A. Just, *Luke*, vol. 3, *Ancient Christian Commentary on Scripture: New Testament III* (Downers Grove, IL: InterVarsity Press, 2005), 48.

Day 3: HEROD THE GREAT

1. Allen C. Myers, *The Eerdmans Bible Dictionary* (Grand Rapids, MI: Eerdmans, 1987), 482.
2. Myers, *Eerdmans Bible Dictionary*, 482.
3. Myers, *Eerdmans Bible Dictionary*, 482.
4. William Barclay, *The Gospel of Matthew*, 3rd ed., *The New Daily Study Bible* (Edinburgh: Saint Andrew Press, 2001), 39.

Day 5: THE DEVIL

1. R. T. France, for example, contends: "To refer to this episode as the temptation of Jesus is doubly misleading. First, the verb *peirazō* (vv. 1, 3) in Matthew always signifies testing (and in its 36 New Testament occurrences it clearly indicates tempting to do wrong only in 1 Cor. 7:5; Jas 1:13–14); see also John 6:6; 2 Corinthians 13:5 for some clear examples of this primary sense." See R. T. France, *Matthew: An Introduction and Commentary*, vol. 1, *Tyndale New Testament Commentaries* (Downers Grove, IL: InterVarsity Press, 1985), 101.
2. Matthew 4:3, *The Common English Bible* (Nashville: The Common English Bible, 2011).

Day 8: THE SCRIBES

1. Earle notes, "The Talmud accuses Him of practicing magic, an accusation similar to that hurled by the scribes." See Ralph Earle, "The Gospel According to St. Mark," in *Matthew–Acts*, vol. 4, *The Wesleyan Bible Commentary* (Grand Rapids, MI: William B. Eerdmans Publishing Company, 1966), 142.
2. James A. Brooks, Mark, vol. 23, *The New American Commentary* (Nashville: Broadman & Holman Publishers, 1991), 75.

Day 9: THE PHARISEES

1. Colin G. Kruse, *John: An Introduction and Commentary*, vol. 4, *Tyndale New Testament Commentaries* (Downers Grove, IL: InterVarsity Press, 2003), 224.

2. Gary M. Burge, *John, The NIV Application Commentary* (Grand Rapids, MI: Zondervan Publishing House, 2000), 281.

Day 10: THE TEACHERS OF THE LAW

1. David Smith, *Mark: A Commentary for Bible Students* (Indianapolis, IN: Wesleyan Publishing House, 2007), 75.

Day 12: THE PHARISEES AGAIN

1. Roger L. Hahn, *Matthew: A Commentary for Bible Students* (Indianapolis, IN: Wesleyan Publishing House, 2007), 125.

Day 13: ONE OF THE TEACHERS OF THE LAW

1. Lamar Williamson, *Mark, Interpretation: A Bible Commentary for Teaching and Preaching* (Atlanta, GA: J. Knox Press, 1983), 226–27.

Day 15: THE JEWS IN THE TEMPLE COURTS

1. Josephus wrote: "And from that time to this we celebrate this festival, and call it Lights." See *Antiquities*, book 12, chapter 7 in Flavius Josephus and William Whiston, *The Works of Josephus: Complete and Unabridged* (Peabody, MA: Hendrickson, 1987), 328.
2. Colin G. Kruse, *John: An Introduction and Commentary*, vol. 4, *Tyndale New Testament Commentaries* (Downers Grove, IL: InterVarsity Press, 2003), 239.
3. If we focus on specific texts, whether the four Gospels of the first century or the Talmud (the writings of the Jewish rabbis) of the fourth century, we will quickly discern that the contrast, and perhaps

even the conflict, between a Christian and a Jewish assessment of Jesus is unavoidable. Jewish readers today will likely experience discomfort or even pain as they read how Jews are portrayed in the Gospel of John. We understand that. In a similar fashion, Christians will likewise experience pain as they read how Jesus is portrayed in the Talmud. We understand that as well. On one level, this is a textual issue. Jews have a right to their revered writings, a part of their ongoing tradition, just as Christians enjoy the same right with respect to the Gospels and their proper interpretation. Though there are clearly difficulties here, and we are not trying to gloss over them in the least, it is best that each community of faith demonstrate kindness, decency, and respect toward the other and take up the very difficult labor of learning how to listen to each other in new and engaging ways.

The Christian church must be especially cautious in this area. Indeed, Judaism poses a significant challenge to the church that, if not handled properly, could undermine its very witness. As the apostle Paul taught: "There is neither Jew nor Gentile, neither slave nor free, nor is there male and female, for you are all one in Christ Jesus" (Gal. 3:28). The gospel message, then, is the *universal love of God* manifested in Jesus Christ. As such, the church can never back away from this vital truth. If it did, then such a move would undermine its very faith—what Jesus Christ was all about in his proclamation of the kingdom of God. Accordingly, if Jews, themselves, became for the church today simply "the other," then what would this regrettable turn of affairs mean but that the church itself had taken the tribal turn in disobedience to its Master. Even if Jews today, or Muslims for that matter, specifically reject Jesus as the Messiah as they practice their own religions, then Christians, by unswervingly following their risen Lord, must love them in return—yes, love them—as the neighbors that they are and remain. Anything less than this would be a perversion of the Christian faith itself. Such a faith would then have become what it was never intended to be: just another religious tribe, one among many.

4. Rodney A. Whitacre, *John*, vol. 4, *The IVP New Testament Commentary Series* (Westmont, IL: IVP Academic, 1999), 273.

Day 16: SIMON PETER

1. William L. Lane, *The Gospel of Mark*, *The New International Commentary on the New Testament* (Grand Rapids, MI: Wm. B. Eerdmans Publishing Co., 1974), 289.
2. Eckhard J. Schnabel, ed., *Mark: An Introduction and Commentary*, vol. 2, *Tyndale New Testament Commentaries* (London: Inter-Varsity Press, 2017), 196.

Day 18: CHIEF PRIESTS, TEACHERS OF THE LAW AND ELDERS

1. See Bengt Runo Hoffman, trans. and ed., *The Theologica Germanica of Martin Luther* (New York: Paulist Press, 1980), 62.

Day 19: JESUS

1. William Arndt et al., *A Greek-English Lexicon of the New Testament and Other Early Christian Literature* (Chicago: University of Chicago Press, 2000), 252 [Entry under διχάζω].

Day 21: HEROD ANTIPAS

1. Walter L. Liefeld and David W. Pao, "Luke," in *The Expositor's Bible Commentary: Luke–Acts*, rev. ed., eds. Tremper Longman III and David E. Garland, vol. 10 (Grand Rapids, MI: Zondervan, 2007), 239.

Day 22: DISCIPLES THEN AND NOW (PART ONE)

1. Vine lifts up the element of aversion in the following observation on μισέω "to hate": "by way of expressing either aversion from, or disregard for, the claims of one person or thing relatively to those of another." See W. E. Vine, Merrill F. Unger, and William White Jr., *Vine's Complete Expository Dictionary of Old and New Testament Words* (Nashville, TN: Thomas Nelson, 1996), 292.
2. Vine, *Vine's Complete Expository Dictionary*, 292. Again, Vine considers μισέω "to hate" in terms of "malicious and unjustifiable feelings towards others."
3. We cannot explore in the limited space here all the questions that arise in terms of when evil, defined as taking away some important value (whether it be property, liberty, or life itself), may be justified as a form of retributive justice and as a protection for society.

4. Kenneth J. Collins and Jason Vickers, eds., *The Sermons of John Wesley: A Collection for the Christian Journey* (Nashville: Abingdon Press, 2013), 431–39.

Day 23: DISCIPLES THEN AND NOW (PART TWO)

1. Michael E. Peach, "World or Cosmos," eds. Douglas Mangum et al., Lexham Theological Wordbook, *Lexham Bible Reference Series* (Bellingham, WA: Lexham Press, 2014).
2. Barclay M. Newman Jr., *A Concise Greek-English Dictionary of the New Testament* (Stuttgart, Germany: Deutsche Bibelgesellschaft; United Bible Societies, 1993), 103.

Day 24: DISCIPLES THEN AND NOW (PART THREE)

1. Joel C. Elowsky, *John 1–10, Ancient Christian Commentary on Scripture NT 4a* (Downers Grove, IL: InterVarsity Press, 2006), 246 ["Commentary on the Gospel of John" II.9].
2. James Strong, *The New Strong's Dictionary of Hebrew and Greek Words* (Nashville: Thomas Nelson, 1996) [Entry 4262; σκληρός sklēroˇs].

Day 25: THE CROWD

1. Gary M. Burge, *John: The NIV Application Commentary* (Grand Rapids, MI: Zondervan Publishing House, 2000), 341.

Day 27: SINNERS

1. James A. Brooks, *Mark*, vol. 23, *The New American Commentary* (Nashville: Broadman & Holman Publishers, 1991), 234.

Day 28: JUDAS

1. Leon Morris, *Luke: An Introduction and Commentary*, vol. 3, *Tyndale New Testament Commentaries* (Downers Grove, IL: InterVarsity Press, 1988), 331.
2. Luke 22:52, *The Holy Bible: New Revised Standard Version* (Nashville: Thomas Nelson Publishers, 1989); *New American Standard Bible* (La Habra, CA: Foundation Publications, for the Lockman Foundation, 1971); *The Common English Bible* (Nashville: The Common English Bible, 2011).

Day 29: CAIAPHAS, THE CHIEF PRIESTS, AND THE SANHEDRIN

1. Manlio Simonetti, *Matthew 14–28, Ancient Christian Commentary on Scripture* (Downers Grove, IL: InterVarsity Press, 2001), 264.
2. Michael J. Wilkins, Matthew, *The NIV Application Commentary* (Grand Rapids, MI: Zondervan Publishing House, 2004), 861.
3. In the fifth century Pope Leo the Great, in commenting on this verse, wrote as follows: "You are oblivious to the command you read concerning high priests: 'Do not let the hair of your heads hang loose, and do not rend your clothes.'" See Manlio Simonetti, *Matthew 14–28, Ancient Christian Commentary on Scripture* (Downers Grove, IL: InterVarsity Press, 2001), 267.

Day 30: PETER

1. For more on the character of Peter, as evidenced in the Gospel of Matthew, see the following: Arlo J. Nau, *Peter in Matthew: Discipleship, Diplomacy, and Dispraise* (Collegeville, MN: The Liturgical Press, 1992).

Day 31: PILATE

1. Robert H. Mounce, "John," in *The Expositor's Bible Commentary: Luke–Acts*, rev. ed., eds. Tremper Longman III and David E. Garland, vol. 10 (Grand Rapids, MI: Zondervan, 2007), 623.
2. Colin G. Kruse, *John: An Introduction and Commentary*, vol. 4, *Tyndale New Testament Commentaries* (Downers Grove, IL: InterVarsity Press, 2003), 352.
3. Joel C. Elowsky, John 11–21, *Ancient Christian Commentary on Scripture NT 4b* (Downers Grove, IL: InterVarsity Press, 2007), 286.
4. In terms of this statement, I am dependent on a conversation that I had with Ben Witherington III, who helped me think through this issue properly. The chronological issues from the time of the Lord's Supper, eaten with his disciples, to the crucifixion of Jesus are challenging given the four accounts of the Gospels. Any misjudgments in this area are clearly my own. Once again, in the arrangement of materials, my chief concern was always thematic.
5. Kruse, *John*, 353.

Day 32: HEROD ANTIPAS

1. Joel B. Green, *The Gospel of Luke, The New International Commentary on the New Testament*

(Grand Rapids, MI: Wm. B. Eerdmans Publishing Co., 1997), 804.

Day 33: BARABBAS

1. This verse does not appear in the earliest manuscripts but is offered as it appears in today's NASB for the sake of filling in the context. See *New American Standard Bible*: 1995 Update (La Habra, CA: The Lockman Foundation, 1995), Luke 23:17.
2. The nature of the offer is clear in the Gospel of Matthew, which reads: "So when the crowd had gathered, Pilate asked them, 'Which one do you want me to release to you: Jesus Barabbas, or Jesus who is called the Messiah?'" (Matt. 27:17).
3. Robert H. Stein, Luke, vol. 24, *The New American Commentary* (Nashville: Broadman & Holman Publishers, 1992), 581.
4. Leon Morris, *Luke: An Introduction and Commentary*, vol. 3, *Tyndale New Testament Commentaries* (Downers Grove, IL: InterVarsity Press, 1988), 341.
5. Arthur A. Just, *Luke, vol. 3, Ancient Christian Commentary on Scripture NT 3* (Downers Grove, IL: InterVarsity Press, 2005), 355.
6. J. Julius Scott Jr., "Cross, Crucifixion," ed. Daniel J. Treier and Walter A. Elwell, *Evangelical Dictionary of Theology* (Grand Rapids, MI: Baker Academic: A Division of Baker Publishing Group, 2017), 223–24.
7. Scott, "Cross, Crucifixion," 224.
8. For more on the details of crucifixion, as practiced by the Romans, see Joel B. Green, *The Gospel of Luke: The New International Commentary on the New Testament* (Grand Rapids, MI: Wm. B. Eerdmans Publishing Co., 1997), 810.

Day 34: THE GOVERNOR'S SOLDIERS

1. Michael J. Wilkins, Matthew, *The NIV Application Commentary* (Grand Rapids, MI: Zondervan Publishing House, 2004), 895.

Day 35: THE CHIEF PRIESTS AND THEIR OFFICIALS

1. The issue of time raised by this verse can be understood, in part, in light of the different reckoning of time between the Gospel of John (the Roman reckoning from midnight and noon) and the synoptic Gospels (the Jewish reckoning from sunrise and sunset).

Day 36: THE CHIEF PRIESTS, TEACHERS OF THE LAW, AND ELDERS (PART ONE)

1. Michael J. Wilkins, *Matthew, The NIV Application Commentary* (Grand Rapids, MI: Zondervan Publishing House, 2004), 897–98.
2. Roger L. Hahn, *Matthew: A Commentary for Bible Students* (Indianapolis, IN: Wesleyan Publishing House, 2007), 332.
3. Craig S. Keener, *The Gospel of Matthew: A Socio-Rhetorical Commentary* (Grand Rapids, MI; Cambridge, U.K.: Wm. B. Eerdmans Publishing Co., 2009), 676.
4. The Gospel of John changed the tense of the verb "to divide."

Day 37: THE CHIEF PRIESTS, TEACHERS OF THE LAW, AND ELDERS (PART TWO)

1. I am making no claims whatsoever that my reconstructions are what the artist himself intended.

Viewers of works of art are free to engage their own imaginations in all sorts of ways, even in playful and creative ones. My comments, then, are simply suggestive of how our text and Tintoretto's painting might point to the deeper truths of the scene. All of this has worked marvelously well for me; it may work for others also.

2. Manlio Simonetti, *Matthew 14–28, Ancient Christian Commentary on Scripture* (Downers Grove, IL: InterVarsity Press, 2001), 290–91.

3. Chrysostom writes: "Jesus teaches us to show the utmost care for our parents even to our last breath. . . . He commits her to the disciple whom he loved. Again, John modestly conceals himself. If he had wanted to boast, he would have also told us why he was loved since it was most likely some great and wonderful thing he had done." See the following: Joel C. Elowsky, John 11–21, *Ancient Christian Commentary on Scripture NT 4b* (Downers Grove, IL: InterVarsity Press, 2007), 318.

4. To illustrate, J. Ramsey Michaels writes: "Does the scene tell us anything further about the identity of 'the disciple whom he loved'? The analogy with Mark and Matthew, where a woman at the cross seems to have been identified as the mother of Jesus' two brothers, James and Joses (or Joseph), could suggest that 'the disciple whom he loved' is one of those brothers, allowed to remain anonymous just as Mary herself is anonymous in this gospel." See the following: J. Ramsey Michaels, *The Gospel of John, The New International Commentary on the Old and New Testament* (Grand Rapids, MI; Cambridge, UK: William B. Eerdmans Publishing Company, 2010), 957.

5. Of the "beloved disciple," Ben Witherington III writes the following: "We also have the story in John 13 about the Beloved Disciple reclining with and beside Jesus, and Peter having his feet washed, neither of which is mentioned in the Synoptic Gospels. All in all it appears that we should think of the Beloved Disciple as the source of much of this material, and that he was a Judean follower of Jesus, not one of the sons of Zebedee, even though his name may have been John." See Ben Witherington III, *The New Testament Story* (Grand Rapids, MI; Cambridge, U.K.: William B. Eerdmans Publishing Company, 2004), 83.

Day 38: JESUS (PART ONE)

1. Second Corinthians 5:21, *The New Jerusalem Bible* (New York: Doubleday, 1985).
2. Of the teaching of Arius and others, James Hawkins pointed out: "God was not always the Father; but there was a time when God was not the Father. The Word of God was not always, but was made 'from things that are not;' for He who is God fashioned the non-existing from the nonexisting; wherefore there was a time when He was not." See James B. H. Hawkins, "Alexander of Alexandria: Translator's Introductory Notice," in *Fathers of the Third Century: Gregory Thaumaturgus, Dionysius the Great, Julius Africanus, Anatolius and Minor Writers, Methodius, Arnobius*, eds. Alexander Roberts, James Donaldson, and A. Cleveland Coxe, vol. 6, *The Ante-Nicene Fathers* (Buffalo, NY: Christian Literature Company, 1886), 297.

3. Anselm writes in terms of the mediator as to why both the divine and human natures are necessary: "The Divine and human natures cannot alternate, so that the Divine should become human or the human Divine; nor can they be so commingled as that a third should be produced from the two which is neither wholly Divine nor wholly human. For, granting that it were possible for either to be changed into the other, it would in that case be only God and not man, or man only and not God." See Saint Anselm, *Proslogium; Monologium; An Appendix in Behalf of the Fool by Gaunilon; and Cur Deus Homo*, trans. Sidney Norton Deane (Chicago: The Open Court Publishing Company, 1939), 245. Moreover, I have translated Anselm's word "satisfaction" as "atonement" as a twenty-first century readership is not likely to understand what is meant by the use of the Anselmic term "satisfaction."

4. Thomas H. McCall, *Forsaken: The Trinity and the Cross, and Why It Matters,* Kindle ed. (Downers Grove, IL: InterVarsity Press, 2012), Kindle Locations 341–42. Thomas Aquinas, in the thirteenth century, noted this point well in his following observation: "by not shielding Him from the Passion, but abandoning Him to His persecutors: thus we read (Matt. 27:46) that Christ, while hanging upon the cross, cried out: My God, My God, why hast Thou forsaken Me? because, to wit, He left Him to the power of His persecutors, as Augustine says." See Thomas Aquinas, *Summa Theologica*, trans. Fathers of the English Dominican Province (London: Burns Oates & Washbourne, n.d.), 3.47.3.

Day 39: JESUS (PART TWO)

1. Eckhard J. Schnabel, ed., *Mark: An Introduction and Commentary*, vol. 2, *Tyndale New Testament Commentaries* (London: Inter-Varsity Press, 2017), 421.
2. Ben Witherington III writes, working with the Greek words of our passage: "In any event, I take καταπετασμα to mean inner veil, as is most natural if one takes ναος in its ordinary sense of inner sanctuary, not merely the temple precincts." See Ben Witherington III, *The Gospel of Mark: A Socio-Rhetorical Commentary* (Grand Rapids, MI: Wm. B. Eerdmans Publishing Co., 2001), 400.

Day 41: MARY MAGDALENE

1. Joel C. Elowsky, *John 11–21, Ancient Christian Commentary on Scripture NT 4b* (Downers Grove, IL: InterVarsity Press, 2007), 349. Emphasis is mine.
2. Elowsky, *John 11–21*, 349.

Day 42: A COUPLE OF DISCIPLES

1. Leon Morris, *Luke: An Introduction and Commentary*, vol. 3, *Tyndale New Testament Commentaries* (Downers Grove, IL: InterVarsity Press, 1988), 356.
2. Joel B. Green, *The Gospel of Luke, The New International Commentary on the New Testament* (Grand Rapids, MI: Wm. B. Eerdmans Publishing Co., 1997), 848.
3. Arthur A. Just, *Luke*, vol. 3, *Ancient Christian Commentary on Scripture NT 3* (Downers Grove, IL: InterVarsity Press, 2005), 382.
4. Green, *The Gospel of Luke*, 849.

Acknowledgments

I would like to thank my wife, Marilyn, for the sacrifices that she has made in support of this work. I am also grateful for a couple of decades-long conversation partners who have taught me much: Jerry Walls in matters theological and philosophical; Ben Witherington III in matters biblical. I would also like to thank Mike Voigts, who encouraged me to go forward despite the obstacles. I am very appreciative of the efforts of Dr. David Watson, who read the full manuscript and offered several helpful suggestions. Beyond this, Brooke Harris showed me how to look at the painting of Tintoretto in a new and fresh way, and Lauren King offered several insightful observations, especially in terms of discipleship. Andrew Miller and Holly Jones were great dialogue partners throughout this effort. My research assistant, the Reverend Andy Newman, has been helpful in so many ways, too numerous to mention here, and I am always grateful. Having received so much from others, I have finally responded.

Printed by Libri Plureos GmbH in Hamburg, Germany